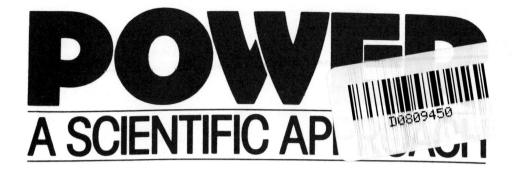

POWER
A SCIENTIFIC APPROACH

FREDERICK C. HATFIELD, Ph.D.
Author of the bestselling
Bodybuilding: A Scientific Approach

CONTEMPORARY BOOKS

Library of Congress Cataloging-in-Publication Data

Hatfield, Frederick C.
    Power : a scientific approach : advanced musclebuilding techniques
for explosive strength! / Frederick C. Hatfield.
      p.   cm.
    Includes index.
    ISBN 0-8092-4433-0
    1. Bodybuilding.   2. Muscle strength.   I. Title.
GV546.5.H39   1989
646.7′5—dc19
                                88-34448
                                  CIP

Cover photograph by Michael Neveux

Published by Contemporary Books
A division of NTC/Contemporary Publishing Group, Inc.
4255 West Touhy Avenue, Lincolnwood (Chicago), Illinois 60712-1975 U.S.A.
Copyright © 1989 by Fred C. Hatfield
Printed in the United States of America
International Standard Book Number: 0-8092-4433-0

99 00 01 02 03 04 QP 28 27 26 25 24 23 22 21 20 19 18 17 16 15 14 13

ACKNOWLEDGMENTS

Thanks to Bill Laich, M.D., Ph.D., Director of Sports Sciences at the CRAFT Medical Research Center in Reseda, California, for his invaluable input on the biochemistry of sports training. I've had the pleasure of working with some truly great athletes. This book is dedicated to them:

Lyle Alzado, L.A. Raiders
Billy Bates, Dallas Cowboys
Kevin Brooks, Dallas Cowboys
Mark Brown, Miami Dolphins
Joe Bradley, Powerlifter
John Brenner, Shot Put
Jim Byrne, L.A. Rams
Ralph Caldwell, San Diego Chargers
Michael Chang, Tennis
Tiffany Chin, Figure Skater
Vinnie Curto, Boxer
Sid Fernandez, N.Y. Mets
Blane Fox, Detroit Tigers
Rich Gaspari, Bodybuilder
Mark Gastineau, N.Y. Jets
Lee Haney, Bodybuilder

Ron Itzaki, Tennis
Dave Keaggy, Powerlifter
Pete Koch, Kansas City Chiefs
Peter Michaels, Shot Put
Mitch Mignano, Weightlifter
Brian Muir, Shot Put
Akeem Olajouwon, Houston Rockets
Tom Platz, Bodybuilder
Mike Quinn, Bodybuilder
Dave Richards, San Diego Chargers
Mark Schmidt, UCLA Football
Chistian Sylvester, 400 Meters
Mike Tully, Pole Vault
Randy Wilson, Powerlifter

CONTENTS

PART I:
WHAT IS STRENGTH AND WHERE DOES IT COME FROM?

1
STRENGTH TRAINING:
A Fresh Look at an Age-Old Topic

Where people of strength gather, their discussion inevitably turns to the methods of training that gave them the greatest returns in strength development. The topic of strength training, therefore, has been bantered about in gyms since gyms were invented. The importance of strength is elemental to anyone's training goals, be they for sports in general, fitness, bodybuilding, or the greatest strength sport of all, powerlifting. So, I implore you to read on. Discover the wherewithal to exceed the record feats of strength of our predecessors. Discover what it will take to achieve massive strength and explosiveness.

WHERE DOES OUR STRENGTH COME FROM?

I have identified no fewer than 23 different sources of strength (see page 2). And the most amazing fact is that only two of these factors are genetically predetermined, meaning that you can do little to augment them. Conversely, you can augment or in some way positively modify the other 21.

Let me give you a brief description of the most significant factors contributing to strength. Then I'll lay a definition of strength on you that'll be sure to turn your head. Together with knowing the sources of strength, knowing what strength really is will give you the knowledge to carry your training light years beyond what you've ever dreamed possible. Certainly far enough to eclipse the records of the great athletes of the past.

FACTORS AFFECTING STRENGTH
Anatomical Physiological Factors

- Muscle fiber arrangement (fusiform, uni-, bi-, and multi-pennate)
- Musculoskeletal leverage
- Ratio of fast- vs. slow-twitch muscle fibers
- Tissue leverage (interstitial and intracellular leverage stemming from fat deposits, sarcoplasmic content, satellite cell proliferation and fluid)
- Freedom of movement between fibers and muscles (scar tissue and adhesions can limit strength)
- Tissue viscoelasticity
- Stretch reflex (muscle spindles)
- Sensitivity of the Golgi tendon organ*
- Endocrine (hormonal levels/functioning)
- Energy transfer systems' efficiency
- Extent of hyperplasia (muscle splitting)
- Proliferation and growth of myofibrils
- Intramuscular/intracellar friction
- Motor unit recruitment*

Psychoneural/Learned Response Factors

- "Psych" (arousal level)
- Pain tolerance
- "Focus" (concentration)
- Social learning (learned inhibitory responses limit strength)
- "Skill" coordination (activation/inhibition of prime movers, synergists, and stabilizers in an efficient sequence; also, position, sequence, direction timing, speed, and effect of force application)

External/Environmental Factors

- Equipment (use of the "best")
- Environment (heat, cold, humidity, precipitation, wind, altitude)
- Gravity
- Opposing and assistive forces (e.g., opponent's efforts)

*May have components logically suited to the Psychoneural/Learned factors category.

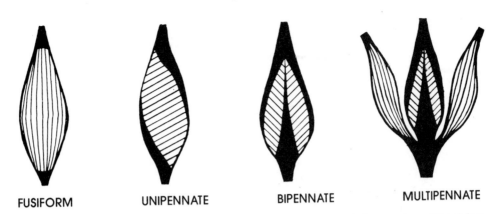

FUSIFORM   UNIPENNATE   BIPENNATE   MULTIPENNATE

Diagrams show kinds of arrangements of fibers of skeletal muscles. (Used by permission of Lea & Febiger, Inc. From Rasch & Burke, *Kinesiology and Applied Anatomy*, 6th Edition, 1978.)

1. *Muscle Fiber Arrangement.* Muscles are an arrangement of muscle cells—called muscle fibers. These fibers can be arranged in unipennate, bipennate, or multipennate configurations. Typically, unipennate muscles (such as the biceps) are adapted for large amplitude movements, and aren't suited for strength, but instead are adapted to speed. Other muscles, such as the psoas muscle (the same muscle tissue as in filet mignon steaks) are arrangements of very short cells in a tweedlike pattern, and are extremely suited to strength, although their movement range at the joint is somewhat limited. Knowing this may assist in improving the efficiency of training speed versus strength movements in some sports, but since there's little you can do about the actual arrangement (it's genetically predetermined), it's traditionally been an overlooked factor by strength athletes in general.

2. *Musculoskeletal Leverage.* Your musculoskeletal system is an arrangement of levers, typically of the third class. This means that the fulcrum—the joint—is at one end, the source of force is in the middle, and the resistance is at the other end. This arrangement is suited for fast movements. The farther away Mother Nature places the source of force (tendon insertion) from the fulcrum, the stronger you'll be. As with muscle fiber arrangement, leverage is a factor which you have no control over, save improved skills mechanics in your respective sports endeavors. Improving your skills mechanics will have the net effect of improving your overall body movements, thereby taking advantage of your inherent strengths while minimizing the detrimental effects of your weaknesses. All wise coaches know this, and that's what practice is all about. For any athlete, the same approach should predominate all weight training movements in an attempt to impart maximum constructive overload to the muscles for greater growth.

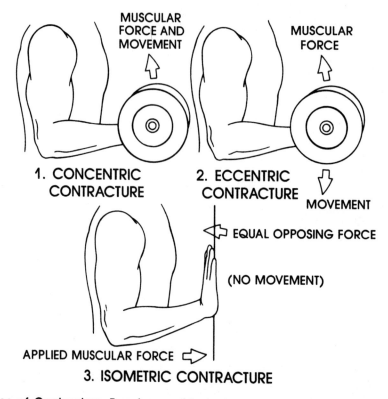

MUSCULAR FORCE AND MOVEMENT ⇧

MUSCULAR FORCE ⇧

1. CONCENTRIC CONTRACTURE

2. ECCENTRIC CONTRACTURE

⇩ MOVEMENT

◁ EQUAL OPPOSING FORCE

(NO MOVEMENT)

APPLIED MUSCULAR FORCE ⇨

3. ISOMETRIC CONTRACTURE

Types of Contracture. Two types of isotonic contracture are concentric (force overcomes resistance), eccentric or negative (resistance overcomes force). Isometric (opposing forces are equal) contracture occurs when muscle attempts to shorten against an unyielding opposing force.

3. *Tissue Leverage.* Called interstitial leverage, mechanical advantages are gained if there's intramuscular fat and fluid filling the spaces between and inside the muscle cells. Care should be taken, though, because such a practice can lead to that "puffy" look that's sure to knock you out of contention in bodybuilding contests. For strength athletes, such as super-heavyweight powerlifters (where sheer mass may be advantageous), it's wise to seek a bit of such leverage provided it isn't carried to an extreme, thereby disrupting your strength-to-weight ratio. For most other athletes, attempts to improve tissue leverage yield no sports advantages.

4. *Enzyme Concentrations.* The enzymes that direct the activity of your muscle cells can be in balances amenable to explosive, strong contracture or for endurance activities. Training specifically for power or for endurance is the stimulus for altering this delicate balance.

5. *Fast- Versus Slow-Twitch Fiber Ratio.* It used to be believed that the ratio of fast-twitch (white) muscle fibers and slow-twitch (red) muscle fibers was a hereditary trait unalterable

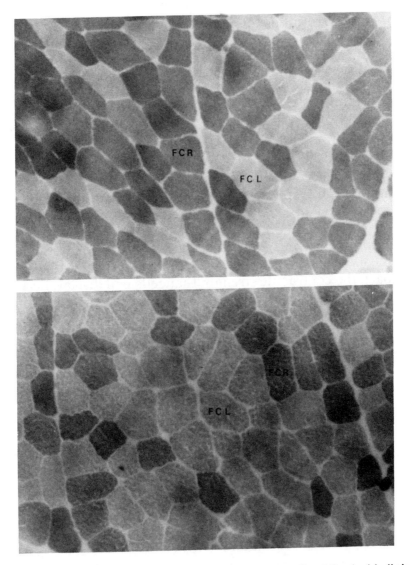

Muscle Fiber Types: The top sample shows predominantly white, fast-twitch muscle fibers (stained dark), while the lower sample is comprised chiefly of red, slow-twitch muscle fibers (light colored cells). Notice that there are different shades of dark and light. These different shades relate to the actual classification of each cell within the fast versus slow categories:

CHARACTERISTICS OF FIBER TYPES

Characteristic	Red (Type I)	Intermediate (Type IIA)	White (Type IIB)
Diameter	Small	Intermediate	Large
Glycogen Content	Low	Intermediate	High
Resistance to Fatigue	High	Intermediate	Low
Capillaries	Many	Many	Few
Respiration	Aerobic	Aerobic	Anaerobic
Twitch Rate	Slow	Fast	Fast

through training. We now know better. Studies show that there's a decided shift in cellular function toward the red (endurance) fibers with long-term aerobic training. This could prove devastating to the careers of power athletes who must depend upon explosively fast movements in their sport. The bottom line is that you must train fast to be fast, and train long to have endurance. Since white muscle cells have a greater capacity for strength and size (hypertrophy), it stands to reason that heavy weights lifted explosively should predominate a strength athlete's training regimen. Of course, you must pay attention to your red fibers too, so a good mix of movement speeds, weights, and rep/set schemes should comprise the truly scientific conditioning program.

6. *Myofibrillar Density.* The number of actin and myosin myofilaments you are able to pack inside each cell determines, in large part, the contractile strength that cells will display. Perhaps the most important contributing factor to overall muscular

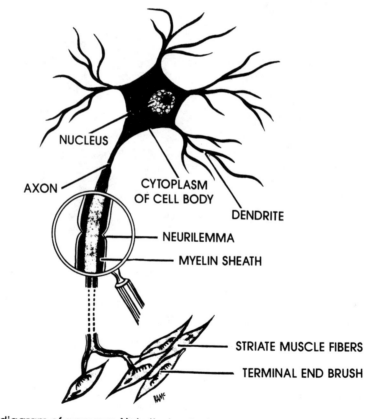

A schematic diagram of a neuron. Note that a single neuron services many muscle fibers, and that the neuron, its axon, twigs, and all of the fibers it services are collectively called a *motor unit*. Each of the fibers of a single motor unit contract together when the excitation threshold is reached or exceeded. (From Morgan and Stellar, *Physiological Psychology*, copyright © 1950 by McGraw-Hill Book Company. Used by permission.)

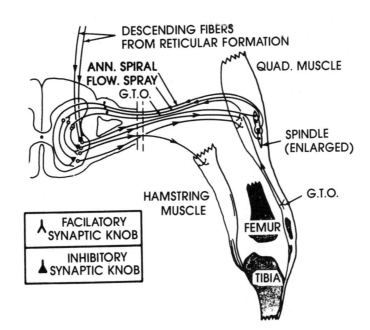

The myotatic and inverse myotatic reflexes act as "autogenic governors" of movement at the knee joint. Notice that supraspinal influence, both faciliatory and inhibitory, is brought to bear on the gamma efferent neuron, thus setting the bias of the spindle. (From deVries, *Physiology of Exercise*, 2nd Edition, Wm. C. Brown Co. Publishers, 1974. Used by permission.)

strength, myofibrillarization is achieved with the use of heavy weights. Light, high repetition training can't improve strength because not enough myofibrils are stimulated to grow.

7. *Number of Fibers Activated.* If you're having a tug-of-war contest, and you have 10 guys while the other team has only two guys, who's going to win? The team with the most guys, naturally. The same with your muscles. The more muscle fibers you can activate simultaneously, the greater your strength output will be. This ability comes from learning. You guessed it—learning how to do this involves the use of heavy weights and explosive movements.

8. *Sensitivity of the Golgi Tendon Organ.* At the juncture of your muscles and tendons, there's a tiny mechanism designed to pick up sensations of too much stretch or stress on the muscles. It relays this message to your brain, and a message is sent back for the muscle to shut down. This is a defense mechanism, designed to keep you from tearing yourself apart with your own strength. The shut-down level is set too conservatively. The way to adjust the threshold at which shut down takes place is through ballistic (jerky movements) training. Be careful, though. Such training must be done under very controlled circumstances because of the dangers inherent in performing jerky movements with heavy weights. I believe that this method

of training is one of the most potentially productive methods for strength improvement, and deserves much closer attention than it's getting from the scientific community.

9. *Psych.* Arousal bordering blind rage produces greater strength output than does calmness. It's that simple. Learn to get psyched! You needn't display your arousal overtly, though—it's an inward trait that can be learned, and practicing lifting the big weights is the way to engage this learning process.

10. *Pain Tolerance.* Pain stemming from extreme exertion and the buildup of lactate in the muscles can be very debilitating. However, studies clearly demonstrate that your training provides you with a greater tolerance to such pain, enabling you to push harder and with greater strength of effort. Foster this ability by pushing past the pain barrier systematically.

11. *Free, Unbound Muscle Cells.* If, over time, you inflict trauma to your muscles, the effect is a buildup of strength-limiting and movement-limiting adhesions and scar tissue. These binding elements can be effectively removed through neuromuscular reeducation procedures, a discovery attributed to Dr. Gary Glum and Joseph Horrigan of the Institute for Neuromuscular Reeducation in Los Angeles. The net effect, of course, is greater strength, greater freedom of movement (range of movement), and the ability for athletes' muscles to grow to their full size potential.

12. *Tissue Elasticity.* All matter in the universe has a propensity to return to its original shape after being stretched. A fancy name for this tendency and the mathematical expression of the extent to which the return phase happens is called its "coefficient of restitution." Or, simply, elasticity. Your bodily tissues—muscles, tendons, connective tissue, bones, and adipose tissue—are no exceptions. Viscoelasticity can assist greatly in exerting force, but only provided your stretch-and-return maneuver is performed sharply—with speed. Once in the stretched position for any measurable length of time, the elasticity wanes. Viscoelasticity can be improved to a small degree, but both age and steroid abuse rob you of it.

13. *Stretch Reflex.* The doctor bumps your patellar tendon with a rubber hammer and your lower leg jerks forward. Why? Because the tendon is attached to your quadriceps muscles, within which are hundreds of specialized muscle cells called muscle spindles. Their job is to signal surrounding cells to contract in opposition to stretch—a defense mechanism designed to keep you from overstretching the muscle or tendinous attachments. You can use this stretch reflex to your advantage through carefully applied ballistic movements in all sports. The wind up in baseball pitching is a classic example. You can

throw much harder by rearing back sharply before the forward arm movement that propels the ball. Holding your arm back for a moment and then coming forward with the ball will produce far less force than eliciting a stretch reflex will. Careful ballistic training augmented with plyometric drills can improve your ability to make use of the stretch reflex effectively.

14. *Coordination.* The ability to integrate your muscles' activities so that all contribute to the movement and none detract is part of the attribute we call coordination. The other part of coordination is ensuring that the right muscles are activated. Synergists, stabilizers, and prime movers must be variably activated, in an efficient sequence, in order for maximum strength to be displayed. This is called skill by some, but it goes beyond that meager definition, for it also involves the interplay of every single one of the other strength components listed above.

DEFINING "STRENGTH"

All of these factors give you a different perspective on strength, don't they? But the scenario is incomplete without a definition of strength. You see, there are several different forms in which strength can be displayed. We all know intuitively that strength is your ability to exert force but *how* it's exerted must also be defined if you really want to know how to improve it.

There are four broad categories of strength, each of which has subcategories. The important point to remember is that each kind of strength requires an altogether different form of training. Each category of strength is not mutually exclusive of the others, since improving one will undoubtedly improve the others to some degree. But to maximize the ones you need in your sport, you need to know the *best* way to train.

1. *Absolute Strength*
   - *Concentric Strength.* Your one-rep maximum in a movement.
   - *Eccentric Strength.* Your one-rep maximum lowering a weight under control (add 40% to your concentric strength).
   - *Static Strength.* Your maximum holding strength in a given position (add 20% to your concentric strength).
2. *Limit Strength.* The same as absolute strength, except that you're "under the influence" of hypnosis, electrotherapy, erogenic substances of any form, or other techniques that elevate your potential for strength output beyond what it ordinarily would be. Absolute strength is achieved through training alone, while limit strength is achieved through whatever means are at your disposal.

3. *Speed-Strength*
   - *Starting Strength.* Your ability to recruit a maximum number of muscle fibers simultaneously.
   - *Explosive Strength.* Your ability to keep the fibers firing over time.
4. *Anaerobic Power*
   - *Local Muscular Endurance.* Your ability to continue submaximal force output over a long period (energy from the lactacid system of muscle energetics).
   - *Strength Endurance.* Your ability to put forth maximum muscular contractures time after time with no appreciable decline in force output (alactacid system).
   - *Speed Endurance.* Your ability to maintain your maximum speed over distances less than 400 m (100 and 200 m most typically exemplify the alactacid system's efficiency while the 400 m dash typifies the lactacid system's efficiency).

Absolute and limit strength call for heavy training, typically above 80%–85% of max level for each lift. Between three and eight reps are called for, according to both experience and research literature, to ensure maximum concentric strength development. However, only two or three reps (each held for 6–10 seconds) is called for in static strength development, and the same holds true for eccentric strength development. Limit your eccentric strength workouts to once weekly or less, since they're extremely taxing on your muscles, and cause massive cellular destruction when carried to an extreme.

Starting strength is achieved through learning. Ballistic training is the only way I've ever found that is truly effective in developing starting strength. Explosive strength, on the other hand, requires a special form of training I developed years ago, called compensatory acceleration training. Simply stated, as you progress through a movement, you must attempt to accelerate the weight so that maximum force is being delivered throughout the movement. Of course, cease the accelerative drive somewhere before the termination of the movement so that injury is prevented from excessive ballistic shock. Again, this form of strength invokes a very strong learning element.

Under the general category of anaerobic power, there are three different attributes: local muscular endurance, speed endurance, and strength endurance. Actually, local muscular endurance is not normally classified as part of the general concept of strength because emphasis is on repetitive muscular endurance such as that displayed in rowing, boxing, wrestling, tug-of-war, and high rep training (more than 50 reps). But strength endurance involves the ability to perform maximum strength—absolute or limit strength movements and speed-strength movements—without displaying any decrement in strength output time after time. A good example of this kind of ability

COMPENSATORY ACCELERATION TRAINING AND PLYOMETRICS WILL:

1. Increase $<Q$
2. Increase $<A$
3. Increase Fmax
4. Decrease Tmax
5. Increase Explosive Strength
6. Decrease Transition Phase
7. Increase Absolute Strength

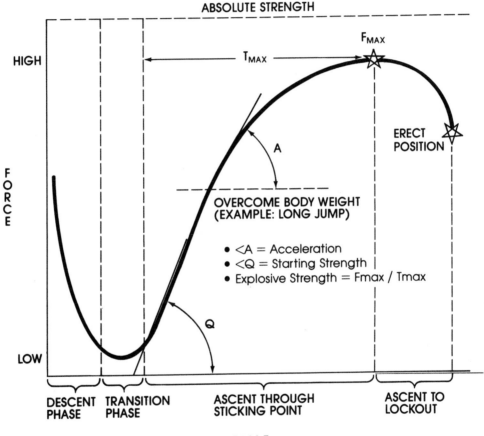

would be the rest-pause system popularized in the Weider magazines years ago. Another would be football linemen, batting heads at full tilt play after play, on into the fourth quarter.

Strength and speed endurance come primarily from changing enzyme concentrations and pain tolerance.

As a final note on strength, please observe graph on page 11, which illustrates any given sports movement. It's a theoretical line, and can be applied to practically all sports movements such as the squat, the long jump, a running step, or any kind of swing, hit, or lift. There are a few points you'll find very helpful in your strength training efforts when you view this graph.

The descending line is eccentric movement, such as the recoil on the toe board just before a long jump. Then the line swings upward indicating concentric force. The transition phase must be extremely short, and that calls for high levels of eccentric as well as static strength. The steepness of the ascending (concentric force) line is an indicator of starting strength. The steeper the line, the greater the starting force. The quickness with which you reach your maximum force (F_{max}) is important in practically every sport.

Notice that no sport movement ever reaches absolute strength output (with the possible exception of powerlifting). There simply isn't enough time to affect maximum muscle fiber recruitment. An absolute strength contraction typically takes over a second or two to achieve, and most sports movements are performed in the twinkling of an eye.

So then, your strength training calls for improving:

1. Your absolute strength levels (all three areas)
2. Your transition time must decrease (eccentric to concentric)
3. You must increase the angle of Q (your starting force)
4. F_{max} must be increased (force actually displayed)
5. T_{max} must be decreased (time it takes to reach F_{max})
6. Explosive strength must be increased

. . . all this to improve one tiny sports movement! For bodybuilders, this exercise in defining strength may seem a bit esoteric, but remember this: Bodybuilders today are better than their forebears because they apply science to their training. Will tomorrow's science carry you beyond the stars of today? I submit to you that it's the *only* way you'll progress!

2

YOUR MUSCLES' COMPOSITION

There are so many things written about muscle physiology that you're no doubt fed up because: (1) they're written for academicians, (2) you don't care about that stuff, or (3) they're written by fools who invariably attempt to pull the wool over your eyes by claiming they know what's happening. My years in the trenches have given me insights I'd like to share with you concerning three sources of strength that relate to your muscles' composition and how they're structured. Although their importance is both acknowledged and vital, scientists and trainers have tended to either overlook them as incapable of being altered or augmented through training, or through just plain laziness or lack of interest.

MUSCLE FIBER ARRANGEMENT

Take a look at the four basic types of arrangements on page 3. *Fusiform* muscles have their fibers arranged longitudinally to the origin and insertion tendons. There are two types of fusiform muscles: long fusiform and short fusiform. Long fusiform muscles are relatively weak but contract a great distance, making them ideally suited to speed. The short fusiform muscles are strong and have a short contractile distance. Long fusiform muscles are typically found in the extremities while short fusiform are found in the intercostal (ribs) region.

The three classifications of *penniform* muscles (unipennate, bipen-

FIGURE 2-1

THE TYPES OF MUSCLE FIBER ARRANGEMENTS

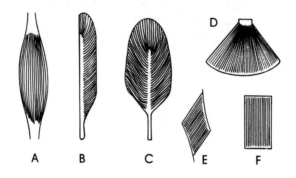

A. Fusiform (biceps)
B. Penniform (peroneal muscles, tibilais posterior)
C. Bipenniform (rectus femoris)
D. Triangular or fan-shaped (temporals, latissimus, pectorals)
E. Rhomboidal or quadrilateral (intercostals)
F. Rectangular or quadrilateral (rhomboids, pronator quadratus)

nate, and multipennate) have their fibers arranged diagonally to the origin and insertion points of the muscle. They're found both in the trunk and extremities. While penniform muscles do not have as great a contractile distance as do fusiform muscles (because of their diagonal arrangement of fibers) they have great strength.

It doesn't take a genius or physicist to figure out that the multipennate muscles are suited to both speed and strength, while the bipennate muscles are most suited to strength. The unipennate muscles aren't quite as strong as the bipennate ones, but have the advantage of being slightly more suited to speed as well.

What's the significance of all this? Simply that by knowing the specific function of each muscle, you have a very important clue as to how to optimize training that muscle!

This is a new concept. Over the years I've been training, I've noticed that some muscles respond better to fast movements performed with a low percentage of max effort. On the other hand, not all muscles act that way. Some respond to training with slow movements with maximum poundages and lower reps.

Intrigued as to why this would happen, I've concluded that there are at least two factors involved in this phenomenon: muscle fiber type and muscle fiber arrangement. Remember: if a muscle is designed to contract fast, you'll probably benefit more if you train with fast movements. If it's designed for strength rather than speed, however, you will no doubt achieve greater strength if you train that muscle for strength.

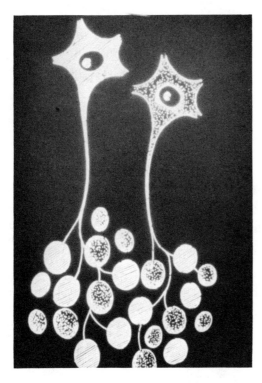

Motor Unit: Each neuron depicted has its specific function with respect to the type of fiber (fast-twitch or slow-twitch) it is associated with. In experiments where cross-innervation was performed, the neuron suited to slow-twitch fibers caused the newly innervated fast-twitch fibers to become slow. Alternately, slow-twitch fibers became fast when attached to a fast neuron.

This may sound like double-talk or perhaps stating the obvious. It isn't. So vast are the implications of this new concept that I dare not tread too heavily at this time into a discussion of them. There are many factors that have to be considered, not the least of which is the kind of joint each type of muscle acts upon.

FAST- AND SLOW-TWITCH MUSCLE FIBERS

Fast-contracting muscle cells appear white under microscopic scrutiny, whereas slow-twitch fibers appear red. Red fibers have much myoglobin, which partially explains why they are fatigue resistant. Myoglobin is involved in the oxidative functions of these cells.

White fibers, although low in oxidative capacity, have a higher ATPase hydrolysis velocity, enabling them to "twitch" more times per second than red, and therefore generate more tension (and more strength). They also have a greater capacity for hypertrophy than do red fibers.

But you probably already knew all this—so much has been written about fast- versus slow-twitch fibers recently. But did you know that strength athletes should not engage in slow, endurance types of activities in any form of a training regimen? That's right. All those 300-pound linemen running laps "to make a man outa them" are actually reducing their explosiveness and strength by running. White fiber is not needed in such training, and gradually becomes slower and weaker in functional characteristics.

Let me remind you that I'm referring to elite athletes, those who aspire to greatness, for it is among them that even minute decrements in performance capabilities can spell the difference between winning and losing. At this level of performance, milliseconds and millimeters mean a lot.

It has been known for a long time that subtle changes in red versus white fiber composition and function could be forced to occur through training. However, recently it has come to light that such changes can be far more important than once believed.

Dr. Gary Dudley (Ohio University) and Dr. Steven Fleck (Olympic Complex, Colorado Springs) reported their research on this important topic in *Sports Medicine*. They found that endurance training reduced a muscle's inherent capability of maximum power output, reduced glycogen content, and altered the mechanical properties of muscle. These changes are all unfavorable to strength athletes. Strength athletes who are serious about their sport, therefore, are well-advised to completely dissociate themselves from any aerobic activities.

The opposite is not true, however. Endurance athletes benefit in several ways from strength training, not the least of which is improved speed of movement.

Muscle Fibers: The two outside fibers are contracted, while the middle one is relaxed. Running atop the fibers are a couple of Alpha motor nerves.

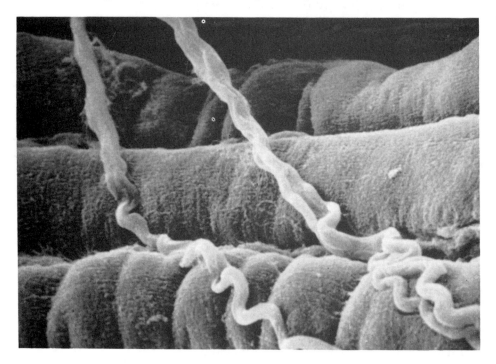

MYOFIBRILLARIZATION

Your muscles contract because of the action of four proteins, actin, troponin, tropomyosin, and myosin, which are arranged in long, thin strands called myofibrils. The more myofibrils each cell has inside it, the greater the amount of force your muscle will generate upon contracture.

The obvious question is, how can you structure your training to force more contractile proteins to be manufactured?

The answer, of course, is *overload*. Forcing your muscles to ever-greater levels of contractile force will create an intracellular need for

FIGURE 2-2

HOW YOUR MUSCLE IS ORGANIZED

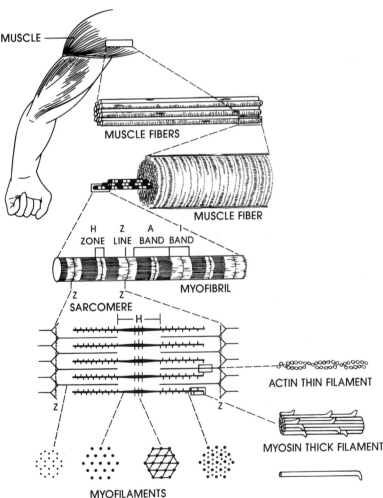

Note that your *muscle* is comprised of *fibers*. Each fiber (cell) is comprised of *myofibrils*. Myofibrils are comprised of *actin* and *myosin*, or contractile protein, which "slide" across each other creating force.

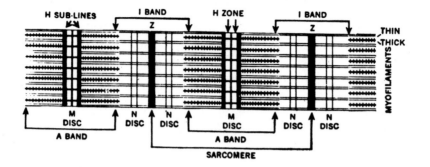

Schematic diagram of a muscle cell's myofibrillar elements. (Used by permission of Lea & Febiger, Inc. From Rasch & Burke, *Kinesiology and Applied Anatomy*, Lea & Febiger, 1978, 6th Edition.)

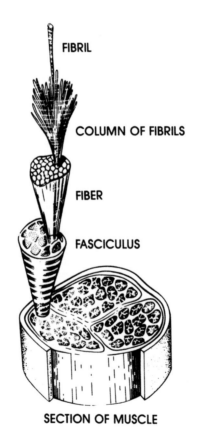

Construction of a section of muscle. An individual muscle fiber contains many fibrils, and a fasciculus contains many fibers. A muscle is a composite of many fasciculii. (Adapted from Sigmund Grollman's *The Human Body*, 2nd Edition, Reprinted with permission of Macmillan Publishing Company. Copyright © 1974 by Sigmund Grollman.)

contractile protein to be manufactured. Your myofibrils, comprised of contractile proteins, thicken, increase in number and increase in enzymatic activities in response to high-tension exercises.

Of course, other changes occur simultaneously within the muscle and nervous system. These changes are spoken of in other chapters of this book. Such changes include a proliferation of satellite cells, connective tissues, ligaments, and tendons. In other words, structural integrity is improved. The greater tension you are now producing with your contracting cells will not jeopardize your musculoskeletal system's structure. Simply put, you're less susceptible to injury.

3

LEVERAGE

Leverage. Now there's a word to ponder! It can mean anything you want: corporate takeovers, power positioning in negotiations, mechanical efficiency, or even real estate speculation deals. Among athletes, it's the single most frequently used excuse for another athlete outperforming you: "Well, that guy was born with great leverage."

Let's explore the leverage concept as it pertains to improved strength in sports. While you can't do anything about changing your body's musculoskeletal levers, you can indeed alter their effectiveness. Furthermore, there are many different forms of leverage at your disposal, and you'll do well to learn what they are for maximizing your ability to display strength.

In sports, it's not always the strongest person who puts the shot the farthest, lifts the most weight, becomes the all-pro tackle, or hits the ball the farthest. Being able to exert maximum force is truly important, but pales in its importance next to:

- Applying force at the appropriate point
- Applying force in the appropriate sequence of movements
- Applying force in the appropriate direction
- Applying force at the appropriate time
- Applying force at maximum speed ("power")
- The ultimate effects of force application

While the mechanical factors of equilibrium, motion, and force are elemental to the entire concept of sport, it is leverage that embodies these concepts and determines the effectiveness of force.

In other words, since strength determines the extent of force you are able to apply, and leverage determines the effectiveness of your application of force, it is important for you to become as strong as possible. If Joe Blow is stronger than John Smith, and both men are of equal skill in their ability to exert leverage, Joe Blow will be the better athlete.

In my view of leverage in sports, the word can almost replace the concept of *skill*. Position, sequence, direction, timing, speed, and effect all weigh heavily in the concept of skill. All weigh heavily in the concept skill. All weigh heavily in the concept of appropriately applied leverage, therefore, all are important in strength.

YOUR BODY'S LEVER SYSTEMS

Your musculoskeletal system is a series of levers. Your joints represent the *fulcrum* of the lever. The *force arm* of the lever is the distance between the fulcrum and point where force is being applied by the muscle. The *weight arm* is the distance from the fulcrum to the weight upon which the muscular force is acting.

There are three kinds of levers (depicted on page 22). Most of the levers in your body are of the third class variety. For example, your gluteals and iliacus muscles flex the hip. Your biceps flex the elbow. Your quadriceps extend the knee. There are some first class levers as well; the triceps' action on the elbow is an example. Another is the action of the gastrocnemius on the ankle joint.

The mechanical advantage of a lever is defined as the ratio of the length of the force arm to the weight arm. Since almost all of your bodily levers have a very short force arm, according to formula, your body is built for *speed*, not strength. The point where the tendon inserts into the bone is the point where force is applied to the bone. Thus, genetics plays an important part in whether you are naturally fast or naturally strong.

However, you can *modify* your inherent leverage through any one of the six points raised earlier (position, sequence, direction, timing, speed, and effect). So, if you desire to exert tremendous force, you must extend your force arm. On the other hand, if you desire to move swiftly you must reduce the length of your force arm and extend your weight arm.

How in the devil can you do that if your insertion points are fixed? It's really quite simple if you think in three dimensions instead of only two. Picture the lever extending *outside* of your body. For example, a wrestler holds his opponent's arm on the mat so he can't move. His efforts would be made far more effective if he were to hold his opponent's arm near the wrist instead of near the elbow. Further, if he

FIGURE 3-1

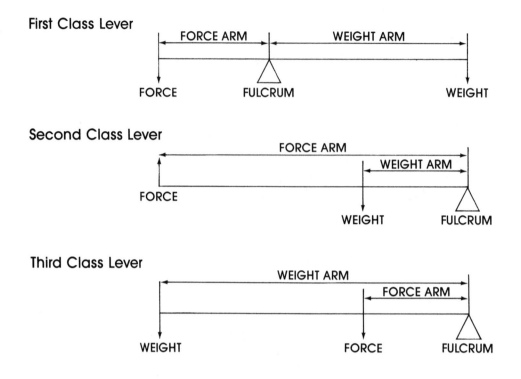

First Class Lever

Second Class Lever

Third Class Lever

were to apply downward force on the wrist perpendicular to the ground instead of doing so at an angle, the amount of force would be greater because the force arm is longest in this position.

On the other hand, if the wrestler wanted to turn his opponent over onto his back, he'd need a shorter force arm (e.g., the half-Nelson) so the force would be greater.

There are many such examples one can draw upon. Holding a dumbbell at arms' length is more difficult than holding it with your elbow bent. Pulling a weight upward close to the body will be more effective than pulling it upward at arm's length in front of your body. The important point to remember in your quest for greater strength is to use your God-given musculoskeletal leverages to their greatest advantage.

You do this by:

1. Keeping your weight arm short
2. Keeping your force arm long
3. Adhering to good mechanics relative to
   • Position of your body's center of gravity
   • Sequence of force applications
   • Direction of force application
   • Proper timing of force application

- Maximizing the speed of force application
- Controlling the effect of the force being applied
4. Never attempting to maximize force at the expense of speed
5. Never attempting to maximize speed at the expense of force

In all the world of sports, *speed* is king. But you cannot become fast in any sports movement without maximum force. And that means one thing: Get awesomely *strong!*

4

ELASTICITY AND YOUR STRETCH REFLEX*

Strength. The word is used endlessly by athletes of every persuasion in the sports world. They use the word as if they know, on the most intimate of levels, what strength is. Moreover, they use it as if they know how to get it and where it comes from.

I hate to pop your balloon, fellow iron freaks, but as you've been reading this book you already know there are at least 11 different kinds of strength. And they come from no fewer than 16 different sources.

Two sources that go hand in hand are your muscles' and other tissues' viscoelasticity and your stretch reflex. Don't belittle their importance. No indeed, not when sports performances are measured in tenths of inches and milliseconds.

Viscoelasticity refers to your tissues' tendency to return to a resting length after they have been stretched—much the same as a rubber band. And the stretch reflex is nothing more than your involuntary reaction to a noxious stimulation of some sort. For example, when the doctor bangs your knee with a rubber hammer your foot kicks forward. Or, perhaps more understandable, you jerk your hand away from a hot stove.

An illustration of the nerve/muscle construction that causes a stretch reflex appears on page 25. Each of your muscles is comprised of muscle cells, of course. But did you know that many of these cells

*Adapted from: Yessis, M. and Hatfield, F. *Plyometric Training*, Fitness Systems, 1987.

FIGURE 4-1

ILLUSTRATION OF A MUSCLE SPINDLE.

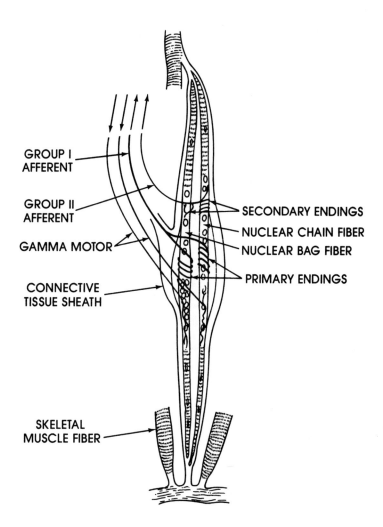

GROUP I
AFFERENT

GROUP II
AFFERENT

GAMMA MOTOR

CONNECTIVE
TISSUE SHEATH

SKELETAL
MUSCLE FIBER

SECONDARY ENDINGS

NUCLEAR CHAIN FIBER

NUCLEAR BAG FIBER

PRIMARY ENDINGS

were actually highly specialized cells called muscle spindles? These spindles provide sensory information about the length and tension within that muscle. They respond to stretch in the muscle by causing an involuntary contracture to oppose the stretch. More of them can be found in muscles controlling fine motor movements than in muscles involved in gross motor movements.

Together with your muscles' and connective tissues' inherent elastic quality, the stretch reflex caused by activation of your muscle spindles can work in your favor in generating greater-than-normal strength. What's more, you can "sharpen" or improve these components of strength through proper training. The form of training most effective in this regard is known as plyometric training.

PLYOMETRIC TRAINING

Plyometrics applies to the display of explosiveness after quick, intensive loading of the muscles. This loading is necessary to pre-tense the muscle with greater force than can be volitionally generated and then using it in the main action. In other words, you make the muscle generate greater force, which can be used in execution of the skill to go further, faster, and higher. Keep in mind that the key elements in sports today are speed and explosiveness.

To fully understand why plyometric training is so effective and why you should use it, it is necessary to examine more closely the relationships between them. To do this, we use a formula to show power, which is a term that can be used in place of explosiveness. In other words, the greater your explosiveness, the greater will be your power and vice versa.

In the formula we see that power (P) is equal to force (f) times distance (d) per unit of time (t):

$$\frac{P = f \times d}{t}$$

However, if we keep distance constant, we can substitute strength(s) for force since the force comes from your strength. Therefore, the formula can be written:

$$P = \frac{s}{t}$$

i.e., the greater the amount of strength that you can display in a certain period of time, the greater will be your explosiveness.

Thus, if you increase strength, power will also go up; if you increase speed and strength remains the same, then power will also increase. However, there is one drawback: If you keep increasing strength but execute the movement slowly, the muscles begin to "learn" slowness and there will actually be a decrease in the amount of power that you exhibit.

The interrelationships between strength and speed can be seen by comparing several sports. In powerlifting, maximal weights are lifted regardless of the amount of time involved. In this case, strength is the main component. However, what occurs in the muscles can still be considered to be explosive. There is maximal recruitment of the muscle fibers and maximal frequency of firing the fibers to display maximal strength. Thus, we can say that there is explosion within the muscle but not within the movement.

In weightlifting, maximal weights are also used but there must also be maximum acceleration and speed, coupled with the strength. Thus, for maximum results you must develop increased strength, together with increased speed or an increase in strength with speed remaining constant.

In throwing a baseball, we utilize a very light object but it must be propelled with maximum speed. In this case, strength is not as important as speed, although keep in mind that with an increase in strength there can also be an increase in speed but only up to a certain point.

Let's examine in greater detail the mechanisms involved in plyometrics to develop explosiveness. First, it is necessary to understand the different types of muscular contractions: Eccentric, isometric, and concentric. In the eccentric contraction, the length of the muscle increases as the muscle undergoes contraction. This type of contraction occurs when the outside force is greater than the force that is being generated by the muscle. Because of this, the outside force lengthens the muscles as the muscle maximally tries to reverse the movement but is unable. The eccentric contraction is sometimes known as a yielding contraction; i.e., the muscle yields to the outside force and lengthens. Most athletes can eccentrically lower 40%–50% more weight than they can lift concentrically.

In the isometric contraction, the muscle contracts but there is no movement. There is some shortening of the muscle fibers but because the outside force is so great, it is not overcome and thus no movement occurs. The isometric contraction is also known as a static or holding type contraction. It should be noted that in this type of contraction the strength developed is 10%–15% greater than can be generated in the concentric contraction.

In the concentric contraction, the muscle shortens when it contracts. In this case, you overcome an outside resistance (weight) and move it a certain distance as the muscle contracts and shortens to produce the movement. This is known as an overcoming regimen, i.e., you overcome the weight being used.

In plyometrics the most important muscular contraction is the eccentric. It is involved in many different ways in many different sports. For example, it is involved in:

- Pre-tension of the muscle prior to a concentric contraction
- A stopping action as when you are running and make a quick stop or in a jump down action in which the eccentric contraction holds you from collapsing
- Receiving a force, as, for example, a football lineman making contact with an opponent who comes at him or in the actions involved in catching a ball
- A repelling action since it re-tenses the muscle prior to pushing an object away from you
- "Blocking," as in the javelin throw after the approach run. You

Text continues on page 35.

VERTICAL JUMPS

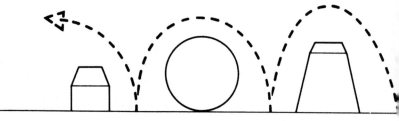

LEFT & RIGHT LEAPS

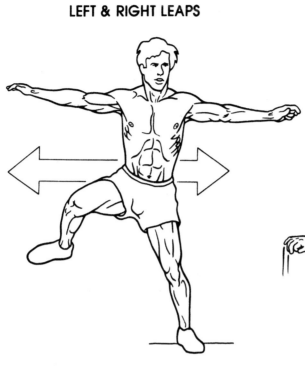

ONE-LEGGED HOPS

OBSTACLE BOUNDING

SIDE LEAPS OVER BENCH (ONE OR TWO LEGGED)

 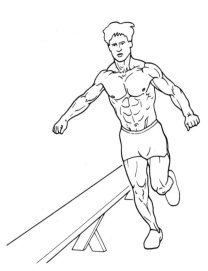

RAPID UP & DOWN HOPS
BETWEEN BENCHES

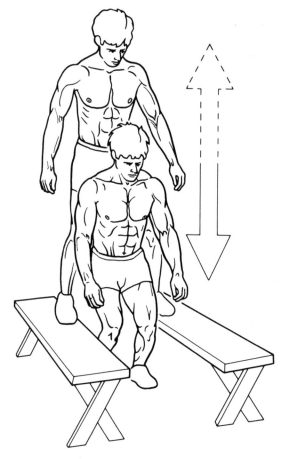

ALTITUDE JUMPS

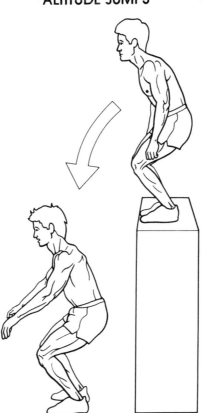

SIDE THROWS

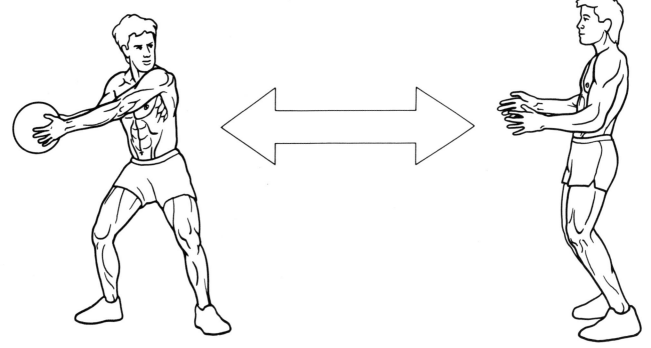

DIAGONAL THROWS UP & BACK

OVERHEAD THROWS

UPWARD CHEST THROW

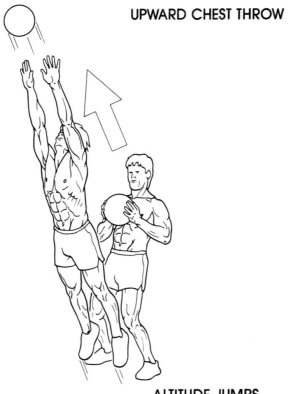

ALTITUDE JUMPS

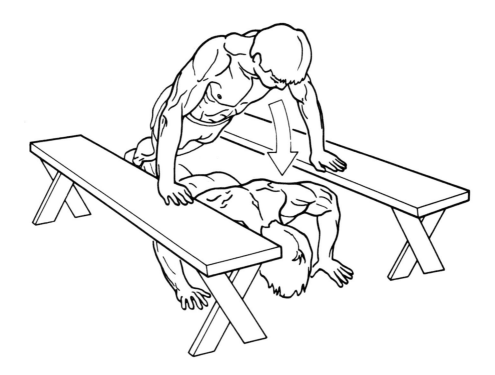

HOP OR JUMP

WALK OR RUN

DEPTH JUMPS (LOW POSITION)

DEPTH JUMPS (HIGH POSITION)

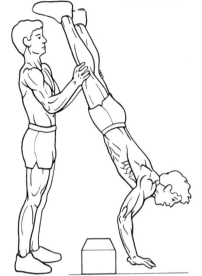

Text continued from page 27.

plant your forward leg to stop horizontal movement and allow the horizontally developed forces to move up into the upper body and then the javelin. Other examples can be seen in the high jump when you plant the push-off leg and in gymnastic vaulting when you hit the take-off board

- Strength gains where it is a very effective way of developing strength by itself or in conjunction with the other muscle contraction regimens. In fact, the eccentric contraction creates the greatest amount of electrical activity, more than the other two types of muscle contractions. As already noted, in some cases the force can reach up to 50% more than in the concentric.

The eccentric contraction also plays a great role in jumping, pushing, and throwing actions. For example, some recent Soviet studies have shown that in jumping movements your results are not limited by the maximum strength shown by the take-off leg extensors and spinal extensors, but by the strength that these muscles show during their stretching, i.e., during their work in the eccentric (yielding) regimen.

In essence, the jumpers execute their skills under the influence of a kinetic energy reserve, which is acquired during the run-up and at the start of the take-off in the so-called amortization stage. In amortization, there is some shock absorbing, which must take place when your foot first hits the ground, and preparation for the following take-off by accumulating the energy of the hit.

The forces generated during the landing are significantly greater than during the push-off stage. Thus, the strength needed most by a jumper is not for extension of the push-off leg, but to prevent excessive flexion of the hip and knee during amortization. If excess flexion of the support leg in this stage is prevented, then the final phase of the take-off, the push-off, is executed successfully.

The reason for this is that in this phase the external forces acting on the jumper's body are substantially decreased and the extensors begin to contract and return to their initial state just as all elastic bodies do. Keep in mind that the muscles are very elastic and resilient and when they are stretched and tensed they exhibit great forces to return to the original state.

Thus, the key in plyometrics is to get a maximum eccentric contraction, which develops maximal tensing of the muscle, and then to have the central nervous system switch this contraction to concentric, which produces the desired movement. Keep in mind that the force developed during the eccentric contraction is greater than what can be generated volitionally. This is so because plyometrics maximizes the limit viscoelastic properties inherent at the time of actin and myosin binding within the muscle's structure.

As mentioned previously, in a volitional contraction it takes approximately six- to eight-tenths of a second to achieve a maximal contraction. However, in sports the entire skill is accomplished in most cases between one- and two-tenths of a second. For example, a sprinter's foot is in contact with the ground for only one-tenth of a second. A high jumper using the Fosbury technique has his foot in contact with the ground approximately two-tenths of a second. Thus, the key to get a maximally explosive push-off is to have the muscles respond with maximal force in the shortest amount of time. This can only be done by first getting a strong eccentric contraction, which must then be converted to a concentric contraction in the shortest amount of time.

5

THE FEEDBACK LOOP

Let's take it from the top. I can't apologize for the complexity of the human body, fellow iron freaks, so bear with me and learn: In all the world of strength, the one technique that holds most potential for improving strength output is through altering the sensitivity of the Golgi tendon organ.

The Golgi tendon organ (so named for its discoverer) is a tiny threadlike receptor located at the juncture of muscle and tendon. Its job is to detect stress or tension from the contracting muscle. When the tension is too great—based on your "motor memory" of previous attempts at lifting that weight—a message is sent to the muscle to shut down.

So, a "feedback loop" exists, a system of neuronal wiring designed to protect you from hurting yourself by lifting too much. Mother Nature, in her infinite wisdom, built this protective mechanism a bit too sensitive, however.

Shutdown occurs too soon for most people. There's a buffer zone that's overly conservative.

Remember the stories, many of which are documented, of the mother, in a moment of panic, lifting a crashed car off her pinned child? Where did that super strength come from? Normally she couldn't have budged that heavy car!

Scientists don't know for sure exactly what happens that gives one such immense strength. However, the best bet at this point is that somehow, the Golgi tendon organ's inhibitory message was prevented

FIGURE 5-1

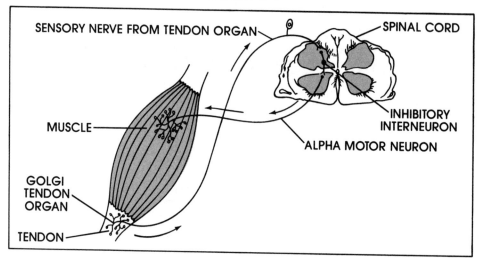

Figure 5-1: The Golgi tendon Organ and the Feedback Loop. Excessive tension or stretch in a muscle activates the Golgi apparatus, which in turn causes a reflex inhibition of that muscle. Follow the arrow, and you'll see the feedback loop. Too much tension and the muscle shuts down. The excitation threshold of the Golgi tendon organ—the "shutdown threshold"—can be altered through proper training.

FIGURE 5-2

THE CONSERVATIVE SHUTDOWN THRESHOLD

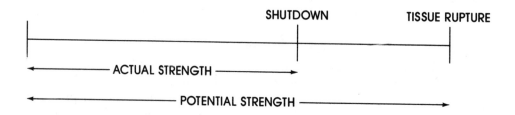

from ever completing its loop back to the muscle. Somewhere, there's a built-in scrambler operating outside the realm of immediate or voluntary functioning.

Panic brought it to the surface.

Can this involuntary strength potential be tapped on a voluntary basis? No one knows, but I suspect so. The answer to this puzzle will yield record performances in every known sport. In the meantime, however, there is a way of pushing the excitation threshold back enough so that far greater strength is indeed possible.

BALLISTIC TRAINING

The question must be asked, "How can I make my tendons thicker? What kind of training—stress application—will make my tendons

BALLISTIC TRAINING TECHNIQUES

Bounce Benches: Lower the weight to within a few inches of your chest, then let it free-fall onto your chest and explode it upward again. Repeat for the required reps and sets (usually about 4–5 reps and 4–5 sets)

Bounce Squats: Follow precisely the same procedure as described above for bounce benches. However, much care must be taken not to free-fall into the rock-bottom position too severely, as your knees are fragile.

Bounce Deadlifts: Again, the same procedure is followed while performing deadlifts as used in benches and squats.

Tendon Jerks: Simply reach down and grab the bar, and without lifting it from the floor repeatedly jerk at it as if attempting to lift it.

The ballistic shock being absorbed by your connective tissue will, over time, induce new growth to the tendons, thereby making them thicker. Just be sure to use these techniques in moderation.

grow?" The answer lies in ballistic training.

Carefully controlled application of jerky movements against your tendons will make tendons respond by growing thicker. Consider this: If your tendon is thicker, its tensile strength is increased. If its tensile strength is greater, it'll take more tension to set off the inhibitory signal. Therefore, greater strength can be displayed without shut-down taking place. Also, unknown changes are thought to occur within the central nervous system (specifically the hypothalamus) that somehow alters the sensitivity of negative feedback levels.

Of course, ballistic training can be dangerous if practiced indiscriminately or too early in your training cycle. It must only be done for a few sessions per month, and only after several months of foundational training.

Above are a few techniques that I've used both in my training and in the training of athletes with whom I've worked over the past few years. The results have been great.

I have been accused by many conservatives of being stupidly extreme in my training techniques. My stupidity, I am told, will invariably lead to unnecessary down time from either direct injury or severe overtraining.

So they say.

In all the years I've been training this way, I have neither been injured nor seen injury happen from ballistic training. I readily admit to its potential harmfulness. You must be careful—don't overdo it. Keep the sessions short, and only for a few weeks at most, preferably right near the end of your training cycle.

Over the years—and I do mean years—there will be a gradual thickening of connective tissue, and an attendant improvement in strength resulting from an augmented shutdown threshold.

6

PAIN TOLERANCE

Vince Lombardi was a dinosaur by today's standards of excellence. He became famous for many of the things he had to say about sports and competition. One phrase that comes to mind is "Fatigue makes cowards of us all." Phooey! I spit on fatigue! Fatigue is the spark that ignites. It is the means to greatness. It is the vehicle to success. Fatigue only makes cowards of the uncommitted!

Fatigue, especially from lactic acid buildup, causes pain. Don't mistake that kind of pain with the kind resulting from injury. I could go on and on with clichés: "No pain, no gain." Or, how about this old standby: "When the going gets tough, the tough get going." All, by my reckoning, fall in the "gimme a break" category.

Let's set the parameters for this discourse on pain. First, there would be no such thing as sport without the existence of pain. Without risk there could be no sport. Since no sport is thoroughly safe, pain must be expected. Whether you *cope* with it or not is your business. Me? I choose to *totally dominate* the situation.

There are means at your disposal that will allow you to dominate, to *use* pain rather than be *subjugated* by it. By mastering pain, by improving your ability to dominate your pain sensations, you will have allowed yourself to gain a much greater measure of strength.

That's right. Pain intolerance limits strength output. Don't you doubt it. Whether you're a wimp or a macho man, pain will bring you to your knees. Pain will make you stop pushing and cry for mercy. It'll make you cease your set and put the weight back on the rack.

Coping with pain is shortsighted, because in the philosophy of sport there is no room for coping strategies. Coping, by definition, means that you are the underdog. You must learn to dominate *all* situations, and your pain tolerance level is of utmost importance in your dominance. Question is, how do you become stronger by dominating pain?

TYPES OF PAIN

There are three broad categories of pain that athletes must expect to face: the pain of extreme effort, the pain of extreme fatigue, and the pain of injury. The first two are a part and parcel of sport, while the third constitutes the element of risk spoken of above. It is the third that we try to eliminate, although its omnipresence is nonetheless cherished and preserved. The other two we just try and put up with despite the discomforts associated with them.

Indeed, the first two are typically thought of as signals to athletes that adaptive stress is being delivered to their bodies, and are therefore positive in their respective displeasure.

This is not always the case. In fact, it is one of the greatest hoaxes in the world of sports and has led to monumentally stupid practices, which collectively have tended to severely reduce the potential for muscular gains.

Consider that postexercise muscle soreness has always been thought of by athletes as the "signal" for development in the location of the painful sensation. All of us have experienced it at one time or another. Indeed, most of you have probably actively attempted to induce it, as if it were the proper way to train.

Most up-to-date scientists realize that postexercise soreness stems from the release of a biochemical called *hydroxyproline* from torn connective tissue. This substance causes the localized pain you experience the following day. It is not a signal of localized development as so many believe. And it is not to be sought after. It is to be avoided because it is, in the long term, counterproductive to your training goals.

Such connective tissue damage is called "microtrauma," and cumulative microtrauma can cause a limiting of your growth potential due to adhesions and tissue scarring. Microtrauma, if left to accumulate over time, becomes *macro*trauma and can cause major injury.

In a very real sense, cumulative microtrauma, and therefore, postexercise muscle soreness, falls into the third category of pain. While it is a result of extreme effort, and often associated with extreme fatigue, it is still injury. An analogy will illustrate what I mean.

If you rub your hands on a rough surface long enough, one of two things will happen. Either you'll develop callouses (a positive adaptive response) or you'll get blisters (a destructive process). One is adaptive growth, the other is injury from too much stress. Similarly, postexercise soreness signals injury, and is an example of a destructive process much the same as blisters are.

The key to avoiding the blisters and getting callouses instead is to know exactly how much pressure to apply and how long it is to be applied. In sports the task is the same. How much stress and how long to apply it are the art and science of our sport.

The belief that your efforts have been in vain unless you experience postexercise soreness has been responsible for yet another very damaging myth in sports. That is the belief that you can shape an individual muscle. You can't do that, and you're wasting time if you try. More importantly, you're backsliding if you seek postexercise soreness as a signal that your funky exercise movements are working.

For example, take the simple bench press movement. With a close grip you feel pain the next day along the origin (the sternum), but with a wide grip you'll experience a mild postexercise soreness out near the tie-in (axillary region), or the outer pecs.

Your illogical conclusion is that wide grip benches are good for developing the outer pecs, and the close grip benches are good for developing the inner pecs. The different pain locations merely signal the fact that mechanical stress in the respective areas was too great, and that microtrauma was inflicted, causing a release of hydroxyproline in the area.

The same reasoning can be applied to Scott curls versus incline curls, or twisting movement curls versus hammer curls. If your bicep has a gap between it and the forearm, there's nothing you can ever do about it. If your bicep is short, it's short. If it's long, it's long. All you can ever hope to do is develop it as fully as possible, accounting for how it "fits" in comparison to other body parts for maximum aesthetic appeal overall by variably developing each body part accordingly. You cannot alter your genetic predisposition for an individual muscle's shape potential.

A SIMPLE SOLUTION TO PAIN

Let's get back to pain in training. How much pain is good? Can you learn to overcome pain? How can you distinguish "good" pain from destructive pain? What about the "no pain, no gain" approach?

Often, cumulative microtrauma will cause movement-limiting adhesions. These same adhesions account for your inability to put on expected muscular size because the muscle cells are literally "bound" together so strongly that outward growth is severely restricted.

Dr. Gary Glum, founding director of the Institute for Neuromuscular Reeducation in Los Angeles, has developed a technique to rid you of these strength-, size-, and flexibility-limiting adhesions. Find a therapist who is skilled at this remarkable therapeutic technique and use his services at least twice yearly.

Of course, the best way to approach this problem is to avoid post-exercise soreness in the first place. To do this, simply approach your training a bit more scientifically. Remember that using too much weight or too many reps and sets is not good in any sport endeavor. The worst training practice in causing overstress is negative movements, or eccentric muscle contracture.

A hot postworkout whirlpool and a vigorous cross-fiber muscle massage following it are also excellent therapies. However, remember that all these techniques can do is prevent or minimize the discomfort associated with tissue damage. Only scientific training can prevent the damage from occurring in the first place.

Injuries, once healed, often leave nerve endings entrapped in the scar tissue that forms. The result is pain upon movement. It is called "useless" pain, because it doesn't serve a useful function insofar as warning you of impending tissue damage is concerned. Again, neuromuscular reeducation is extremely beneficial in treating this kind of common problem. So too is flexibility training, particularly dynamic flexibility training and proprioceptive neuromuscular facilitation (PNF) stretching. (Another more understandable term for PNF stretching is "partner resistance stretching.")

Various injuries can cause chronic pain. This kind of pain is often very debilitating to your training, and should be dealt with. There are several ways of dealing with chronic pain:

- *Mental Rehearsal.* By performing a movement perfectly, you can effectively eliminate often unwanted, pain-producing movements.
- *Progressive Relaxation.* By alternately relaxing and contracting each individual muscle, especially the painful area, you can learn to minimize the amount of involvement (and therefore, the amount of pain it causes) of that muscle.
- *Systematic Desensitization.* A painful muscle often makes you cower upon having to perform a movement that involves the use of that muscle. By systematically performing the steps you must go through to accomplish the movement, you can make the movement more automatic and thereby reduce the pain.
- *Transcutaneous Electrical Nerve Stimulation.* Called TENS or TNS (transcutaneous electrical nerve stimulation), this electrical stimulation technique "tricks" your brain into feeling no pain by effectively blocking that specific neural signal from going to the brain.
- *Ultrasound.* Sound waves of specific frequencies stimulate blood flow to a muscle, blood vessels open, and extracellular fluid is removed, thereby helping a muscle to relax.
- *Rest, ice, compression, and elevation (RICE).* Of course, this should be your first approach to any sort of chronic pain

associated with injury. Rest gives injuries a chance to heal, and ice reduces inflammation and swelling as do elevation and compression.

FATIGUE AND COWARDICE

Perhaps the most common form of pain to lifters and other athletes is the pain of intense effort and fatigue—the first two classes of pain mentioned earlier. Take note of these important distinctions between the different sources of pain. Pain isn't limited to the mental and physical anguish of injury.

The pain associated with effort or fatigue can, and often does, become debilitating. Such pain becomes a signal that you're pushing too hard, leads you to believe that you're in trouble, and becomes an anxiety-provoking experience, thereby increasing muscle tension, heart rate, respiratory distress, and sensitivity to painful training. This vicious cycle perpetuates anxiety, and your training can become a nightmare. Eventually you quit in sheer terror of the task before you. Maybe Vince was right.

While the methods cited immediately above are helpful in combating this sort of cycle, the responsibility is ultimately yours: Do you want to succeed badly enough to endure the pain? Are you willing to make the sacrifice? Do you realize that such pain can actually be used to your advantage? Do you understand the difference between adaptive stress and injury-provoking stress? Do you have the will to exceed the bounds imposed on you by convention?

To acquire these traits, you must first acquire passion.

7

HYPERPLASIA: MUSCLE SPLITTING

For years scientists told us that genetic endowment alone would determine the number of muscle cells each of us would ever have and that we could do nothing to increase that number. Now, they're not so sure.

Imagine the possibilities: More muscle cells! Bigger muscles! Perhaps, but perhaps not. Let's take a closer look.

WHAT IS HYPERPLASIA?

During the late sixties and early seventies, European scientists discovered that the muscle cells of some animals adapted to severe overload by splitting in two. This compensatory response is called *hyperplasia* and is generally accompanied by increases in the size of the surrounding muscle cells that didn't split.

Needless to say, this discovery rocked the scientific community back on its heels. Subsequent research during the early and mid-seventies revealed the exact mechanisms that cause hyperplasia, but to this day scientists have been unable to determine conclusively whether such muscle cell splitting can occur in humans.

THE MECHANISMS OF HYPERPLASIA

As an athlete you are no doubt aware that slow movements are a major source of the size-building stimulus in most training regimens.

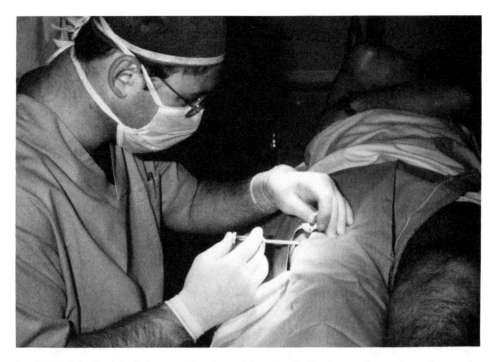

Dr. Bill Laich, Sports Science Director at the Craft Center, pulls a plug of muscle from an athlete's vastus lateralis muscle. The plug will be frozen, sliced, and stained for electron microscopic scrutiny.

ISO-tension movements, peak contraction movements, continuous tension movements, and heavy-duty training methods all require relatively slow contraction from the working muscles. The results of such training are what we all refer to as *hypertrophy*—an increase in the size or quantity of various muscle components without an increase in the overall size of muscle cells.

According to some recent studies, however, by engaging strictly in hypertrophy training, you may be robbing yourself of the very stimulus that can promote hyperplasia.

A group of scientists working under the direction of Swedish exercise physiologist W. J. Gonyea discovered that a cat's muscle cells would undergo hyperplasia only if the cat were involved in a weight-training program that incorporated both high-speed and high-tension exercises.

So how does this relate to you as an athlete? No one really knows, but some interesting possibilities exist. Some studies have used the electron microscope to observe the structural changes in muscle cells after exercise. This technique requires a *biopsy*—taking a plug of muscle tissue, freezing it, then slicing it super thin for microscopic examination. The typical hypertrophied muscle shows not only larger individual cells but a closer packing of the cells.

Champion swimmers' deltoids were scrutinized by electron microscopy, and the findings of that study stand to this day as the most compelling argument for the occurrence of hyperplasia in humans. While the swimmers' total muscle size was obviously greater than the average person's, the individual cells comprising their deltoids were smaller and more numerous.

The empirical conclusion that can be drawn from this startling fact is that hyperplasia took place in the deltoid muscles, giving them greater overall size and strength.

Why the split cells did not achieve the level of hypertrophy possible in unsplit cells remains, for the moment, an intriguing mystery. Some scientists speculate that this inability to achieve a hypertrophied state results from each cell having only half the number of nuclei it had before splitting. The cells' nuclei regulate virtually all their many functions, including their potential for growth.

WHAT CAN WE LEARN FROM ANIMAL RESEARCH?

Cats, rats, and other animals are different from humans in some very important ways. For example, have you ever seen a heavily muscled rat? With few exceptions, lower animals are incapable of developing the kind of muscle hypertrophy that humans can. It seems quite possible that compensatory cell splitting is the animals' unique way of adapting to the stress of overload training.

Forget size for a moment and consider speed of muscle contraction. Rarely will you see a slow cat! Animals that display capabilities of muscle hyperplasia are generally faster afoot and in reaction time than humans, a fact that can be explained by comparing differences in the anatomy and the chemical makeup of cells between the respective species.

Rats, for example, have 11 different kinds of muscle cells, as opposed to four in humans. On the basis of cell variety alone, the possibilities of speed of movement and contraction, reaction time, endurance, and other muscle functions are probably much greater in such animals than in humans.

These differences notwithstanding, the swimmers' deltoid study comes out more intriguing than ever! Is it possible to get those split cells to grow larger? If so, has that muscle's size potential increased in proportion to the increased cell count? And what about the strength factor? Judging from the increased performance capabilities of the swimmers, hyperplasia seems to account for increases in all three areas of muscle function!

HOW CAN ATHLETES PROMOTE CELL SPLITTING?

Whether hyperplasia occurred in the swimmers' deltoids remains speculation at present. Conclusive evidence of hyperplasia taking

> ## TIPS FOR THE EXPERIMENT-ORIENTED ATHLETE
> - Hyperplasia, the splitting of muscle cells, may be a reality for humans, but present bodybuilding methods apparently don't promote it.
> - Laboratory animal studies, together with research on champion swimmers, suggest that high-speed/high-tension exericse is the only way to promote hyperplasia.
> - While high-tension/slow-speed movements make the muscle bigger, they also tend to make it slower in contraction speed.
> - Hyperplasia does not occur in laboratory animals engaged in high-tension/slow-speed training.
> - It is unknown whether hyperplasia can increase the ultimate potential for a muscle's size in humans or if it can even take place in humans in the first place.
> - To derive the benefits of potential hyperplasia, you should incorporate both traditional muscle building exercises as well as compensatory acceleration training, which requires explosive movements against heavy resistance.

place in human muscles will come only when scientists can observe the process actually happening. For now, though, the empirical evidence at least is promising.

Animal studies have clearly shown that hyperplasia can take place only if there is both sufficient intensity as well as speed of movement. Unlike the average bodybuilder, who performs primarily slow-speed exercises, swimmers engage in relatively fast movements against both weighted resistance (when they are training with weights) as well as the natural resistance of the water. Since biopsies of bodybuilders' muscles have not shown the same structural alterations resulting from imposed stress as swimmers' muscles, it seems reasonable to conclude that if hyperplasia did indeed take place in the swimmers' deltoids, it was a result of their specialized training.

While slow movements with heavy weights made laboratory animals bigger, such exercise also tended to result in slower muscle contraction. No cell splitting was observed under these conditions. When the animals were forced to move quickly with the heavy weights, however, both size and speed were dramatically increased and cell splitting occurred.

If you want to maximize your chances of promoting hyperplasia, the evidence suggests that high-speed training is the only way to do it. There are many components to a muscle cell. Most have the potential to develop in size and number, but only in response to highly specific overload. Your job as an athlete is to determine exactly what kind of stress to apply to your muscles to promote development in the precise manner for your sport.

There's no doubt that you will find, just as I have over the years, that a great *variety* of training methods must be incorporated to maximize muscle development. Promoting hyperplasia may become a part of the answer for some athletes of the future. But for now this interesting phenomenon remains only a possibility, leaving the old-standby methods of hypertrophy training your primary concern.

8

TIES THAT BIND

Moving heavy iron is more than tough. It's dangerous. In my quest for world records, I blew both my rotator cuffs. The cuff, a group of four relatively small, but important, shoulder muscles that control inward and outward rotation of the humerus, is particularly vulnerable to the kind of trauma gymnastics, weightlifting, and powerlifting inflict.

I was involved in all three at one time. Now, mercifully, I only powerlift. That's because that is all I *can* do now. My rotator cuff muscles, now hanging on precariously, would never make it through another German giant on the high bar or another limit snatch.

For the first several years of my exclusive career in powerlifting, I couldn't bench too well. I didn't want to, frankly, because I didn't want to get cut on again. I had lost most of my range of motion in both shoulders, and was unable to perform even a simple maneuver like pulling my wallet out of my hip pocket—handy in restaurants.

Then I met Dr. Gary Glum. As editor-in-chief of *Sports Fitness* magazine, I was on a constant lookout for exciting, new angles for stories. Glum had a thing going he called neuromuscular reeducation. The bodybuilders and elite athletes I trained were literally raving about Glum's treatments. I figured I'd pay the guy a visit. Perhaps a story would come of it.

I brought a registered physical therapist of some reknown with me to interview Dr. Glum. Dr. Jeff Everson (now editor-in-chief of *Muscle & Fitness* magazine) had a ruptured pectoral muscle that needed care. With a degree in physical therapy, and years of in-the-trenches experience under his belt, Everson was an apt guinea pig for Glum's handiwork.

I mean, what did I know about the new chiropractic? My degree is in exercise science, with no experience in caring for injured people. Little did I realize that Glum had taken chiropractic to a level previously only dreamed about. He was into all those things that normal chiropractic physicians were into, but he was also into making it possible for elite athletes to achieve peak athletic performance capabilities as well.

I watched as he worked on Everson. "Holy ——!" Everson cried. "What the hell you doin' to me?"

Glum wasn't reassuring at all. "Quit griping!" he muttered. "The proof will be in the pudding." He continued to do his thing on the skeptical Everson. Me? I wasn't impressed at all, either.

Then the treatment was over. Relieved beyond words, Everson dragged his beaten body off Glum's torture rack. His range of motion was greatly improved and he felt much stronger.

"It feels much better!" Everson offered.

Now Everson is a trained scientist. I decided to give this guy another test—this time on me. If Everson was impressed, I reasoned, then I should at least listen.

The next week found me on the same couch upon which Everson sweated so impressively.

I didn't make the same mistake Everson did though. I brought a bullet to bite on. I subjected myself to Glum's gloom. I got up. My rotator cuffs—I have zippers atop both shoulders to prove it—had been very limited in range of motion and strength. After Glum's NMR treatment, my ROM was 100%. I went home and bench pressed 30 pounds more than I had ever done before. 30 pounds! Do you know what that means to a competing athlete? Two hard years of advanced training can't put that much on your benching strength!

Over the next several months, I dug as much information as I could from Glum and his partner and co-developer of NMR, Joe Horrigan. These guys were really on to something revolutionary.

WHAT IS NEUROMUSCULAR REEDUCATION?

Over years of hard training, microtrauma build up and build up, becoming macrotrauma. Minute scarring takes place between muscle cells and can severely limit both range of motion and contracture strength.

In my own case, scarring from the rotator cuff operations had been so severe that my ROM and strength were severely limited. In fact, any movement close to my limit of flexibility resulted in severe pain stemming from nerve endings that had become entrapped in the scar tissue.

In short, I was operating far below my potential. Most athletes who

Neuromuscular reeducation (NMR), a system of soft-tissue and neuronal stimulation developed by Dr. Gary Glum (shown), is unbelievably taxing. Note the elbow pressure! It works.

have trained for years are operating under the same limitations. Adhesions and scar tissue contribute to loss of strength, flexibility, and skill.

Neuromuscular reeducation removes all (or most of) these range-limiting adhesions and breaks up scar tissue. In a sense, NMR is similar to rolfing, a form of sports massage. However, NMR goes far beyond this age-old technique.

The technique involves reestablishing appropriate motor control over your movement patterns which are, upon completion of the NMR treatment, considerably different than they were. After months or years of performing sport skills with your strength and movement patterns disrupted by adhesions and scar tissue, your motor patterns adjust to these disruptions. Once they're removed, you have what is essentially a "new" body, with far different movement capabilities than previously noticed. Your motor memory—how you attempt to perform your sports skills—needs to be altered to accommodate your new-found strength and ROM.

Therein lies the true value of NMR. Let me give you one typical example of how NMR works. Let's take a baseball player. His eye/hand coordination is honed to a fine edge over the years. He can hit the ball well, batting over .300. Rotator cuff problems, which are common in baseball, have been hampering his hitting and throwing for several agonizing months.

He has three options: (1) get cut, (2) use various modalities (such as ultrasound, rolfing, or just plain rest), and (3) NMR.

The first option, surgery, would lay him up for months. He'd have a difficult time reestablishing his former skill level, if ever. His ROM would never fully return under most typical rehab programs following rotator cuff surgery, and he'd be catapulted back to the minors or cut, in the other, more final sense of the word.

The second option often helps, but only temporarily. If the cuff is damaged, there's little that will restore it in any permanent fashion. This player would be hampered over the remainder of his career with recurring bouts of pain. Indeed, his career would most probably be terminated prematurely.

With NMR, however, it is possible to restore ROM and eliminate shoulder pain immediately. Simple impingement from too much tissue inside the shoulder capsule causes a lot of pain. And small tears or strains in any of the rotator cuff muscles will only get worse over time. NMR can both eliminate impingement and restore damaged tissue. Most often, cuff problems stem from an array of tissue scarring and adhesions throughout the entire shoulder joint complex. There are over a dozen muscles involved, and if all of them are affected, the net result is often felt in the cuff.

By removing the source of the problem, rather than treating only the symptoms, cuff problems can often be eliminated permanently. Our baseball player would experience immediate relief of the pain, and have his skill at batting and throwing left intact by the immediate readjustment of his motor control mechanisms to his newfound strength and range of motion.

Now I see Glum regularly. At age 46, I'm supposed to feel the effects of years spent under heavy iron. I don't feel any ill effects at all, and in fact feel far better than I ever did while competing in weightlifting or gymnastics.

I reckon I can continue for a few more decades.

9

ANAEROBIC POWER

Everyone knows what "aerobics" means. All the pencilnecks chime in, "with oxygen!" Proudly they strut around with socks down around their ankles (calves too small to support them) and new Reeboks. "We're in shape!"

But except for a gym-hardened few, the word "anaerobics" has little meaning to people, except for a possible fleeting cognition relating to "opposite of aerobics." Yet, did you ever stop and reflect upon the fact that virtually 95% of everything you do in your life is anaerobic?

So how come so much emphasis is given to aerobics? The ol' ticker, my friend, your heart. Little else is improved through aerobics, though, and whatever lifestyle benefits accrue from the tedium of aerobic training are beyond me. But, as you know, I'm into hard-core *power. Mass.* No skin-tight leotards for this iron freak!

Enough sarcasm—I don't mean to debate the relative merits of aerobic training and aerobic conditioning. What I'd like to do instead is discuss the benefits of improving your *anaerobic* fitness. Who knows? Maybe I'll start a whole new fad! Imagine! Generations of li'l iron pumpers! The joggers will be looked upon as strange for a change.

ANAEROBIC POWER

Let's get real specific for a moment, and define in more exact terms what I mean by anaerobic power.

55

ENERGETICS OF ANAEROBIC AND AEROBIC PATHWAYS

The energy for muscular contraction is derived from ATP (adenosine triphosphate). As contraction continues, the stores of this organic compound are broken down to produce inorganic compounds and energy (ATP → ADP + P + E). This is the energy used for contraction. However, these ATP stores are quickly depleted, and another organic compound called *creatine phosphate* (CP) is broken down so that the energy released in its breakdown can combine with the ADP to resynthesize ATP for additional energy for contraction. This reaction is summarized as follows: CP → C + P + E. Again, however, this process cannot continue, because the CP is also quickly depleted. At this point, glycogen is broken down to yield the energy required to replenish the stores of creatine phosphate (CP) so that it can in turn be broken down to resynthesize ATP. As the glycogen is broken down, lactic acid and energy are released. It would now appear that the process is complete; that is, the organic phosphates are continuously resynthesized. The stores of glycogen are also being depleted, however, and lactic acid, a waste product that retards contraction, is accumulating as a result of the glycogen breakdown. The equilibrium of this process, therefore, is not maintained; if it were, muscular contraction could last only about 30 seconds due to the buildup of lactic acid and the depletion of glycogen. Thus far in the process, no oxygen has been used to produce contraction. Therefore, the process to this point is referred to as the *anaerobic* glycolytic pathway.

Oxygen being introduced into the process allows two more chemical reactions to occur. Oxygen combines with about one-fifth of the built-up lactic acid to produce energy. This energy is used by the liver to convert the remaining four-fifths of the lactic acid back into glycogen. The water and carbon dioxide produced in the first reaction are passed off via the circulatory system and expelled by the lungs during normal breathing. The entire chain is summarized in the figure below. It should be clearly understood, however, that both the processes summarized here and in the figure are just that—summaries. The reader is directed to any good exercise physiology text for the complete group of reactions that occur. The portion of the reactions summarized that involve the utilization of oxygen is called the aerobic pathway. Work can now continue indefinitely, provided that sufficient oxygen is present to interact with the lactic acid.

As work becomes progressively intense, and the circulatory system becomes incapable of supplying sufficient oxygen to oxidize the lactic acid, fatigue sets in. A buildup of less than a few tenths of 1% of the lactic acid concentration in a muscle results in muscular pain and a cessation of contraction. This fatigue is the most commonly experienced type, and is normally accompanied by an *oxygen debt*. Expressing it another way, the amount of oxygen it would take to oxidize the built-up lactic acid is "owed" to the system, and one's "tolerance" for an accumulated debt is generally proportional to his aerobic fitness. More will be said on this subject later, specifically with regard to other mechanisms involved in fatigue.

1. Organic Phosphate $\rightarrow$ Inorganic Phosphate + Organic Phsophate + Energy
      ATP $\longrightarrow$ P   +   ADP   + Energy
   (Adenosine   (Phosphate)   (Adenosine
   Triphosphate)   Di-Phosphate)

2. Organic Phosphate + Organic Phosphate $\rightarrow$ Organic Phosphate + Organic Mineral
     CP   +   ADP $\longrightarrow$ ATP   +   C
   (Creatine   (Adenosine   (Adenosine   (Creatine)
   Phosphate)   Di-Phosphate)   Tri-Phosphate)

3. Glycogen $\rightarrow$ Lactic Acid + Energy for resynthesis of CP
        (i.e., for putting 'P' from 1 and 'C' from 2 back together)

4. Organic Mineral + Inorganic Phosphate + Energy $\rightarrow$ Organic Phosphate
    C   +   P   + Energy $\longrightarrow$ CP

5. 1/5 Lactic Acid + O_2 $\rightarrow$ CO_2 + H_2O + Energy for resynthesis of remainder
                     Lactic Acid

6. 4/5 Lactic Acid + Energy (from 5) + O_2 $\rightarrow$ Glycogen

During high intensity training your energy requirements are met in large part by metabolic processes that do not require oxygen consumption. Thus, the ability of your muscles to consume adenosine triphosphate (ATP) begins to exceed that of the aerobic mechanism. In other words, your oxygen delivery system is limited in its ability to bring oxygen to the working muscles, so other metabolic processes must take up the energy slack.

In the process of anaerobic work (work that takes place without the presence of sufficient oxygen) a tremendous oxygen "debt" is incurred.

The phosphagens (ATP and creatine phosphate—CP for short) are the immediate sources of anaerobic energy. However, the phosphagen pool is very limited, and can only sustain (at best) a brief anaerobic burst of muscle contracture. Anaerobic energy must come from some other source. That's anaerobic glycolysis.

So far, the above discourse is pretty straightforward. Easily understood by any dedicated iron freak, right? But to understand where most of your anaerobic energy comes from you'll have to understand this concept of anaerobic glycolysis far more fully.

Energy During Maximum Muscle Contracture

How long does an average maximum lift take? Maybe two or three seconds, right? Well, by the time you've maximally tested your muscle's strength of contracture for one brief second, you're already into the third stage of muscle energetics—the glycolysis stage (see accompanying sidebar on page 56.

Within 1.26 seconds, for example, 80% of your muscle's ATP is derived from CP degradation (step #2 in sidebar), and 20% from anaerobic glycolysis (step #3 in sidebar). And, by the time your muscle has contracted for a period of 2.52 seconds, fully 50% of your ATP comes from anaerobic glycolysis (Eric Hultman & Hans Sjöholm, 1983).

By the time you've contracted maximally for six seconds, your power output has begun to decrease despite the fact that your muscle's CP content is still at least 65% of its basal level. Continuing beyond six seconds, your CP content diminishes, your ATP diminishes, and acidosis, the buildup of lactic acid, begins to severely hinder work.

It's pretty obvious, then, that your inability to generate maximum muscle power after six seconds or so stems from a multiplicity of factors rather than from a depletion of any single energy source.

Anaerobic Power Defined

Anaerobic power, then, can be defined in lay terms as your ability to continue to perform maximum muscle contracture over time. Fatigue, the mortal enemy of athletes not capable of withstanding severe oxygen debt and the metabolic corollaries, is often very misunderstood in this regard. Fatigue used to be thought of as a decrease in intracellular pH resulting from lactate accumulation (Hill & Kupalov, 1929). Not necessarily. By 1970, the view was that decreased creatine phosphate (step #2 in the sidebar) was the main contributory factor in fatigue, limiting maximum force output (Spande & Schottelius, 1970).

More recently, with the aid of nuclear magnetic resonance imaging techniques, it was discovered that a decrease in a muscle's tension-producing ability was directly proportional to increases in hydrogen ions and of free ADP (a metabolic byproduct of ATP degradation—

step #1 in sidebar) rather than resulting from either lactate concentrations or CP content (Dawson, Gadian & Wilke, 1978).

Two Swedes, Eric Hultman and Hans Sjöholm, reporting their research at the International Symposium on Human Muscle Power (McMaster University, Hamilton, Ontario, 1984), believe that anaerobic power—the ability to continue maximal work—stems from several factors, including: decreased ratio between ATP and ADP, decreased muscle pH, and depletion of ATP (by as much as 60%). The biochemical processes that bring about fatigue, according to Hultman and Sjoholm, are the formation and breakdown of the muscles' actin-myosin cross-bridges.

The cross-bridges are activated by the breakdown of ATP molecules. ATP breaks down into ADP and P, giving off energy in the process. It's that released energy that ultimately causes the cross-bridges on the actin-myosin myofibrils to "contract." Muscle contracture, then, is a result of thousands of microscopic cross-bridges grabbing, releasing, and regrabbing their way across one another, causing the actin and myosin to "slide" across one another.

Cross-bridging is stopped by (to repeat):

1. A lowering of your intramuscular pH—your cellular environment becomes too acidic from the buildup of lactic acid. Lactic acid inhibits other enzymes within the cell that are supposed to assist in the energy transfer system of the cell.
2. The regeneration of ATP is slowed below a critical threshold necessary to maintain contracture. You're using up your ATP too quickly during intense muscle contracture for resynthesized ATP to be effective in maintaining contracture.

HOW CAN YOU IMPROVE YOUR ANAEROBIC POWER?

Mind you, all of these enzymatic reactions are taking place in seconds. Pushing heavy weights for 8–10 reps and 5–6 sets (for example) reduces your intracellular environment to a junkpile of metabolic wastes and enzymatic poisons.

The critical question for all anaerobic athletes is whether there is a way of improving their anaerobic power. There is. You can delay the processes involved in fatigue, and you can speed the recovery process markedly by following these suggestions:

- Pay attention to your mineral balances, especially your calcium/magnesium and sodium/potassium ratios.
- Ensure that you've adopted a long-term commitment to sound nutrition, as it is only over time that you can achieve efficiency in intramuscular energetics.
- Use branched-chain amino acids to assist in maintenance of an

adequate amino acid pool (blood-borne aminos) for protein turnover during and following training.

- Inosine is known to activate enzyme activity (specifically, pyruvic acid) allowing cellular activity to progress until more ATP can be biosynthesized.
- By far the most important way to improve anaerobic power, however, is to engage in high-intensity training of the white (fast-twitch) muscle fibers. That's where most of the enzymatic activity is taking place, and where your anaerobic powers are the greatest.
- The use of buffers, alkaline substances, to reduce your blood acidity can assist in improving anaerobic power, especially in untrained or out-of-shape athletes. The longstanding buffer of choice is baking soda (sodium bicarbonate).
- Substances that scavenge ammonia (a toxic by-product inside muscle cells) appear to assist in rapid recovery both during and following intense training/competition.
- Kinotherapy—active rest during the recovery phase following intense training—causes a compensatory effect in the fatigued centers of the central nervous system. Simply exercise antagonistic muscles mildly during rest periods (e.g., electrical stimulation on triceps following a biceps workout).
- Massage therapy, performed properly, can facilitate recovery in several ways, such as by reactivating peripheral circulation, decreasing muscle tension, and eliminating toxins.
- Several other techniques can help, such as oxygen therapy, chemotherapy, psychological therapy, acupressure, ultrasound, and a host of other potentially rejuvenating techniques.

Highly trained athletes are known to be capable of tolerating lactate levels as much as 30% higher than untrained individuals. The mechanism presumed to contribute to this improved tolerance is *motivation*. However, it's just as certain that greater ability to improve ATP/ADP ratios, resynthesize ATP, and reduce lactate buildup will contribute to improved anaerobic power as well. That takes high-intensity training supported by sound nutritional practices.

It seems to me that if you're serious about your sports training, you'll begin to get acquainted with your most important attribute— your anaerobic power. It is this attribute that will give you the edge you need in gaining strength. And then you will discover that the true secret to sports training is your ability to *recover*!

REFERENCES

Hill, A. V., and Kupalov, P. (1929). Anaerobic and aerobic activity in isolated muscle. *Proceedings of the Royal Society of London: Series B*, 105, 313–328.

Hultman, E., and Sjöholm, H. (1983a). Energy metabolism and contraction force of human skeletal muscle in situ during electrical stimulation. *Journal of Physiology* (London), 345, 525–532.

Hultman, E. and Sjoholm, H. (1983b). Substrate availability. In H. G. Knuttgen, J. A. Vogel, and J. Poortmans (Eds.), *International Series on Sport Sciences. Biochemistry of Exercise* (Vol. 13, pp. 63–75).

Jones, N. L., McCartney, N. and McComas, A. J. (1986). *Human Muscle Power*, Human Kinetics Publ., Champaign, IL.

Spande, J. I., and Schottelius, B.A. (1970). Chemical basis of fatigue in isolated mouse soleus muscle. *American Journal of Physiology*, 219, 1490–1495.

PART II
CONCEPTS IN STRENGTH TRAINING

10

GETTING STARTED IN A WEIGHT TRAINING PROGRAM

You've made the commitment to excel. You realize that in order to do so, you're going to have to pay the price of discipline. Hard work. Sweat. Long hours in the gym. No time for anything else.

Hold it right there.

Anybody ever hear the phrase, "smart work"?

Sweat, hard work, long hours? Perhaps. Sometimes. But above all, you have to work smartly! That—and *only* that— will assist you in your quest to excel in sports.

To me, working smart means stripping all the less-than-worthwhile exercises from your training regimen. It means *following* a carefully constructed training regimen. It means giving careful attention not only to what you do in the gym, but to how you do it. That goes for your diet as well. What you eat is indeed important, but when you eat it, how much you eat, what you use for supplements, and how you've scheduled your eating and supplementing to match your training intensity over weeks of time all are critical steps toward excellence.

I hope that you'll learn from what follows that strength training is utterly sophisticated. You can't go into a gym and simply pump heavy iron and come out expecting to be appropriately stronger. No indeed! You may have improved your absolute strength or limit strength by doing so, but that form of strength is of little importance to most athletes (except powerlifters). Of far greater importance to you is following the sequential steps outlined several times throughout this book.

You'll notice that Step I involves developing a solid foundation of absolute or limit strength in all of your muscles. Step II asks you to really zero in on those muscles and movements that are of critical importance in your sport and maximize the respective levels of limit strength. Then, Step III requires that you begin concentrating on explosive strength and (finally) starting strength. Steps IV and V involve plyometric exercises and overspeed exercises in order to really "hone" your explosive strength and starting strength to a fine edge within the context of your actual sports skills.

But none of these general instructions tells you exactly what exercises to do, how often to do them, how much weight you should use on the bar, and other practical information.

Moving heavy iron isn't the answer. It's only an initial step toward achieving your sports goals. Don't make the mistake of falling into the musclehead trap of assuming that brute strength equals better sports performance.

DETERMINING YOUR MUSCLES' MAXIMUM FORCE

Your muscles' maximum force capability means how much weight each can move through its range of movement for a single repetition. Competitive weightlifters and powerlifters are the only people who should ever truly test themselves this way. You don't have to, and you shouldn't. It's dangerous.

The chart on page 65 should guide you instead. For example, when you're able to do 10 repetitions with a weight in any exercise, you're probably using in the neighborhood of 80% of your muscle force capability to do so. Or, if you're only able to do five repetitions before your muscle becomes too fatigued to go any farther, you're using approximately 90% of your total strength. The chart is pretty accurate for most people, so don't even bother trying to determine your maximum strength by lifting as much as you can one time. Simply use the chart and then approximate your muscle's total strength from it.

HOW MANY REPS AND SETS SHOULD I DO?

A *repetition* is one movement with the barbell or weight machine. A *set* is a group of repetitions. There is a science behind determining the proper number of reps and sets you should do, and it depends on what your training *goals* are.

Take another look at the chart on page 65. You will see that for each goal (power, size, strength, or endurance) there is a range of repetitions noted. These guidelines are scientifically determined by looking at the changes that occur inside a muscle cell after several weeks of training in a certain way.

DETERMINING YOUR TRAINING INTENSITY PER OBJECTIVE, AND HOW MANY REPETITIONS/SET YOU SHOULD DO

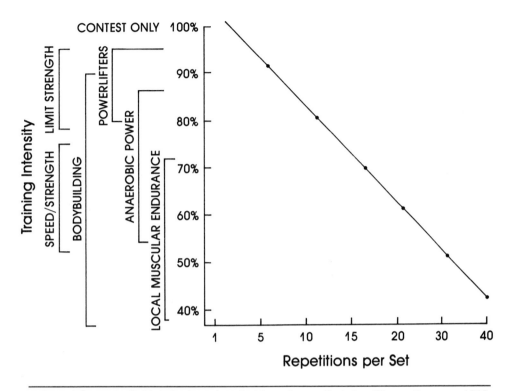

Adapted from Hatfield, F.C. *Complete Guide to Power Training*, Fitness Systems, 1983. Used by permission.

You will notice that high reps with a light weight produces muscle changes related to endurance, whereas lower reps with a heavier weight produces stronger muscles. Bodybuilding, which concentrates on muscle size, is most effectively accomplished with a variety of rep schemes in order to affect a number of cellular changes rather than just one.

When your muscles become too fatigued to accomplish another set at the intensity level noted on the chart above, then you have done the right number of sets. Typically, you will be able to perform three to five sets before you become too fatigued to do another while still maintaining the proper level of intensity (that is, the proper percentage of your maximum).

You should rest for about three to five minutes between sets to allow your muscles to recover a bit and to allow your heart rate to come back down to a manageable level.

For the first few weeks of exercising, you should not try to achieve the guidelines for reps and sets listed. Instead, work into it slowly,

THE PEAKING CYCLE FOR POWER SPORTS

	Cycle One (3-4 weeks)	Cycle Two (3-4 weeks)	Cycle Three (3-4 weeks)	Cycle Four (3-4 Weeks)
I	FOUNDATION TRAINING: OVERCOMING WEAKNESSES (LIMIT STRENGTH)			
II		FUNCTIONAL STRENGTH: SPORT RELATED (LIMIT STRENGTH)		
III			COMPENSATORY ACCELERATION (EXPLOSIVE STRENGTH)	
			BALLISTIC TRAINING (STARTING STRENGTH)	
IV		PLYOMETRIC TRAINING		
		JUMPING/HOPPING	WEIGHTED JUMPS/HOPS	SHOCK
V				OVERSPEED DRILLS

STEPS

LOAD (TONNAGE) PER WORKOUT
WORKOUT INTENSITY (HEAVIER WEIGHTS)

CARDIOVASCULAR TRAINING
ANAEROBIC POWER (SPEED & STRENGTH ENDURANCE)

LIMIT STRENGTH TRAINING
SPEED/STRENGTH TRAINING

GENERAL CONDITIONING
SKILL & BODY CONTROL

TRAINING OBJECTIVES

performing only a bit more than what you were used to doing. Soon you will be able to perform at maximum effectiveness—don't rush it!

CHOOSING THE PROPER EXERCISES

Stand in front of a mirror and give your physique a critical look. Arms too small? Abdominal muscles loose and bulging? Chest flat? Skinny legs? Shoulders stooped and rounded? Or, if you're an athlete, critically evaluate your sport's physical requirements. Need explosive legs? Enduring arms? Strength for lifting, throwing, jumping, or swinging a bat?

When you have listed all of your conditioning goals, you have, in effect, mapped out the two important guides in determining what exercises to do. First, you have given yourself a guide for picking the proper number of reps and sets to do (for strength, power, endurance, or size); and second, you have identified the muscles you want to work on.

But knowing which muscle and which exercise isn't enough. You must also be able to choose which machine or implement to use in order to achieve your goal most efficiently. There are virtually dozens of machines and exercise apparatuses from which to choose, and the selection process can be quite confusing!

When deciding on the exercises you need to reach your conditioning goals, you must remember that each exercise will cause you to become a bit more fatigued. You will not be able to do more than around 10 exercises in any given workout because your fatigue level will not allow it. So, choose your exercises wisely, making sure that each will deliver maximum results. One or two exercises per body part and 10 exercises per workout is sufficient.

HOW OFTEN SHOULD I WORK OUT?

Remember the old saying, "Fools rush in where angels fear to tread"? Don't rush into a training program determined to get instantaneous results. Working out too often and too hard will not get you to your goals any faster. In fact it may just slow you down or discourage you altogether! Sore or injured muscles and joints are no joke! And training too hard or too often is the surest way of causing them. At the risk of boring you with old sayings, here's a final one: "Slow and steady wins the race."

The time it takes for your muscles to recuperate between workouts can vary, depending on muscle size (larger muscles take longer), age (older people recover more slowly), training intensity (heavy training for strength requires longer recuperation time than does lighter training for endurance), and fitness level (the better shape you are in the shorter the recovery time necessary between workouts).

On the average, you should be able to train each muscle three times per week. Monday, Wednesday, and Friday is the most typical training schedule. If you have more than 10 exercises to accomplish, you may want to use a *split routine*, which requires daily workouts.

For example, a typical split may look like this:

Monday, Wednesday, Friday	Tuesday, Thursday, Saturday
Chest	Lower back
Shoulders	Sides
Upper arms	Abdominals
Forearms	Hips
Upper back	Thighs
	Lower legs

FLEXIBILITY AND WARMING UP

Every workout should be preceded and followed by flexibility and warmup/cooldown exercises. Stretching and general warming up exercises prepare your muscles for your strenuous workout; stretching and cooling down after your workout helps prevent postexercise muscle soreness and allows your heart rate to return to normal slowly.

Here is a great way to conduct your workout sessions:

Stretching

Your shoulders, spine, and hip joints are the ones most vulnerable to injury from overexertion. Slowly stretch the muscles associated with these joints, avoiding jerky or bouncing movements. Each muscle should be stretched for about one minute, avoiding any painful sensations while doing so. A complete stretching session should last for about 10 minutes.

Warming Up

A slow jog around the gym or jogging in place for about four or five minutes will gear up your body for your weight training workout by raising your overall body temperature a degree or two. Another great warmup exercise is jumping rope. Also, before performing each weight training exercise, you should warm up the specific muscle(s) that the exercise is for by performing a set or two with extremely light weights.

Exercise Session

After thoroughly stretching and warming up, perform your planned workout.

Cooldown

After working out, again jog in place or around the gym for about two or three minutes. Follow the short jog with a minute of rapid walking. This will allow your heart rate to return to normal gradually, thereby preventing "blood pooling" in any specific muscle group.

Stretching

A brief session of stretching following your workout helps to prevent undue muscle soreness from heavy training.

LOWER BACK STRETCH

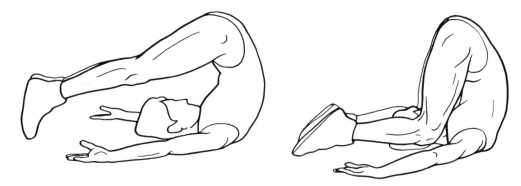

GROIN STRETCH

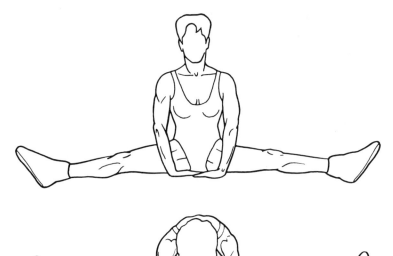

GROIN & THIGH STRETCH   HAMSTRING STRETCH

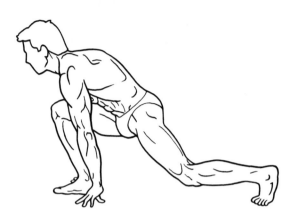
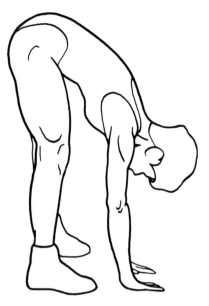

GROIN STRETCH

THIGH STRETCH

NECK STRETCH

CALF STRETCH

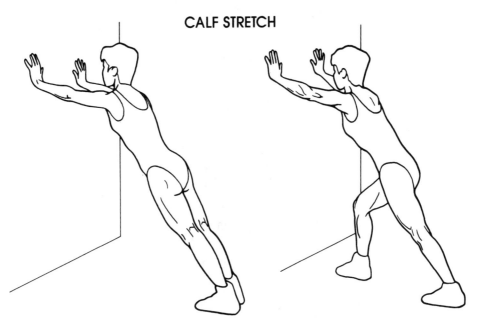

HIP JOINT STRETCH

GROIN & HAMSTRING STRETCH

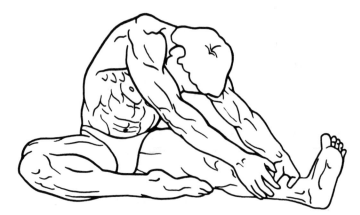

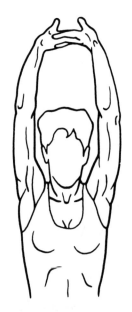

SHOULDER STRETCH

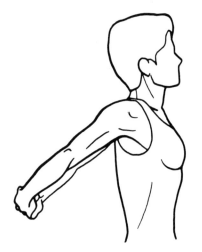

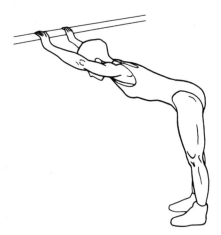

CHEST & SHOULDER STRETCH

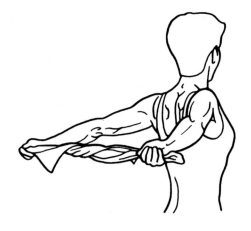

LOWER BACK STRETCH

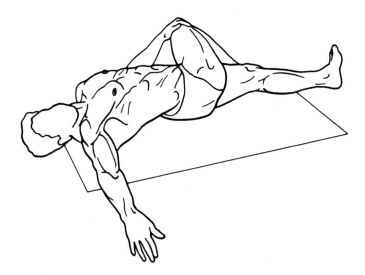

LOW BACK STRETCH

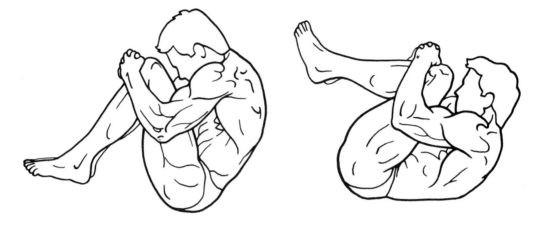

BREATHING

If you should hold your breath during a particularly heavy lift, you may run the risk of shutting down blood flow to the brain. That can cause *anoxia*—a shortage of oxygen in the brain. So, a simple rule of thumb while exercising is *don't hold your breath for long periods!*

Most experts agree that you should inhale while lowering the weight or at the top of the lift and exhale when lifting the weight. But this is often too difficult to do because the heavy weight causes pressure to build up in the lungs and it's difficult to control your breathing pattern. Besides, the pressure in your lungs helps to stabilize your chest and shoulder muscles so that they can exert maximum force more easily.

So, it is often advisable to hold your breath for a *short* period during the phase of the lift when you are just beginning to contract the muscle. The added stability afforded by thoracic pressure will make the lift a bit easier. On the way up, however, begin to exhale to release the pressure.

During light sets in which 10 or more repetitions are being performed simply breathe normally—do what comes naturally. Thoracic pressure rarely becomes a problem with lighter weights.

THE FOUR TECHNOLOGIES OF FITNESS MACHINES

Some sociologists believe that the fitness boom is a backlash resulting from the inactivity forced on modern man by the age of technology. People *want* to be fit, and are doing so in increasing numbers the world over. It's a bit ironic that the fitness industry is itself becoming more and more "high tech." They're actually making it easier for us to get back in shape.

Necessities of life do not control how or whether we remain fit. Instead, science does it for us, and quite effectively at that. The denizens of the drawing board—those stalwart biomechanicians who have our best interests at heart—have produced four different technologies from which we can choose in our efforts to excel in sports.

Let's return now to the first time you ever walked into the gym. Remember? You probably heard noises from chains clanking over pear-shaped sprockets, air releasing from valves, the squishing of fluid being forced through tiny apertures, and, probably most of all the clang of heavy iron hitting the floor—a veritable cornucopia of fascinating biotechnology. Still, you hoped that someone would put you on the one that hurt least. Let's look at the four basic forms of fitness equipment that the technocrats who rule the fitness marketplace have devised while playing their game of one-upmanship with each other.

Constant Resistance Devices

The term *constant resistance* means that the weight does not change during a movement. The resistance remains constant from the beginning of an exercise movement to its completion. When you lift a barbell or dumbbell the weight remains the same. When you lift a weight attached to a cable and pulley system, the weight remains the same, too, providing the pulley is round rather than elliptical.

This form of weight training (or *resistance* training) has one major drawback. It doesn't correct for musculoskeletal leverage changes that occur during an exercise movement. When you lift a weight your leverage changes during the joint movement. For example, when you perform a deep knee bend with a barbell resting on your shoulders, the amount of muscular force you have to exert near the bottom of the squat movement is far more than what it is near the top of the movement. The reason is that your musculoskeletal leverage improves the closer to the erect standing position you come.

The improved leverage means that you don't have to work as hard during the *easy* phase of the movement, and therefore benefit somewhat less than you do during the *hard* phase. Remember the most important law of conditioning: Your muscles need *stress* to grow bigger, stronger, or more enduring. With some of the beneficial stress gone the exercise is a bit less effective than it might be.

However, constant resistance exercises have their advantages also. Your body is really a complex machine. The muscles are connected by an infinitely complex network of nerves, all of which ultimately feed information to the brain. Many fitness scientists believe that constant resistance training is more *natural* and therefore more effective in the long run.

In other words, the changes in musculoskeletal leverage during the movement of an exercise is the way the human body works, and exercising it that way will give you better results. As we shall see, however, there are also those who believe that we can improve upon what Mother Nature hath wrought.

Variable Resistance Devices

When you hoist a weight by pulling on a cable that goes over the top of a pulley and attaches to it, you're engaged in constant resistance training. But if the pulley isn't round, or if the hole in the pulley isn't in the center, the amount of weight you lift at different points throughout your movement will change. This is true because the lopsided pulley—the offset cam—changes the leverage for you.

Scientists during the latter part of the 1800s found that they could vary the resistance this way, and in fact make the variance coincide with the natural variance in each joint's leverage. In other words, they were able to make the amount of weight increase or decrease to coincide with the increase or decrease in musculoskeletal leverage during an exercise movement.

As with constant resistance training, however, variable resistance training has its advantages as well as disadvantages. One major disadvantage is that the movement is not *natural*, and therefore causes "confusion" in the brain centers that interpret the force and movement pattern. The result, according to some experts, is that muscular gains in strength and size are slower in coming and are limited in their final potential.

Another major disadvantage—one shared with all machines, regardless of their underlying technology—is that because the movement pattern is directed for you, surrounding muscles that act as *stabilizers* and *assistants* are not stressed and therefore never have the chance to grow. Machines are constructed so that when you push the handles or pull on the cables you effectively isolate the target muscle or muscle group. This is not the way Mother Nature intended things to be. In every body movement you use far more than one muscle, many of which are meant to help control the movement pattern or assist in moving the resistance. Others act as stabilizers of the trunk or limbs so that the main muscle(s) can act more efficiently. None of these other important muscles are provided with sufficient stress to force them to adapt and become bigger, stronger, or more enduring when using machines that control the weight for you.

This disadvantage is the chief reason why serious athletes and bodybuilders most frequently opt for free weights (dumbbells and barbells) in their training. Of course, there are several exercises that do not lend themselves to free-weight training, and machines then become most desirable. In fact, a great majority of professional athletes and bodybuilders use a *combination* of machines and free weights in their training, but key primarily on free weights.

But let's get back to variable resistance technology. There are many forms of variable resistance for exercise equipment. Cams and elliptical pulleys are but one. Another that has become extremely popular is the Dynamic Variable Resistance technology developed by Universal Gyms.

Universal Gyms' DVR machinery operates on the same theory as does Nautilus's and Paramount's offset cams, but uses instead a rolling lever system. As you lift a weight on Universal's machines, the lever arm becomes shorter or longer by action of a rolling fulcrum point. Like the offset cam, the rolling fulcrum allows you to match your musculoskeletal leverage changes to the variations in resistance afforded by the machine. This is the major advantage of all variable resistance devices.

To understand why varying the resistance through an exercise movement is advantageous, recall one of the most important basic principles of conditioning—the overload principle. You can maximize the level of stress you place on your muscles by making them work as hard as possible throughout the full range of motion in any given exercise. That is precisely what variable resistance machines do.

To illustrate this important advantage, let's use the same exercise discussed earlier, the deep knee bend, or squat. You lower your body to a squatting position and begin to raise back up to a standing position. Near the bottom of the squat your leverage is poorest, and you can move less weight than near the top where leverage is best. That means that your leg muscles are only benefiting near the bottom because the stress is greatest there. The stress on your leg muscles becomes less and less as you ascend back to a standing position. In fact the stress becomes so little that virtually no gains in strength, size, or endurance are likely. Why? Because you have not stressed your muscles more than what they are used to.

With variable resistance machines, the stress is increased throughout the ascent from the squat position and matches the improvement in your musculoskeletal leverage. The result is that you are now receiving ample overload stress to make your muscles work more than what they are used to, and growth occurs.

Literally scores of other forms of variable resistance devices have found their way into the fitness marketplace. Springs, rubber bands, surgical tubing, and a host of other home-use and spa-quality contraptions all make your job of picking the best equipment for you more difficult.

Springs. Stretching a spring gets harder the more it's stretched. So long as the increasing difficulty matches your improving leverage through an exercise movement, it will be effective as an exercise device. This rarely happens though, and springs are therefore relegated to a position of lesser effectiveness as a form of resistance.

Rubber Bands and Surgical Tubing. The most popular form of stretch resistance is manufactured by Soloflex. Their machine uses elastic bands for its source of resistance. If you want more resistance, you simply add more elastic bands. Devices such as the Soloflex apparatus, hand-held elastic stretch devices, and the like are no more effective than the spring devices mentioned above, and their popularity is due to their low cost and the mammoth marketing campaign behind them—not their effectiveness.

The biggest drawback of variable resistance devices of all sorts, apart from their unnatural feel, is that it is quite impossible to perfectly match the variance in human musculoskeletal leverage by manipulating the resistance you apply. People come in all sizes and shapes, and their leverage systems vary as much. That makes it quite impossible to match human leverage with machine leverage, making the concept of variable resistance theoretical at best. Rolling lever systems such as Universal's, and offset cams such as Paramount's, Nautilus's, and others come closest, however. Remember that all of these devices are effective.

Accommodating Resistance Devices

The fitness industry's war of one-upmanship rages on. The newest form of resistance to hit the marketplace is called *accommodating resistance.* Like variable resistance devices, accommodating resistance machinery is designed to allow you to exert maximum resistance throughout the full range of movement in each of your exercises. In so doing, you are able to maximize the amount of exercise stress your muscles receive.

But there is a big difference—accommodating resistance does so by *controlling the speed* of your exercise movement, while variable resistance devices operate on the theory that the amount of resistance changes to match the leverage changes in your body.

When you push on a bar that can move only at a fixed rate of speed, it doesn't matter what your leverage is, you will be able to exert maximum force in any position. Even though you can exert more force at the top of a squat movement than you can at the bottom, with accommodating resistance technology you will be able to maximize the amount of muscular force being applied throughout the entire squat movement.

Of course, the advantage gained in being able to apply maximum overload force throughout the entire range of each exercise movement is that you are now able to increase the amount of *time* that adaptive overload is applied in each exercise. But is that really an advantage?

Some exercise scientists say no, and that the accommodating resistance technology is no more than another marketing gimmick to improve sales. But if you heed the arguments of their inventors, *time* is a critical element of overload; almost as important as *tension*. *Tension* (resistance that is stressful enough to cause muscles to adapt) together with sufficient *time* over which it is applied go hand in hand to produce superior gains, they say. A true statement to be sure, but it implies that the time over which overload is applied with other machines of the constant resistance and variable resistance varieties is inadequate.

Such is not the case, so it's fair to say that all three technologies are very effective. Each has its distinct advantages, and shares others. The same can be said of their disadvantages.

The one feature that all accommodating resistance device manufacturers claim as the chief advantage of controlled speed exercise is the fact that ballistic movement is eliminated. This, they say, both improves the quality of overload throughout the exercise movement as well as eliminates the element of danger resulting from overextended joints and uncontrolled movements.

As with variable resistance devices, however, accommodating resistance movements are unnatural and therefore limited in their effectiveness. It seems that the brain isn't adapted to accepting the unnaturalness of controlled speed—ballistic movements are the way nature intended muscles and joints to work. Taking a look at how controlled speed training is accomplished may give you a clue as to why some scientists believe this to be true.

The Cam II and Cam III machines manufactured by Kaiser use compressed air to control movement speed. The advantage of using air is that it can be moved very rapidly to and from a storage reservoir, making it possible to finely control resistance at any point in an exercise movement rather quickly. As fatigue sets in, for example, reducing the amount of air pressure by routing some air back to the storage reservoir makes it possible to continue exercising. This can be accomplished by the press of a button or pedal conveniently located on the machine.

Mini-Gym uses a combination of clutch plates and flywheel to control movement speed. Reducing or increasing the amount of friction between the clutch plates accomplishes this goal. Unlike the Kaiser equipment, you are required to stop exercising to adjust the tension (speed).

Yet another accommodating resistance apparatus uses fluid cylinders similar to an automobile's shock absorbers. By adjusting the hole diameter through which the fluid passes you can vary the speed of movement. The most noteworthy example of this sort of technology is found in the Hydra-Gym line. Their equipment can, like Kaiser's, be adjusted during a movement.

Practically all rowing machines on the market use fluid in the same way that Hydra-Gym does. Exercise bicycles, on the other hand, use the same sort of technology as Mini-Gym: friction. A relative newcomer to the world of exercise technology, the Stairwalker, employs friction also. This ingenious device allows you to walk upstairs fast or slow without having to return to the bottom for another set! It resembles a miniature escalator.

The Bullworker became famous as the exercise device used aboard the Apollo spacecraft. It too uses friction as its source of resistance. A rope wound around a central rod is pulled during exercise. The more winds of the rope, the more friction. Manual treadmills use friction to control walking or running speed. Electric treadmills of the sort used in scientific laboratories use the speed of the electric motor to control running or walking speed.

The plethora of devices finding their way into today's fitness marketplace are testimony to the incredible popularity the fitness lifestyle enjoys. It's safe to say that nearly all of these devices work. They all can, if used *properly* and *consistently*, afford you with a level of fitness greater than what you started with. Most offer miraculous results, but in the final analysis it's *you* who must do the work. *No machine yet developed can do that for you.*

Static Resistance Devices

When there is no movement resulting from muscle contraction your muscles are said to be *statically* contracting. The term *isometric exercise* was coined to describe this form of stress. During the fifties and early sixties, this form of exercise was heralded as a major technological breakthrough in exercise science. In bandwagon fashion, athletes the world over adopted isometric exercise as a major technique to increase their strength. The public obligingly followed their lead.

It wasn't too long, however, before the truth was learned. Isometrically contracting a muscle, pushing or pulling on an immovable apparatus, made you strong *only in that position!* In order to become stronger throughout the entire range of movement, you would have to pull or push at every angle throughout the entire range. Of course, this was impossible from both a practical standpoint as well as from a technological standpoint. No one has the time nor the energy to spend doing this. Neither did the isometric rack manufacturers have the technology to efficiently permit this. The isometric movement died a quiet death.

It seems that the nerves running from the brain and spinal column to the muscles are not capable of delivering an electrochemical impulse in ranges of movement other than which they are made for. To make a muscle bigger, stronger, or more enduring, the exercise scientists found, you must stress the muscle through the entire range of movement.

Still, static muscle contraction does make you stronger in the position it's applied, and therefore has some uses in sport training. Because of the extreme stress such training has on the heart—blood flow is all but stopped in the statically contracting muscle—isometric exercise is not recommended for those with heart problems or high blood pressure.

Some Other Noteworthy Devices

There are many fitness devices on the market that are designed to deliver cardiovascular benefits, chiropractic (spinal) wellness, and sports skill. Often, these devices are difficult to categorize on the basis of the four technologies of fitness equipment discussed here. Let's review some of them, as you will surely run into many of them in your quest for fitness.

Any time you use your own body weight as a source of resistance, you are using constant resistance technology. Pushups, pullups, jumping jacks—even stretching—fall into this category. Sometimes special apparatuses facilitate calisthenic exercise. The *dancer's barre, chinup bars, twisting platforms, hand springs, slant boards* for situps, *jump ropes, inversion machines,* and *miniature trampolines* are but a few of the well-known calisthenic apparatuses on the market today.

Some calisthenic exercises are designed to improve endurance (either cardiovascular or in a single muscle group), strength, or flexibility. Others, as is the case with the *Nordic Track* ski simulator and the *roller ski shoes,* are designed to deliver both cardiovascular benefits as well as sport skill. Another example of sport skill calisthenics is agility drills. Even running and jogging are considered calisthenic exercise because you're required to use your own body weight. Adding *heavyhands* or *ankle weights* makes the task of running more stressful.

Viewed in this light, then, *calisthenic exercises are actually a special case of constant resistance technology.* The reason is quite simple: your body has weight, and if that weight is sufficiently stressful, it delivers overload to the muscles. Since there are no springs, offset cams, shock absorbers, or other devices attached to vary or otherwise control movement, calisthenics follow the dynamics of constant resistance weight training.

The most important point to remember about calisthenics is that if your muscles do not receive more stress than what they are used to receiving, you are essentially wasting your time. *You will not benefit from nonstressful exercise.* If a calisthenic movement is too easy then simply begin using weights—free weights (dumbbells and barbells) or machines. Weight training takes up where calisthenics leave off.

The remainder of this chapter focuses on actual training exercises. Each exercise will be discussed fully, both in regard to what muscles are affected and which machines work best. Remember that all of the technologies employed in weight training have advantages and disadvantages. You must select your exercises and apparatuses so that you will benefit to the maximum degree.

CHEST
Target Muscles
Clavicular Pectoralis (upper chest)
Sternal Pectoralis (lower chest)

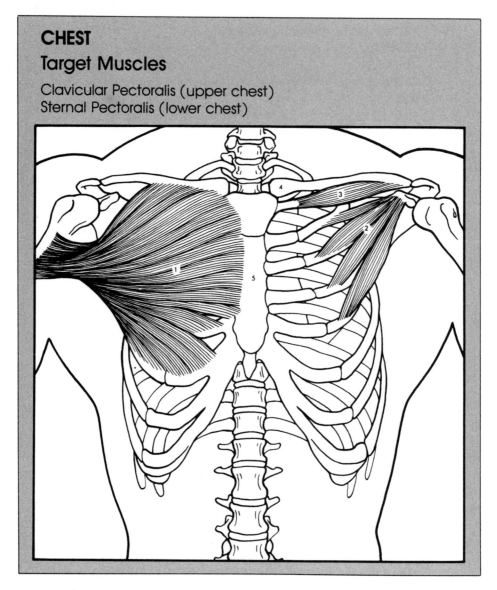

1. PECTORALIS MAJOR
2. PECTORALIS MINOR
3. SUBCLAVIUS
4. CLAVICLE
5. STERNUM

PULLOVERS

Free Weight Exercises. *Bench presses* with dumbbells or a barbell are performed while lying on a bench (supine position). Both upper and lower chest benefit from these exercises, and they are considered the best way to develop the chest. One drawback you should be aware of is that the triceps (back of upper arm) and front deltoid (front shoulder) muscles are also affected, and can sometimes limit your bench press efforts. A great way to get maximum isolation of the chest muscles is to do *flyes* with dumbbells. The major advantage of bench presses and flyes is that surrounding muscles that help balance and control the weight are also developed, a consideration important to athletes. This exercise *must* be performed with a *spotter* (a partner) standing ready to assist in case you fail to make the lift. The exercise can be extremely dangerous!

PEC-DECK

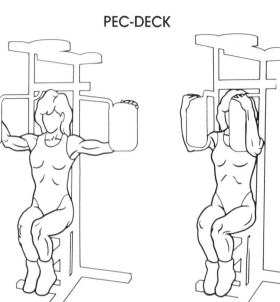

PUSHUPS

Machine Exercises: Bench presses can be performed on Universal's DVR machine, Paramount, Soloflex, Marcy, or DP equipment. All are similar to regular bench presses done with the free weights, except that the path of the exercise movement is controlled for you (''helping'' muscles receive little or no benefit). There are some equipment manufacturers (e.g., Nautilus, Kaiser, Universal) who make a machine called the *pec deck*, which allows you to isolate the pectoralis muscles while in a seated (rather than supine) position. All are quite effective, but free weight exercises are generally regarded as the most effective way to develop the chest.

BENCH PRESS

INCLINE BENCH PRESS

SHOULDERS
Target Muscles

Deltoids (front, middle, and rear shoulders)

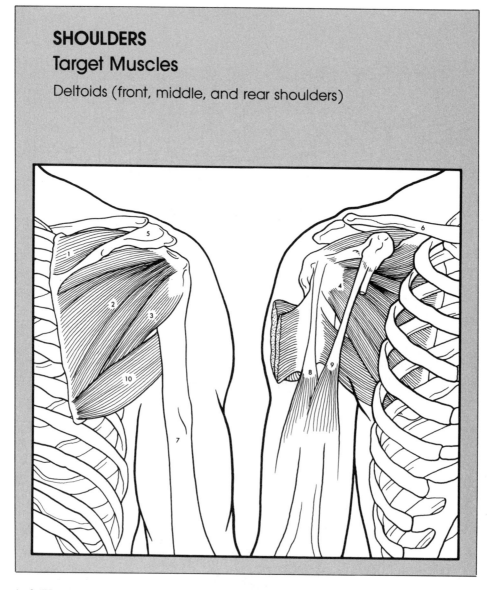

1. SUPRA-SPINATUS
2. INFRA-SPINATUS
3. TERES MINOR
4. SUBSCAPULARIS
5. SPINE OF SCAPULA

6. CLAVICLE
7. HUMERUS
8. BICEPS BRACHII—LONG HEAD
9. BICEPS BRACHII—SHORT HEAD
10. TERES MAJOR

DIPS

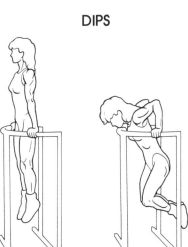

Free Weight Exercises. *Lateral raises* with dumbbells (raising the two dumbbells sideways to head height) and *upright* rows with barbell (with hands close together, lift the barbell to your chin) are the two favorite shoulder exercises among bodybuilders and athletes. To center more on the front shoulder muscles, raising the dumbbells or barbell forward to head height works best. And, to affect the rear deltoids, *inverted flyes* (with dumbbells in hand, bend forward and raise the dumbbells sideways) are recommended. Again, experts feel that free weight exercises are the most efficient because of the control that must be exercised over the weights.

Machine Exercises: Several companies, including Universal, Nautilus, Marcy, DP, Paramount, and others, have seated or standing *military press* stations among their equipment. This exercise affects the shoulders (primarily the middle deltoid), but you will almost always be limited in your efforts by the weaker tricep (back of upper arm) muscles. Nautilus, Kaiser, and a few others feature a seated deltoid raise machine (middle deltoid), which works quite well in achieving maximum isolation of the target muscles. Almost all of the major equipment manufacturers have a low pulley attachment that allows you to do upright rows or one-side-at-a-time lateral raises with a cable system. These exercises are also quite effective. No single machine stands out as better than the rest when it comes to effectively exercising the shoulder muscles.

FRONT DUMBELL RAISES

SEATED DUMBELL PRESS

BENT OVER ROWS

UPRIGHT ROWS

UPPER ARMS
Target Muscles

Biceps (front of upper arm)
Triceps (back of upper arm)

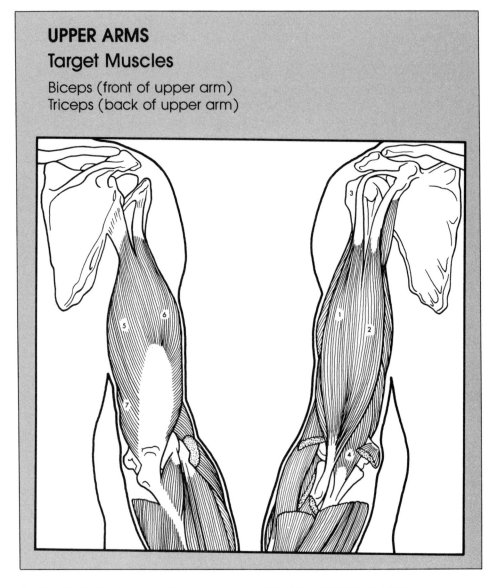

1. BICEPS BRACHII—LONG HEAD
2. BICEPS BRACHII—SHORT HEAD
3. HEAD OF HUMERUS
4. BRACHIALIS
5. TRICEPS—SCAPULAR HEAD
6. TRICEPS—LATERAL HEAD
7. TRICEPS—MEDIAL HEAD

ALTERNATE DUMBBELL CURLS

SCOTT CURLS

CONCENTRATION CURLS

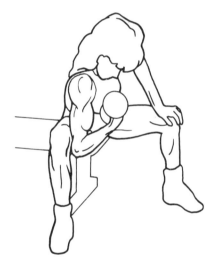

Free Weight Exercises. *Bicep curls* (bending the elbows with dumbells or a barbell in hand) and *tricep extensions* (while lying on your back, straightening the arms to an overhead position) are the most effective exercises for the muscles of the upper arms. Many muscles in the shoulder girdle help and control during the execution of these two popular exercises, making them exceptionally suited for athletes and bodybuilders. Several variations of these two basic movements have become popular, including several performed with machines.

Machine Exercises: Nautilus, Paramount, Marcy, and Kaiser (to name a few) have developed *Scott curl machines* (also called *preacher curl machines*) for the biceps. Several, including those mentioned, have adapted the machines to also accommodate *tricep pushdowns*. The popular name for these machines is the *double arm machine*. All are quite effective, but share the common disadvantage of not being adjustable enough to fit very short or very tall users. As with all machines, variable resistance, accommodating resistance, and constant resistance technology are employed. Your choice of which is most suited to your needs depends on your training goals, but mostly upon personal preference.

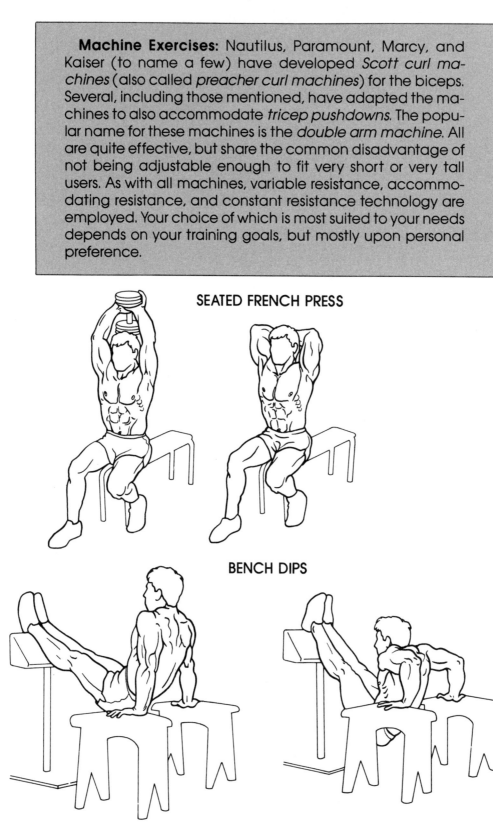

SEATED FRENCH PRESS

BENCH DIPS

E-Z BAR CURLS

SEATED CABLE CURLS

SUPINE TRICEP EXTENSIONS

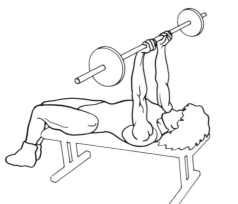

TRICEP PUSHDOWNS

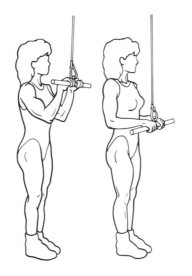

TRICEP CABLE EXTENSIONS

FOREARMS
Target Muscles

Radio-ulnar pronator and supinator muscles
Flexors of the fingers
Wrist flexors and extensor muscles

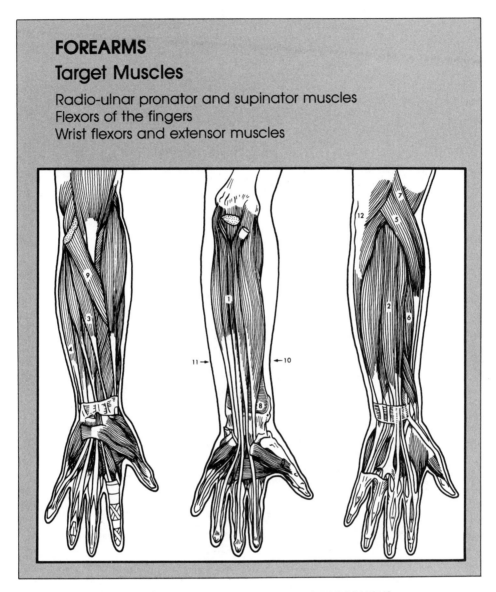

1. FLEXOR PROFUNDUS DIGITORUM
2. EXTENSOR COMMUNIS DIGITORUM
3. FLEXOR CARPI RADIALIS
4. FLEXOR CARPI ULNARIS
5. EXTENSOR CARPI RADIALIS LONGIOR
6. EXTENSOR CARPI RADIALIS BREVIOR
7. SUPINATOR LONGUS
8. PRONATOR QUADRATUS
9. PRONATOR RADII TERES
10. RADIUS
11. ULNA
12. ELBOW

REVERSE FOREARM CURLS

FOREARM CURLS

Free Weight Exercises: With the forearms resting on a bench, and palms facing upward (for wrist flexors) or downward (for wrist extensors) raise the barbell upward by flexing the wrist (palms upward) or extending the wrists (palms downward). Even with very light weights, your forearms will feel a deep burning sensation, a signal of development taking place. The same sensation is experienced with forearm pronations (forearms rotating to a palms-down position) and supinations (forearms rotating to a palms-up position), both of which employ the use of a dumbbell handle with weights on one end only, called *Thor's Hammer*.

Machine Exercises. The only machine for the forearms to hit the market is called *wrist rollers*. This device, made by Marcy, Paramount, and others, is simple rope tied to weights at the bottom and a roller at the top. The object is to roll the rope around the roller, which in turn raises the weight. It's effective, but cumbersome and expensive—free weights are more versatile. This device develops the wrist extensor muscles—flexors, pronators, and supinators are left unaffected. There are many *gripping* devices on the market that develop the finger flexors (located in the forearms). These include springs, rubber balls, and various other squeezable devices that employ constant resistance technology (weights). All are very good, and there seems to be no discernable advantage as to the type chosen. The free weight exercises are best, primarily because of their versatility.

GRIP SPRINGS

TENNIS BALL SQUEEZING

WRIST ROLLER

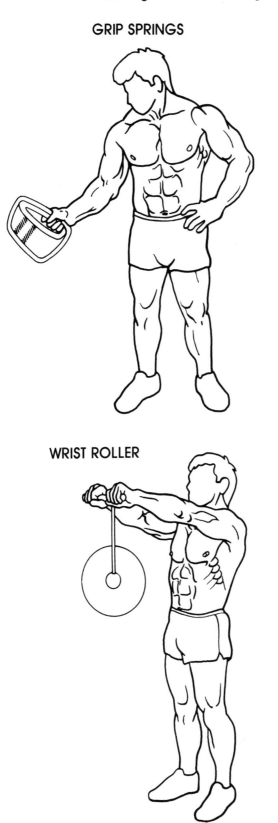
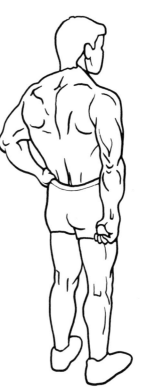

UPPER BACK
Target Muscles

Latissimus dorsi (arm depressor muscles)
Rhomboids (downward rotators of the scapulae)
Trapezius (shoulder elevators)

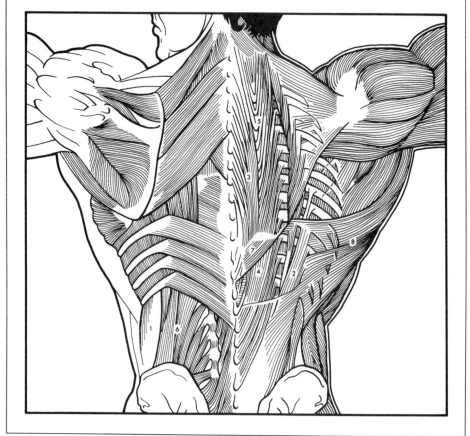

1. INTERNAL OBLIQUE	7. TRAPEZIUS (SECTIONED)
2. ILIO-COSTALIS ★	8. LATISSIMUS DORSI
3. SPINALIS DORSI ★	9. LEVATOR ANGULI SCAPULARIS
4. LONGISSIMUS DORSI ★	10. RHOMBOIDEUS MINOR
5. TRANSVERSALIS CERVICIS ★	11. RHOMBOIDEUS MAJOR
6. QUADRATUS LUMBORUM	12. SERRATUS POSTICUS INFERIOR

★ MUSCLES OF THE ERECTOR SPINAE

LAT PULLDOWNS

BACK EXTENSIONS

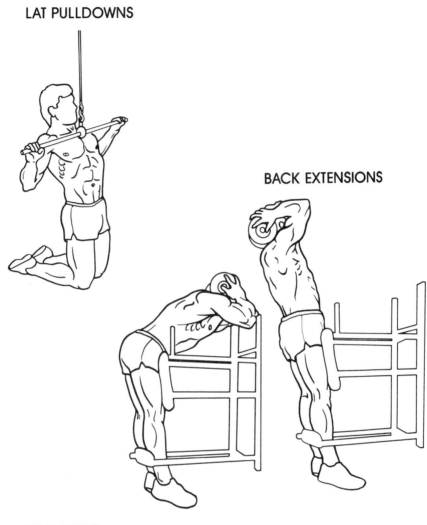

BENT ROWS

STIFF—LEGGED DEADLIFTS

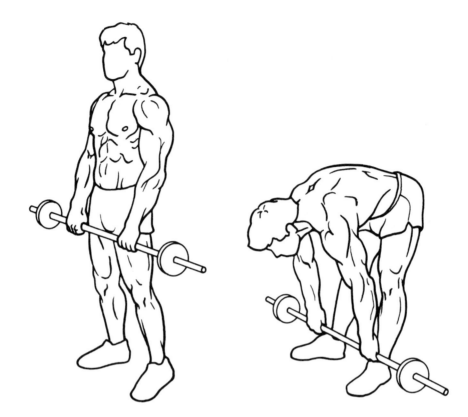

Free Weight Exercises. Chinups, a calisthenic movement, is the most popular exercise for the latissimus dorsi muscles (called *lats* for short). Doing them, of course, assumes that you can lift your own body weight! *Bent rows* are done for the rhomboids, and involve bending forward and pulling a barbell to your chest in such a way that the elbows are at 90 degrees from your body. Your ability to perform this movement is often limited if your biceps are weaker than your rhomboids, however, and *inverted flyes* (bending forward and raising two dumbbells to the side) are performed when bicep weakness limits your ability on the bent rows. Holding a barbell in front of you and resting against your thighs while shrugging the shoulders upward (called *shrugs*) develops the trapezius muscles. A burning sensation brought on by fatigue signals effectiveness. You'll feel it on top of your shoulders close to the neck.

Machine Exercises. *Lat pulldowns* are performed by pulling down on a bar attached to a cable overhead. The cable is attached to weight stacks on most machines. Universal, Marcy, Paramount, and several other manufacturers make such a device, and all employ constant resistance. When your body weight prohibits you from performing pullups, lat pulldowns are the best way to develop the lats. Also, when you are so strong that your body weight isn't sufficient for maximum stress, lat pulldowns again are the answer. Nautilus and a few other manufacturers make a *pullover* machine, which is also designed to exercise the lats. It too is effective. Nautilus, Marcy, Paramount, and others make a *shrug* machine that requires you to rest your forearms in a padded lever device which, when the shrug movement is executed, raises a weight stack. This device almost always hurts your forearms where the pads rest on them, and is not very popularly used as an alternative to the more comfortable and effective barbell shrug exercise.

CHINUPS   SHRUGS

LOW CABLE ROWS

HIGH PULLS TO A CLEAN

DEADLIFT

LOWER BACK
Target Muscles

Erector Spinae (two long muscles located on both sides of your spine)

Free Weight Exercises. *Back extensions* and *deadlifts* are the two most popular low back exercises. The first is executed while hanging face down over a waist-high bench with feet secured under a padded bar. Simply bending at the waist and then raising up with a small weight held behind the head effectively develops the erector spinae muscles. Deadlifts (bending down and picking up a barbell to the erect position) also effectively develops the lower back. Care must be used in the latter exercise so that not too much stress is placed on the relatively fragile spine. Slipping a disc can be a career-ending injury!

Machine Exercises. Very few equipment manufacturers make low back machines. Can the reason be that low back problems are so prevalent that lawsuits would become a problem? There are a couple of notable exceptions, however. One is the Nautilus *low back machine* which, incidentally, is quite safe. A padded lever against your back raises a weight stack when you extend your body backward. As with all Nautilus' equipment, variable resistance technology is employed. It's a great device for general toning or low back endurance, but not nearly as suited to developing strength, size, or power as are the free weight exercises.

CRUNCHERS

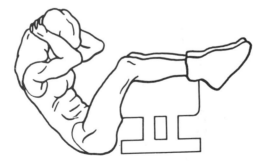

ABDOMINALS
Target Muscles
Abdominals (stomach)

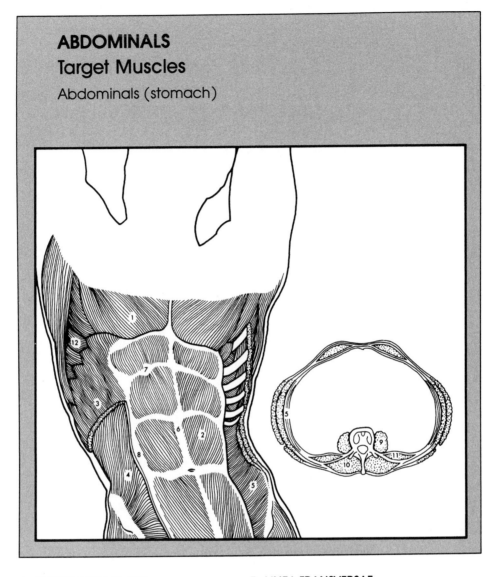

1. PECTORALIS MAJOR
2. RECTUS ABDOMINIS
3. EXTERNAL OBLIQUES
4. INTERNAL OBLIQUES
5. TRANSVERSALIS
6. LINEA ALBA
7. LINEA TRANSVERSAE
8. LINEA SIMILUNARIS
9. PSOAS
10. ERECTOR SPINAE
11. QUADRATUS LUMBORUM
12. SERRATUS

Free Weight Exercises. Everyone knows what *situps* are, but did you know that they are *dangerous*? Most people perform situps in the hopes that their belly will flatten. In the process, they all but ruin their lumbar spine by action of a very strong hip flexor muscle called the *iliopsoas*. This muscle is the primary muscle involved in a sitting-up movement. All the abdominals do is stabilize the trunk by statically contracting. The best calisthenic exercise for the abdominals is the *crunch*—a partial situp performed with the hips already fully flexed. Lie on your back with your feet over the top of a bench and "crunch" your torso by drawing your ribs toward your pelvis with the abdominal muscles. You can hold a weight behind your head for added stress. It's a very effective exercise.

Machine Exercises. After Fitness Systems Equipment Company came out with its abdominal crunch machine, several others followed suit. Nautilus's abdominal machine requires you to raise your knees and pull down with your shoulders against two resistance sources. It's an inferior design because it stresses the iliopsoas (and therefore the lumbar spine) too much. Universal has a similar device, which eliminates the lumbar spine problems of Nautilus, but the range of movement is limited. Fitness System's machine is by far the best on the market (and it's now being manufactured by Weider Health & Fitness, Inc). It features a full range of motion for the abdominal muscles, and allows no stress on the spine or shoulder girdle. The abdominals are completely isolated. This is one example where machines have a decided advantage over free weights or calisthenics.

REVERSE CRUNCHERS

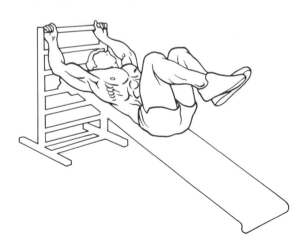

WEIGHTED SIDE BENDS

SIDES
Target Muscles

Internal and external obliques (sides)
Quadratus lumborum (lateral flexor of spine)

Free Weight Exercises. Holding a dumbbell in one hand, bend to the weighted side and then raise back to an erect position. This movement will develop the internal and external obliques on the unweighted side. Performing the same movement with the weight held on the opposite side completes one set of *side bends.* It is by far the most effective exercise for the muscles of the side, including the deeply located quadratus lumborom, an extremely important muscle for improving the stability of the lumbar vertebrae.

Machine Exercises. Holding the handle of a cable attached to a low pulley works identically to the free weight side bends described above. Many equipment companies make a *twisting platform* that is designed to tone the muscles of the sides. Holding on to a set of handles or a dancer's barre in front of you while standing on the circular platform, you simply twist from side to side, relying on your body's inertia to provide overload stress to the internal and external obliques.

Unfortunately, the stress is too little to do any real good, and most importantly, the lumbar vertebrae take a severe beating with this side-to-side twisting! In this writer's opinion, it is a dangerous exercise and ought to be outlawed! In fairness, however, it should also be pointed out that when the twisting movement is done *gently,* the spinal movement can actually *benefit* the spine! To receive such benefit, a twisting platform isn't necessary. Just standing and twisting is good enough.

LOWER LEGS
Target Muscles
Gastrocnemius (calf muscles)

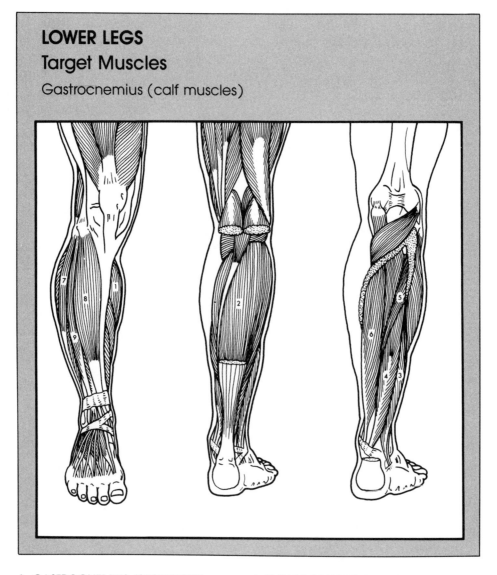

1. GASTROCNEMIUS (SECTIONED)
2. SOLEUS
3. PERONEUS BREVIS
4. FLEXOR LONGUS HALLUCIS
5. TIBIALIS POSTICUS
6. FLEXOR LONGUS DIGITORUM
7. PERONEUS LONGUS
8. TIBIALIS ANTICUS
9. EXTENSOR LONGUS DIGITORUM
10. GASTROCNEMIUS (SECTIONED)

Free Weight Exercises. Performing *toe raises* with a weight on your back develops the calves. But because your calves are very strong (owing to their great leverage) it is difficult to hold enough weight on your back to provide sufficient stress to force them to develop. The obvious alternative is to use machines.

Machine Exercises. All leg press machines, requiring either a seated or lying position, are suited to toe raises. All you have to do is press the weight to a straight-leg position, rest the edge of the foot pedal on your toes, and extend your ankle joint. Unfortunately, this can be dangerous if the foot pedal slips off your toes! They are *not* recommended! A host of professional gym equipment companies (all of which are small in comparison to Marcy, Nautilus, Paramount, or Universal) make specialized apparatuses for toe raises. Exactly why the large equipment manufacturers don't make such equipment is a mystery, considering the popularity of the exercise.

STANDING CALF RAISES
(BARBELL)

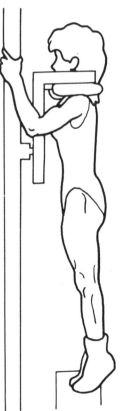

STANDING CALF RAISES (MACHINE)

SEATED CALF PRESSES

DONKEY RAISES

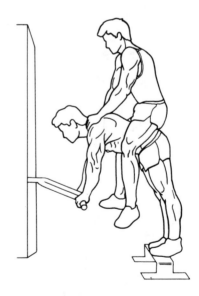

HIPS

Target Muscles

Gluteus maximus (your butt)
Gluteus minimus (under your hip pocket)

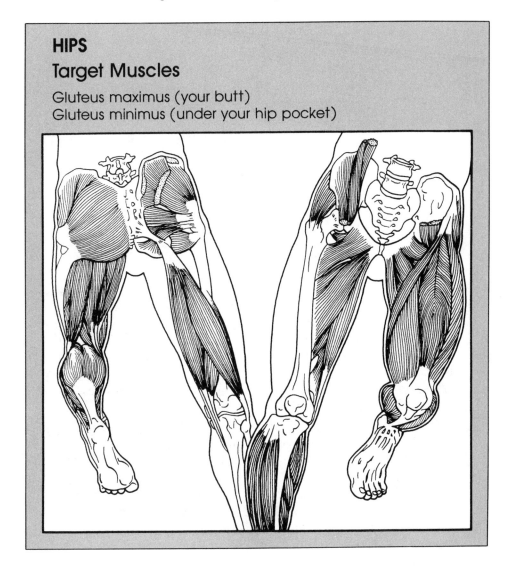

BACK SQUATS

FRONT SQUATS

Free Weight Exercises. *Stiff-legged deadlifts* and *squats* effectively develop the gluteal muscles. In the process, the hamstrings and quadriceps of the upper legs and the erector spinae of the lower back are also exercised very effectively. Despite the fact that the gluteal muscles are not completely isolated in these two exercise movements, they are nonetheless very effective in strengthening and toning the target muscles. In fact, no other exercises employing free weights or machines are as effective as are squats and stiff-legged deadlifts.

Partial squats never touch the gluteal muscles, and neither does the Stairmaster, despite their advertisements. Why? Because the hips have to be flexed almost all the way before the gluteals ever become stretched enough to afford a moving force! Climbing stairs (e.g., the Stairmaster) works the thigh muscles only—not the gluteals. But, climbing stairs three at a time and with weights on your back would be effective gluteal developers.

Machine Exercises. Several companies have developed reasonably effective gluteal machines. Nautilus' *hip and back machine*, like those made by Marcy and a few others, work to the extent that tone can be achieved in the gluteal muscles. But none compare to squats and deadlifts where strength, power, and endurance are the objectives. The gluteus minimus can be effectively isolated and developed quite well with the *in-and-out thigh machine* made by Marcy and Paramount. The outward movement (hip abduction with outward rotation) gets the gluteus minimus.

FRONT LUNGES

SIDE LUNGES

**INWARD (OR OUTWARD)
CABLE KICKS**

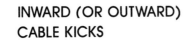

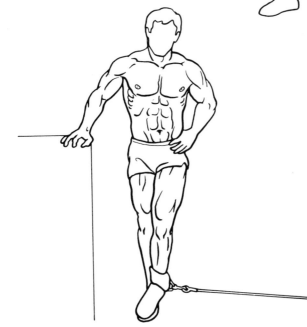

MACHINE SQUATS

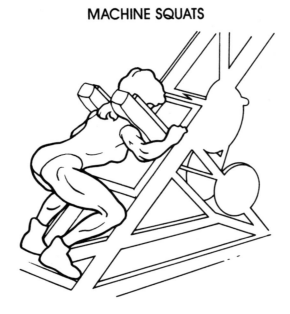

HACK SQUATS

THIGHS
Target Muscles

Quadriceps (front of thighs)
Hamstrings (back of thighs)
Adductors (inside of thighs)
Abductors (outside of thighs up near the hips)

Free Weight Exercises. As noted in the discussion above dealing with exercises for the hips, *squats* are excellent for the gluteals, hamstrings, and quadriceps. The adductor and abductor muscles of the inner and outer thighs also act strongly in squats, providing assistance and stability during the movement. When done correctly, squats are by far the best exercise for all of the muscles of the thighs. No machine comes even close.

Machine Exercises. Almost all of the major equipment companies manufacture *leg curl* and *leg extension* benches that attach to a weight stack and are operated with any one of the three technologies of weight training. These exercises effectively isolate the hamstrings and quadriceps, respectively. In fact, they isolate them so well that very little weight can be lifted in these movements, making these exercises suitable only for toning, size, and endurance—not strength. If you want strength, you must do squats. Leg press machines, requiring you to lie on your back and push a weight up, or sit and push a weight up via lever action are effective thigh developers. Nautilus, Universal, Marcy, Paramount, and a host of other manufacturers make such leg press machines. The in-and-out thigh machines manufactured by Marcy and Paramount are good for the gluteus minimus (hips) and the adductor muscles located on the inside of your thighs. Low pulley arrangements, on practically all commercial gym machines, are effectively used for the adductors and abductors (inside and outside of the thighs), employing an ankle strap to allow leg kicks in all directions.

LEG CURLS

LEG EXTENSIONS

11

THE PERILS OF MACHINE TRAINING

As you travel the path of least resistance toward your dream of someday achieving Olympian status in the fun world of competitive sports, beware the perils of . . . machine training!

Who was it that said, "The easy way out and easier is *not* the way to athletic success"? No, it wasn't a bodybuilder of note, but it was the next best thing (and I do mean thing). It was a football player. Not your ordinary football player, mind you. It was all-pro lineman Bob Young, speaking to *Sports Illustrated.*

The path of least resistance. Hmmm. Conjures up images of cute little Nautilus machines straddled by yet cuter little fillies in tights Those machines are high-tech looking, and most of them "track" the weight to make it easier for you to perform the exercise "correctly." Well, fellow iron freaks, that ain't necessarily correct, and in my opinion, when it comes to peak performance in sports or bodybuilding, the highest tech is the lowest tech.

Machines that "track" the weight for you may allow you to exercise each muscle or limb movement through a path of least resistance, but isn't the point of exercising to make your muscles work through a path of *maximum* resistance?

As I travel around the world of sports, I observe all manner of exercise techniques being performed on all manner of equipment. Most often, my gut reaction is that people everywhere take the path of least resistance.

Well, weight training performed at the highest levels isn't fun, folks.

Nautilus's offset cams were a design feature that started a revolution in the exercise equipment industry.

It's unbelievably grueling, tedious, and complex. Of course, the fun comes in when the outcome becomes apparent. The process, however, is anything but fun! And, while it can indeed be done with machines that track the weight through the path of least resistance for you, it cannot be done at the highest levels of perfection without the lowly dumbbell and barbell.

Dr. Pat O'Shea, the man who wrote the first college text ever on weight training, makes 10 points concerning the perils of machine training. He was directing his comments toward sports training in general. So, from the ivory towers of Oregon State University, Dr. O'Shea speaks. Listen and learn.

1. *No machine can provide full range multiple joint movements as closely as free weights.* In many sports, especially those requiring gross motor skills as opposed to fine motor skills, it is often quite assistive if the movement pattern of the skill is replicated against opposing resistance. This kind of replication is not possible with machines that "track" the weight for you.

2. *Motor skill engrams aren't established with machines as well as with free weights.* Your muscles' neuromuscular function depends in large part upon sensory input provided by many different types of proprioceptors. These proprioceptors sense movement, pain, temperature, limb position, velocity, and so forth. All such input is critical during skill learning and practice, and free weight training appears to facilitate a more "natural" feel that is conducive to skill acquisition. Machine movements, on the other hand, are unnatural feeling, and hinder skill acquisition.

3. *The carry-over value of free-weight training is superior to that provided by machine training.* Movements such as the snatch,

clean & jerk, squat, and bench press are gross body movements that have wide applicability to many different sports movements. This is so in the snatch, clean & jerk, and squat because they are "complex" exercises, utilizing several joints and muscle groups in synchrony. In the case of the bench press, all pushing movements require a similar movement pattern. Machine movements with predetermined patterns of motion cannot replicate this kind of carryover as efficiently. In the words of Dr. O'Shea, "The greatest positive transfer of training comes from athletic type exercises which allow *power* to manifest itself to a greater degree."

4. *Machine training won't help you to develop a high level of fluid, dynamic full-range athletic strength.* In all the world of sport, you'll never be required to lay on your back and push a weight. Never will you sit and crunch a couple of padded levers in front of you. These movements are, according to Dr. O'Shea's way of thinking, foreign to the concept of integrated athletic movement. In sports, synchronous activation of synergists, stabilizers, and prime movers must occur simultaneously with inhibition of antagonists. More often than not, these kinds of complex movement patterns must take place over a very complete spectrum or range of motion, something that most machines cannot begin to simulate.

5. *The body is a homogeneous unit that engages in ballistic movements, particularly those generated by strong hip thrust.* It's strange to me that almost all machine companies try their best to eliminate the element of ballistics from their contraptions. Ballistic movements are part and parcel of almost every sport there is. Ballistic training is therefore vital to any athlete's conditioning program. Almost all throwing, kicking, hitting, and swinging movements require hip thrust, which stems from powerful leg, hip, and midsection movements. Nothing of the sort can be gained from machine training.

6. *Machine training doesn't provide for training variety and variability.* You can perform movements in an endless array of movement patterns, speeds, directions, and timing sequences with free weights. Machines absolutely prescribe these elements for you. For bodybuilders, most of whom enjoy doing a variety of movements for each body part, any machine can give them but one, whereas free weights give them the entire spectrum of options. For athletes, such variation is essential because of the variability encountered in real-life sport settings.

7. *Machines don't permit the mind and body to develop in synchronization.* If your mind says, "Do this!" but your machine tells you to do something else, which it invariably does, then where are you? Simply, you haven't made the mind–body link

that permits maximum strength expression possible. There are physical and neural forces operating that must be in sync before maximum training adaptation can take place. For example, the factors of position, direction, sequence, timing, speed, and effect of force application must be under the athlete's control, not the machine's. Only then can the mind—your nervous system and thought patterns—meld with muscular force output to create truly skilled and effective movement.

8. *Machine training does not stress the psycho-endocrine systems.* In your mind you must be able to say to yourself, "I'm strong! I'm explosive! I can meet any physical challenge!" This kind of self-psych technique forces your endocrine system to pump out various hormonal secretions that gear you for a "fight or flight" response. Free-weight training challenges this system in a manner that machine training, which is built to be "safe," simply cannot do because all the challenge has been designed out of the machine. Machine companies hate lawsuits stemming from overchallenging the user. Yet, without challenge, neither the mind nor the body can adapt efficiently.

9. *Machine training does not provide for positive training experience.* Lifting weights is fun. Moving a lever isn't. It's that simple, folks, and if you don't believe me, go tax yourself to your strength's limit and feel the exhilaration of the experience. Some clever guy once referred to it as "the joy of effort"—the late, great Tate McKenzie, I believe.

10. *Machines don't provide for continuous long-term motivation.* It's motivating to be able to observe progress in lifting. Lifting reflects your strength levels, and because it's challenging and because they're universally accepted as the standards of strength, the Olympic lifts and the power lifts provide a motivational kick that simply cannot be replicated with machines. All machines are different, and there is no universal basis for comparison of strength levels. Anyone in the world can test their strength in one of the lifts and feel assured that they compare thus-and-so with anyone else in the world.

Folks, I know all the arguments, pro and con, relating to machines versus the use of free weights. Most of us do, and it seems neverending that this kind of discussion must take place in the first place.

I guess it's like the difference between a good pair of running shoes and a cheap pair. Like the difference between a Rolls Royce and a Ford. Like the space shuttle and the Kitty Hawk experiment. Machine training gets results, sure, but if you're into exceeding all bounds of sports excellence, it takes the very best science has to offer. Nothing has yet been invented that surpasses the lowly dumbbell and barbell for high performance training in the world of Irondom.

12

ACTIVATING TOTALLY: Isokinetics and Compensatory Acceleration

A few years ago, some devilishly clever fellow invented a device that allowed the user to exert maximum force against a bar throughout a full range of motion. He called his new device an *isokinetic* machine. The invention was gobbled up by the machine industry moguls, and heralded as the greatest innovation in weight training the world had ever seen.

Reams of research reports followed, all attesting to the incredible advantages of isokinetics over the now all-but-dead concept of iso-metrics, and even over the old standby techniques of isotonics. Most of the research was ill-conceived, however, and unfortunately too, it was done with primary and vested interests at stake. The researchers often had to prove the efficacy of isokinetics or not get paid! Too much loot was at stake!

Many of the claims set forth by these investigators are indeed quite true. Many are not. It is now well known that isokinetics are indeed a tremendous *adjunctive* exercise modality, but not an efficient *solitary* one. It is my belief also that the vast majority of the early researchers interested in isokinetics missed what may well be the point of greatest significance. It appears that the greatest effect of isokinetic training may reside in the nervous system rather than in the muscle (vis à vis growth in size or strength) itself.

My own investigations into isokinetic effects indicate that, over an eight-week period of training both isokinetically as well as with conventional weight training methods typically used in a peaking

FIGURE 12-1

SPEED OF MACHINE OVER PEAKING CYCLE

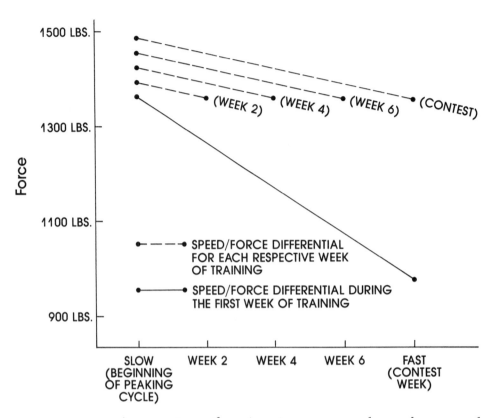

program, maximum strength gains (as measured on slow speed isokinetic movement) do not increase nearly as dramatically as do the gains in power output (as measured by high speed isokinetic movement). The figure above illustrates this point dramatically. Notice that there will be increases in strength from week one through week eight (illustrated are gains from 1,325 pounds to 1,475 pounds).

The slowest speed setting on the isokinetic machine allows movement at approximately the rate of one foot per second—plenty of time to elicit maximum motor unit recruitment during the movement (in this case the squat movement is plotted). However, when the speed setting is moved to two feet per second, there appears to be insufficient time to get such total recruitment, and the total force applied is significantly diminished with the increased speed (or, decreased recruitment time).

By gradually increasing the speed of movement over an eight-week period, I found that, while strength increased somewhat, the increases in one's ability to get maximum recruitment increased dramatically. By the end of a peaking period, the typical lifter was able to exert just as much force at the fastest speed setting as he was able to exert initially on the slow speed setting! This, friends, is very much the definition of *power*! Power, in athletes' terms, is the ability to get as many motor units (or muscle cells) as possible enervated to contract in a sudden burst of movement.

The strength gains noticed over the eight-week period are not unusual, and normal peaking procedures generally account for such strength increases. But never have I noticed such marked increases in *power* through the use of conventional weight training methods in so short a period. The addition of isokinetic training seems to be the key to these tremendous increases in power. This effect is hypothesized to be the result of learning. One literally "learns" to elicit maximal motor unit involvement. The mechanism remains unclear, however. It may be that the excitation thresholds of certain motor units are substantively lowered so that they're recruited more easily. It may be, alternatively or additionally, that greater amounts of electrochemical discharge became possible, thereby equaling or surpassing the relatively high excitation thresholds of some infrequently used motor units. The answer remains to be found.

To clarify what has happened, let's apply some simple mathematics to the squat. A lifter may perform five sets of five repetitions in this exercise, but how much of the total energy expenditure is actually beneficial? What percentage of the total number of reps actually constitutes sufficient overload to force an adaptive process in the organism? I suspect that at least 75% of his efforts are wasted! Consider that a lifter only "strains" in the lower 25% of the range of movement in the squat. (The upper ranges of movement involve better leverage, and therefore the weight feels lighter—so light that little benefit from overload is derived.) Furthermore, only the last two reps are difficult enough to constitute significant overload—the first three are easy because fatigue hasn't set in yet. So, what are we left with in terms of total overload? Somewhere around 75% wasted movement, and 25% useful overload.

What if someone came up with a method of getting nearly 100% efficiency from every rep and set of squats? That would require that overload be applied throughout the entire range of motion for every rep and every set. If this were possible, theoreticians tell us, there may well be a chance that previously unused (or untaxed) motor units would have to become involved owing to the greater requirements placed on the muscle. There are only two practical ways of accomplishing this training objective: isokinetically, and through compensatory acceleration.

Compensatory acceleration is similar to isokinetics, except that rather than controlling the speed of movement so that total effort can be applied throughout the range of motion, one compensatorily speeds up his own movement in such a way that increased leverage is accommodated for. In other words, as a lifter ascends out of a deep squat position, his leverage advantage increases. Unless he were to push harder and harder (accelerate), the overload factor would necessarily diminish commensurately with the lessening of the load. So, rather than lose this opportunity to overload by slowing down, the lifter speeds up! The result is, as it was with isokinetics, increased efficiency in achieving adaptive overload. Now, what took a lifter four workouts to accomplish in the gym, it takes a lifter using compensatory acceleration only one workout!

COMPENSATORY ACCELERATION IN DEPTH

Let's look at compensatory acceleration training from two more perspectives: safety and greater explosive power.

Fewer Injuries

The fact that you are able to achieve sufficient overload to force the desired adaptive process to occur in the muscles and tissues of the body even on the first few reps and sets means that you can use lighter weights than what was heretofore considered conventional or necessary. The use of *moderately* heavy weights (e.g., around 60%– 80% of your maximum capacity) is sufficient, providing you are compensatorily accelerating the weight throughout the movement. And, the use of slightly lighter weights is good for the reason that heavier weights predispose you to commensurately more (and more severe) injuries.

Power Is Increased

The standard definition of power is force times distance per unit of time (fd/t). Thus, moving a weight from point A to point B in as short a period of time as possible would constitute an appropriate test of power. Moving your body from point A to point B in similar fashion would also be a test of power. The fact that you are pushing as hard as you can every inch of the way through a movement, compensatorily accelerating the weight all the while, means that you are exercising power. One's ability to achieve maximal contracture instantaneously (i.e., the ability to recruit as many motor units of the muscle as possible in a given moment) is a *learned* response. Repeatedly calling upon your muscles to contract explosively in this manner actually "trains" them more easily to respond explosively in subsequent training bouts.

There is mounting evidence that such explosive movements against an external resistance as weight training involves can also "deinhibit" the muscle. That is, the Golgi tendon organ (located at the juncture of muscle and tendon) will be delayed somewhat in sending its message of stretch to the brain. When this message is interpreted by the brain as "Whoa! You're pulling too hard!" the brain sends a message to the contracting muscle to shut down. This inhibitory response limits strength. By delaying this message through compensatory acceleration training, you're actually allowing your strength potential to increase!

When to Use Compensatory Acceleration

All major limb movements can be trained with this technique. When training shorter movements, as in curls, crunches, or other muscle groups that act synergistically or in stabilization, compensatory acceleration is not advisable or practical. But, movements such as squats, bench presses, and cleans or high pulls are excellent candidates for compensatory acceleration training.

The primary goal in training synergists and stabilizers is strength rather than power. Thus, heavy sets of eights are normally most productive. Further, the movements involved in such exercises are generally very confined or short in distance, and do not lend themselves to accelerative techniques.

In conclusion, compensatory acceleration training works. Power-lifters who are using this technique have never failed to add well over 100 pounds to their squat, for example, in just three months or less. Many football players I have trained claim that they're coming off the mark far more explosively than they had ever done before, and basketball players are vertical jumping as much as five or six inches higher than ever.

The technique requires very concentrated effort on your part. You must concentrate! Concentrate on exploding every inch of the way through the movement—not just initially or at the top, but all the way.

13

SPEED/STRENGTH TRAINING: SOVIET STYLE

My training partner, Dave Keaggy, and I traveled to the Soviet Union to procure, steal, beg, cajole, or otherwise do whatever was necessary to find out, once and for all, what the devil's going on over there! How come those guys are so much better at weightlifting than our guys?

We came back with so much information that it will take several years to really understand it all. Dave Keaggy worked out an adaptation of Soviet strength training for power athletes. With both ourselves and the guys we train with as "guinea pigs," we were able to incorporate many of the Soviets' most productive training techniques into our own power training.

First, however, let me tell you about a method of training that the Soviets developed. They call it speed/strength training, and it consists of a combination of various types of bar (weightlifting) exercises, jumping exercises, and shock exercises.

THE CHIEF ELEMENTS OF POWER

The Soviet scientists believe that the chief elements of speed/strength (power) are: explosive strength, absolute strength, starting force, and reactive ability. These elements relate to different aspects of a power movement. For example, look at Figure 13-1, and notice that each of these four elements is represented in a simple movement like the standing broad jump.

How do these four elements relate to what strength athletes do in

FIGURE 13-1

LONG-JUMP FORCE CURVE

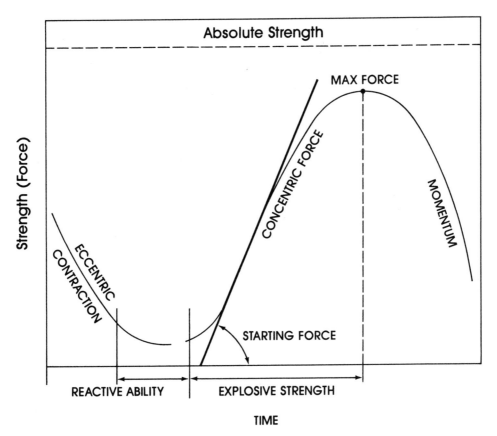

training, in competition, or both? To me, the answer is rather simple—it's what I've been "preaching" for a long time now. Here is what I believe the Soviet research can contribute to our powerlifting efforts in a nutshell: get *powerful!* Limit strength alone simply may not cut the mustard. But let me be a bit more specific:

- Starting strength is needed for coming out of the deep squat position, off the chest in the bench press, and off the floor in the deadlift. However, *explosive* strength is needed to complete these movements.
- Absolute strength (the maximum ability of a muscle to exert force) diminishes rapidly after the first two seconds of maximum effort. This necessitates completing the lift or movement within that time frame; therefore, explosiveness is essential.
- Reactive ability is important during training because it "teaches" your muscles to react with maximum starting force. In other words, deinhibition occurs during explosive training (fast

"touch-and-go" movements), and muscle fiber recruitment is greatly enhanced.

Of course, starting force (the number of cells you can recruit at the moment of contracture) is very important, and, as indicated in the preceding point, is dependent upon touch-and-go training in the various exercises suited to your sport. Proper weight training is most critical, but there are some methods that greatly assist such training. This is where the Soviet jump and shock methods of training come in.

How Do You Train for Power?

When I was an Olympic lifter, I was coached by the great Joe Mills. He believed that power was a way of life. For instance, he didn't just stand up—he exploded from his chair. He did everything to the absolute max. He had a funny tale to explain his philosophy. As a young man, he and a few friends went drinking one night and he drank all of them under the table. Then, on the way home, they all decided to see who could pee the highest. Ol' Joe reared back and got a flying start, and released the purposely pressurized stream at the height of his jump. Of course, he won by several yards. The others with him just didn't stand a chance! They didn't understand the concept of power. Joe believes that power and life (and weightlifting) are one and the same. So do I, and I am thoroughly pleased that I had such an apt coach.

In case the point of all this has passed you by, let me say it another way. You have to think speed! Every movement you make must be calculated, yet as explosive as possible, and for guys like Joe Mills, that's easiest to do when you have put your life's energy behind your training.

Take a look at Figure 13–2. There you will see how the Soviets advocate peaking for an athletic event (such as the long jump, for example). I have given some of their techniques a bit of trial, and believe that the complex method of training (combining bar exercises, jumps, and depth jumps) is most suited for the last half of most athletes' peaking period (the last six weeks). Here's how a typical workout might look:

1. Warm up with sequence jumps (like a kangaroo) for two to three sets of five jumps
2. High bar squats done with compensatory acceleration: 5 × 5 or 3 × 3
3. Sequence jumps for distance with dumbbells in hand: 2 × 10
4. Depth jumps: 2 × 10
5. Short, explosive running drills: two sets of runs

FIGURE 13-2

EFFECTS OF RUSSIAN TRAINING METHODS

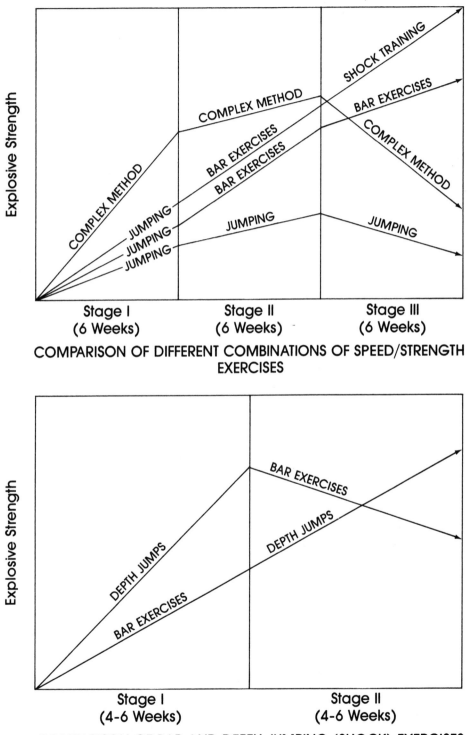

COMPARISON OF DIFFERENT COMBINATIONS OF SPEED/STRENGTH
EXERCISES

COMPARISON OF BAR AND DEPTH JUMPING (SHOCK) EXERCISES

The descriptions of these training methods are outlined in the accompanying sidebar.

SOME PRACTICAL APPLICATIONS OF SPEED/STRENGTH TRAINING

As a powerlifter, I sometimes found myself deciding at the last minute to enter a contest. For me, "the last minute" meant within six weeks. That's how long it would take, at peak training efficiency, for me to get the most out of my body.

Peaking for a powerlifting contest within six weeks required some very careful, stepwise poundage incrementing. The juggling act—as described in Figure 13–3—required a push followed by a backing off period; then another push followed by another backing off. And so forth for six weeks. Each push was higher in intensity than the previous one. In this fashion, I was able to peak without overtraining.

For athletes in any power sport, this same kind of careful arrangement of intensity balanced by rest in your training (especially weight training) is the fastest way I've ever seen for improving strength in the short run. There may be more productive methods for long-term strength gains, but none so productive for quick gains.

Jumping exercises, an integral part of the Soviet's speed/strength training program, serve a variety of functions that are crucial to power output. They facilitate the stretch reflex in the muscles and assist to strengthen ligaments, tendons, and connective tissue. Jumping helps maximize the development of young athletes beyond what the athletes could achieve without such training (e.g., greater growth potential). They "teach" the athlete to increase the starting force and reactive ability of his muscles, and they aid in achieving a greater degree of coordinated muscle activity.

Jumping exercises include such techniques as long jumps for 100 yards (for strength endurance), short jumps for 30 yards (explosiveness), jumps over short, intermediate, and tall obstacles (such as benches, vaulting bucks, etc.), jumps onto tables or tall bucks, and one-legged hops over obstacles, such as hopping over a long bench back and forth for the length of the bench. Weights are used with many jumps.

Their so-called **shock exercises** are actually a specialized form of jumps. They're done off the top of a tall object with an immediate rebound out of the bottom of the jump. Another method is to vertically jump several times, hitting the bottom between each jump and rebounding out with

Yet another practical application of the Soviet system of speed/strength training can be seen in Figure 13–4. The curve represents my squat back in the days when 900 pounds was my limit. Everyone has a strength curve for every exercise they do. Your task is to determine how much weight you must train with for peak effectiveness. Peak effectiveness will always be at the top of your curve. You will find that your strength curve for almost any exercise will peak between 50%–80% of your maximum.

A final application of speed/strength bears mention. The place is Seoul. Carl Lewis and Ben Johnson meet for the big showdown. Forget the fact that Johnson was disqualified for using steroids for a moment. Look beyond that, and focus on the dynamics of that great race. Figure 13–5 illustrates, in remarkable detail, the three stages of a 100-meter race:

- Stage One: Starting strength out of the blocks and explosive strength to accelerate to top speed.

greater and greater force. The idea behind such shock (or depth) jumps is to stimulate maximum contraction capabilities (starting force). The Soviet scientists believe that an athlete's *will* is not capable of producing such sharp stretch reflexes, and that normal training procedures simply aren't as effective in promoting power.

The mechanical stretch (viscoelasticity) of all soft tissues (including muscle, tendons, connective tissue, and ligaments) is improved through such measures, and this relates to improved reactivity during explosive sport events.

Bar exercises, of course, are designed to increase absolute strength. When the situation warrants it, size and muscular endurance are also improved through the use of bar exercises. The Soviet's concept of bar exercises is not much different from ours in this respect, but they seem to have no clue as to the tremendous variety of exercises that are possible. This is immediately obvious by the fact that in the Soviet Union there are few weight-training machines designed to provide maximum isolation—they have only archaic, poorly designed multiple-station gyms that look like a backyard assemblage of junk iron. Perhaps 80% or more of all the exercises they perform are done with a regular Olympic-style bar and weights. But then, it is entirely conceivable that they have opted for this condition—bar exercises are known even among Western athletes to be generally more productive overall than are machines.

FIGURE 13-3

SIX-WEEK SOVIET STRENGTH PROGRAM

Week 1

Workout 1 — $\dfrac{70}{2}$ $\dfrac{75}{2}$ $\dfrac{80}{2}$ 6

Workout 2 — $\dfrac{70}{2}$ $\dfrac{75}{2}$ $\dfrac{80}{3}$ 6

Workout 3 — $\dfrac{70}{2}$ $\dfrac{75}{2}$ $\dfrac{80}{2}$ 6

Week 2

Workout 4 — $\dfrac{70}{2}$ $\dfrac{75}{2}$ $\dfrac{80}{4}$ 6

Workout 5 — $\dfrac{70}{2}$ $\dfrac{75}{2}$ $\dfrac{80}{2}$ 6

Workout 6 — $\dfrac{70}{2}$ $\dfrac{75}{2}$ $\dfrac{80}{5}$ 6

Week 3

Workout 7 — $\dfrac{70}{2}$ $\dfrac{75}{2}$ $\dfrac{80}{2}$ 6

Workout 8 — $\dfrac{70}{2}$ $\dfrac{75}{2}$ $\dfrac{80}{6}$ 6

Workout 9 — $\dfrac{70}{2}$ $\dfrac{75}{2}$ $\dfrac{80}{2}$ 6

Week 4

Workout 10 — $\dfrac{70}{2}$ $\dfrac{75}{2}$ $\dfrac{85}{5}$ 5

Workout 11 — $\dfrac{70}{2}$ $\dfrac{75}{2}$ $\dfrac{80}{2}$ 6

Workout 12 — $\dfrac{70}{2}$ $\dfrac{75}{2}$ $\dfrac{90}{4}$ 4

Week 5

Workout 13 — $\dfrac{70}{2}$ $\dfrac{75}{2}$ $\dfrac{80}{2}$ 6

Workout 14 — $\dfrac{70}{2}$ $\dfrac{75}{2}$ $\dfrac{95}{3}$ 3

Workout 15 — $\dfrac{70}{2}$ $\dfrac{75}{2}$ $\dfrac{80}{2}$ 6

Week 6

Workout 16 — $\dfrac{70}{2}$ $\dfrac{75}{2}$ $\dfrac{100}{2}$ 2

Workout 17 — $\dfrac{70}{2}$ $\dfrac{75}{2}$ $\dfrac{80}{2}$ 6

Workout 18 — $\dfrac{70}{2}$ $\dfrac{75}{2}$ $\dfrac{105}{1}$ 2

Top numbers indicate percentage of current maximum single lift; bottom numbers are reps. Last number by third fraction indicates number of sets at that poundage. Use ultrastrict form for each rep. Don't miss workouts.

- Stage Two: Distance you can hold top speed (usually less than 20 yards, beginning at 40–50 meters)
- Stage Three: Speed endurance is taxed in the last 40–50 meters, and all sprinters begin to slow down.

The 10-meter splits noted in the table accompanying Figure 13–5 clearly indicate that Johnson won the race during the first 60 meters, displaying superior speed during each of the six splits. Thereafter, the race was narrowly in favor of Lewis, who showed superior speed endurance.

Johnson's superior acceleration and top speed were too much for Lewis, and he won in 9.79 seconds to Lewis' 9.92 seconds.

Contrary to popular opinion, Johnson's starting strength out of the blocks was only a minimal contribution to his win over Lewis. By far

FIGURE 13-4

RELATIONSHIP AMONG MOVEMENT SPEED, LOAD AND POWER IN THE SQUAT*

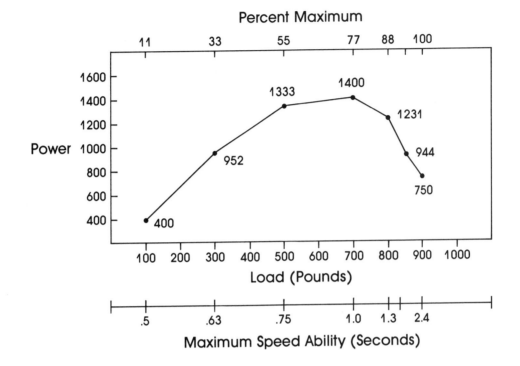

*Assumes squat distance equals two feet and maximum effort is expended to achieve maximum speed at each load

This graph illustrates that your training intensity (the percentage of your maximum) should always be close to the top of the curve—where *power* is maximized! For ballistic training, keep it closer to 55%, and for absolute or limit strength training, your intensity should be closer to the 80%-85% level.

the most important factor was his accelerative ability—that is, his starting strength *per individual step*—over the first 60 meters.

Simple mathematical interpolation shows that Johnson's 40-yard dash time was 4.419 seconds, while Lewis' 40-yard dash time was 4.527 seconds.

I am definitely not impressed. I've witnessed many, many athletes (especially in shot put, baseball, weightlifting, and powerlifting) capable of better 40-yard dash times than that! One baseball player I trained, for example, was capable of a 4.2 second 40-yard dash! A top shot putter also trained by me was able to complete a 5-meter dash (in sneakers and without starting blocks) in 1.03 seconds! Both are radically superior to Johnson's capabilities.

Why should this be? Johnson (and all 100-meter dash athletes) must

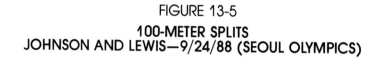

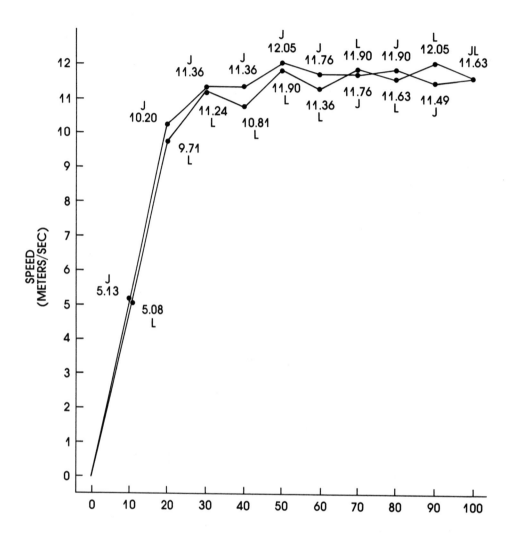

FIGURE 13-5
100-METER SPLITS
JOHNSON AND LEWIS—9/24/88 (SEOUL OLYMPICS)

Meters per Sec		25-Meter Times		10-Meter Times		Meters	Cumulative Times		Margin (Sec)
5.08	5.13	3.445	3.370	1.97	1.95	10	1.95	1.97	.02
9.71	10.20			1.03	.98	20	2.93	3.00	.07
11.24	11.36			.89	.88	30	3.81	3.89	.08
10.87	11.36	2.205	2.150	.92	.88	40	4.67	4.81	.12
11.90	12.05			.84	.83	50	5.52	5.65	.13
11.36	11.76			.88	.85	60	6.37	6.53	.16
11.90	11.76	2.150	2.120	.84	.85	70	7.22	7.37	.15
11.63	11.90			.86	.84	80	8.06	8.23	.17
12.05	11.49	2.120	2.150	.83	.87	90	8.93	9.06	.13
11.63	11.63			.86	.86	100	9.79	9.92	.13
L	J	L	J	L	J	Meters	J	L	

train for speed endurance. Doing so ultimately detracts from starting strength and explosive strength, the two most essential ingredients in both accelerative force and top speed. Power athletes, on the other hand, need only concern themselves with one giant blast of muscle contracture. The muscles, as you have discovered in the first chapters of this book, differ between these classes of athletes in their biochemical, neural, and metabolic properties.

14

IMPULSE-INERTIAL TRAINING

Locked in the brains of apparently normal folk are fantastical concepts which only heaven knows whence they came. Steve Davison is apparently normal. You know, kinda smart but nothing one might call brilliant. Average height and build, family, pet dog, car in need of repair. He's average—until you begin to pick his brain, that is. His brain is definitely not normal. Some years back, Steve found the key to unlock a portion of his brain, and out spilled one of the most amazing concepts for sports training I've ever come across.

He called his invention the impulse–inertial exercise system. I believe that this system holds one of the keys athletes, as well as rehabilitation specialists, have sought for countless years. Impulse–inertial exercise will radically improve the one attribute that might make its practitioners great: *starting strength*—the ability to "turn on" instantly and maximally.

IMPULSE-INERTIAL EXERCISE

So incredibly effective is the impulse–inertial training system for improving starting strength that Steve Davison has dedicated his life to marketing it on a full-time basis. His company, EMI, Inc., based in Atlanta, has sold dozens of his devices over the past few months, mostly to rehab specialists. But they've found their way into sports training at the highest levels—at the CRAFT Center in Reseda, for instance. I bought one of Steve's machines and interfaced it with some rather sophisticated computer technology. What Dr. Bill Laich and I have discovered relative to its value in sports staggered us.

You know how I've been preaching "compensatory acceleration training" and "ballistic training" for years now. I've said many times that CAT and ballistics were the *only* ways an athlete could ever hope to improve his explosiveness and starting strength. Well, in a sense, impulse–inertial training is a special form of ballistic training. The effects of gravity have been completely eliminated, however, and what's left is "pure" inertia, which the user must overcome.

Overcoming the mass of the gravity-free sled on the device requires you to decelerate it with eccentric contracture of the target muscle. Then, to move the sled in the opposite direction, to accelerate the mass, you contract your muscle concentrically. But all this happens in the twinkling of an eye. And with very low mass, the machine is almost totally safe: no maladaptive stress, only adaptive stress. The real key is in the effect such training has on one's nervous system.

By repeatedly decelerating and accelerating the mass of the sled, you "train" your neuromuscular system to approximate that all-important checkmark.

POOR   GOOD   GREAT

Checkmark training involves the strength curve described in Chapter 5. The great athlete's strength curve looks like a checkmark.

Now, try an experiment. Place a 10-pound weight on your toes. Hurt? Naw! Now drop it on your toes from a height of five feet. Yeow! Why the difference? The weight stayed the same but dropping it produced far more force.

The difference, friends, is what's called *ballistics*. The plate rests on your toes with a force equal to one *gee* (force of gravity), or 10 pounds. The weight dropped from a height of five feet landed with an impact of 89.4427 foot-pounds per second. And, if the weight hit your toes edge first, the force would have been magnified tremendously. Look at the formulae for determining this force on page 138.

That 10-pound weight, when dropped from a height of five feet, lands with a force of nearly 90 pounds, or .16 horsepower!

That's all very interesting. I went through all that yucky math just to prove a point (for those of you who are interested in the mathematics of strength). The point is that with impulse–inertial exercise

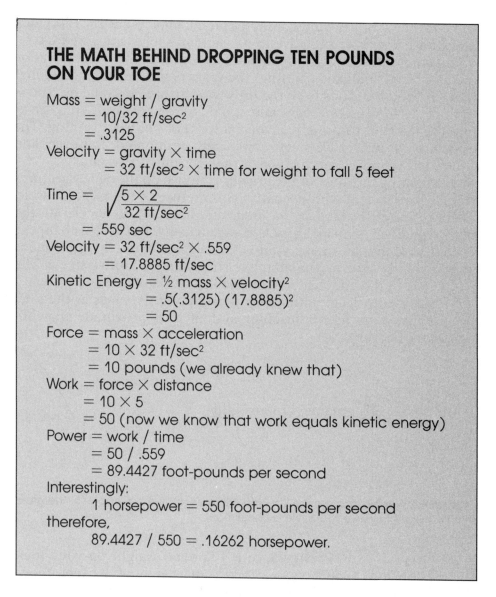

THE MATH BEHIND DROPPING TEN POUNDS ON YOUR TOE

Mass = weight / gravity
$\quad$ = 10/32 ft/sec^2
$\quad$ = .3125
Velocity = gravity × time
$\quad$ = 32 ft/sec^2 × time for weight to fall 5 feet
Time = $\sqrt{\dfrac{5 \times 2}{32 \text{ ft/sec}^2}}$
$\quad$ = .559 sec
Velocity = 32 ft/sec^2 × .559
$\quad$ = 17.8885 ft/sec
Kinetic Energy = ½ mass × velocity^2
$\quad$ = .5(.3125) (17.8885)^2
$\quad$ = 50
Force = mass × acceleration
$\quad$ = 10 × 32 ft/sec^2
$\quad$ = 10 pounds (we already knew that)
Work = force × distance
$\quad$ = 10 × 5
$\quad$ = 50 (now we know that work equals kinetic energy)
Power = work / time
$\quad$ = 50 / .559
$\quad$ = 89.4427 foot-pounds per second
Interestingly:
$\quad$ 1 horsepower = 550 foot-pounds per second
therefore,
$\quad$ 89.4427 / 550 = .16262 horsepower.

technology, you can magnify the amount of force your muscles produce by several dozen times!

Let's go through a bit more math, and you'll see what I mean. For example, let's say that we have an impulse–inertial machine and you have a 10-pound weight on the nongravity sled. You are moving the sled two feet back and forth at the rate of three reps per second.

$\quad$ Travel time = .333 sec
$\quad$ Distance = 4 inches (.333 feet)
$\quad$ Acceleration = 30 gees
$\qquad$ = 960 ft/sec^2

If you accelerate the sled over a distance of four inches, as we're assuming, then we have a force equal to 30 times the normal gravitational force of 10 pounds

Velocity = 25.1714 ft/sec

Kinetic energy = 99 pounds

Force = 300 pounds (10 pounds $\times$ 30 gees)

Power = 3000 ft/lbs per second (99/.33)

Horsepower = 7.27

Fellow iron freaks, you are not strong enough to voluntarily contract your muscles with that amount of power! Instead, you do it with *non*volitional impulse. Your nervous system compensates for your lack of strength and allows you to overcome the mass in one explosive burst of muscle recruitment.

Picture jumping off a ladder. Your body travels eight feet downward at 32 ft/sec^2 and you hit the ground with over a ton of force! That's many times more than you can squat voluntarily. For a brief fraction of a second, your muscles contract eccentrically to overcome the tremendous force of impact.

Mother Nature watches over you.

This tremendous force is used to overload your muscles, tendons, and ligaments in such a way that you become stronger faster. Not in an *absolute* or *limit* sense of the word strength, but instead in the *starting* strength sense.

And that spells greatness in any athlete's handbook.

With impulse–inertial exercise, you can isolate any muscle or muscle group, and you can simulate any sports skill requiring ballistic force. That's something you can't even do with a dumbbell or barbell in any consistent matter.

My opinion? This new technology makes sense. I bought two of them, so I can do both sides simultaneously. I even hooked the machines into my computer! I recommend that any athlete use this technology. It's not only great for improving starting strength, but also of immense benefit in rehabilitating from injury.

15

THE SIMPLICITY OF PERIODICITY

In the neverending struggle to compete, to annihilate your competition, you have to learn how to get the most out of your training efforts. Balancing short periods of high intensity against periods of low intensity, and progressing toward the competition season with a rationally planned sequence of stages designed to improve your level of skill and conditioning is called *cycle training*.

Cycle training has been given much attention in this country over the past year or so, particularly in the scientific journals. One reader who obviously has been befuddled with all the technical jargon in one of the more scientific strength and conditioning journals wrote:

> Help, Dr. Squat! I believe that by cycling my training I can become a better athlete, but I'm damned if I can understand how to do it after reading the volumes written about it in the *National Strength & Conditioning Association Journal*! Can you shed a bit of light on this subject in *layman's* terms?
>
> A Confused College Strength Coach

Well, CCSC, join the club! The cute little graphs, bobbles, and bows adorning the technically written journal articles obviously weren't written with you in mind. Some scientists, hidden away in obscure, glistening towers in Academe, that wonderful, holy land where true thinkers reside, may understand that stuff, but I sure don't. So, I share your frustrations, believe me!

I shall, notwithstanding, attempt to remove the mystique from this

Starting and explosive strength displayed over four quarters of play equates to *strength endurance*. Football players, like most power athletes, need *no* special cardiovascular training. In fact, they should avoid it.

beautifully simple concept which the Soviets call *periodized training*. We traditionally call it cycle training, but the periodicity—the scheme used to segment the year's worth of training—is very similar in any case.

Let's say you're a pro football lineman and you want to get ready for mini-camp in May, and then really pull out all the stops for preseason camp. You're borderline, and want to give it your best shot. Sound like a familiar scenario? Sure it is—all athletes in practically every sport have similar short-term goals.

Take a look at the accompanying two charts on page 142. I've simplified them as much as I can without losing the overall perspective. Consider the charts as a "roadmap" to your goal. If you follow the prescribed route, you won't get lost.

According to the Soviets, the year is divided into *macrocycles* for example: the off-season, preseason, and competition periods), *mesocycles* (a phase of training within a macrocycle, such as the "general fitness" stage, or the "power development" stage), and *microcycles* (how you vary your training intensity, volume, or exercise selection on a week-to-week or workout-to-workout basis).

I choose not to use such terms, since they are not part of the average American's vocabulary. Instead, to simplify things and to make them perfectly clear, let's call a spade a spade. For our football player, we have *mini-camp preparation* (a macrocycle) within which there are five steps (the mesocycles) of preparation. By varying your training intensity within each stage of preparation you can avoid staleness, overtraining, and injury.

Of course, for different athletes and different sports the objectives of each period—each cycle, whether it's macro, meso, or micro—will vary. For example, with our football player mini-camp preparation is

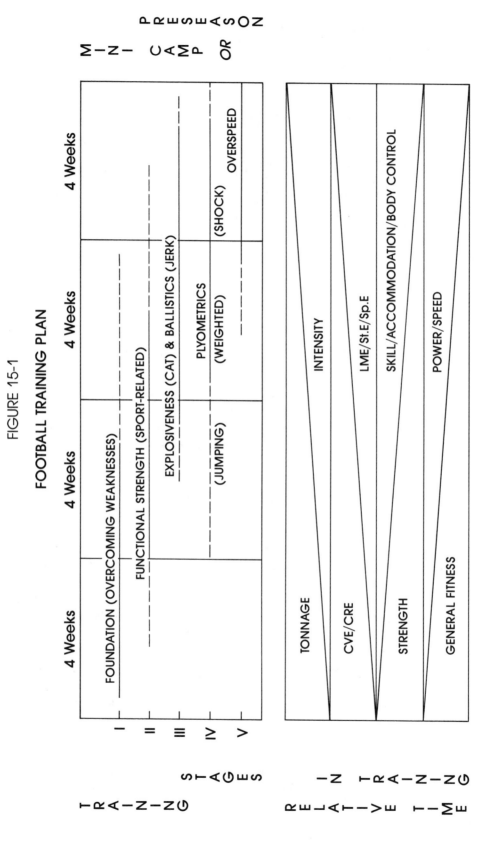

FIGURE 15-1

FOOTBALL TRAINING PLAN

divided into five stages, the ultimate objective of which is to perform the test items (e.g., strength tests, 40-yard dash, etc.) and the skill items (e.g., the drills) so well that the coaching staff is blown away by your abilities:

1. Stage one: Laying a solid foundation of strength and general fitness
2. Stage two: Gaining sport-specific strength and fitness
3. Stage three: Gaining explosiveness through highly specialized exercise methods
4. Stage four: Taking your explosiveness to the limits through specialized plyometric exercises
5. Stage five: Honing limb and body speed to a fine edge through overspeed drills

Of course, the five stages overlap, allowing you to continue work on deficiencies while beginning the next step up the intensity ladder: preseason camp preparation, which is identical in scope to that of mini-camp, except that your objective now becomes far more focused on football skills related to your position. In general, your progress should reflect the following changes in overall program content:

- Tonnage decreases over the program's time period
- Intensity increases
- Cardiovascular work decreases
- Local muscular endurance, speed endurance, and strength endurance (collectively referred to as anaerobic endurance) work increases
- Work on skills and body control increases
- Work on absolute strength decreases
- Work on power and speed increases
- Work on general fitness gives way to more specific fitness

These above factors relate to football, but they are as adaptable to any sport. Your job as an athlete or coach is to identify the variables—the attributes—you need, when you need them to be in place, and how to go about getting them.

The stepwise procedure you set up is your roadmap, your cycle, your periodicity of training protocol. It really is that simple. But it's frustrating to me that so many coaches and athletes fail to grasp the simplicity because they've been given a scientific treatise to decipher.

16

ENDURANCE AND STRENGTH: Ne'er the Twain Shall Meet

Irondom has made claims which, for years, went unheeded by Academia. The list is long. Claims like, "weight training can improve flexibility," "weight training doesn't interfere with a child's growth," or "squats are not bad for the knees, they're good for the knees" fell on deaf ears.

Over the past few years, however, the intrepid Sleuths of Academe have been getting their act together. Many of the beliefs we have held have, one by one, been adopted by the scientists. What we knew intuitively and through years of practical insight, researchers slowly came to the same conclusions through painstaking observations and statistical analyses.

There is one observation that we've known about a long time which scientists are finally beginning to realize. And it does my heart a world of good to see it happening. For, in one fell swoop, scientists have laid waste to the surreptitious claims of Nautilus freaks and dinosaur coaches alike. Remember the Nautilus line: slow movements for one set to failure? And, remember the coaches' sentiments regarding long distance running for their strength athletes: "It'll get you through four quarters of play and make a man outta ya"?

What disturbs me most, though, is the current practice of certain athletes who spend hours on the cycle ergometer or jogging in order to reduce body fat.

So that you don't lose interest in what I have to say here—and it is important—let me give you the bottom line first. Explosive movements with the weights is the only way to develop great strength and power. Not only that, but engaging in slow, endurance-type movements will prevent you from reaching your maximum potential in strength, explosiveness, and muscular size.

There. I've said it in clear, concise language so that there will be no misunderstandings. Now let's backtrack and have a look at the research supporting these contentions, and some of the far-reaching implications from a practical perspective. These observations may very well impact on your career as a strength athlete more than any single piece of advice you've ever come across.

WHAT THE RESEARCH SHOWS

I do not want you to wade through volumes of research findings, irrelevant data, or obscure esoterica to get to the truth of the matter regarding the significance of my above-stated observations. Instead, let me list them for you in terms that you will understand:

1. Maximum power output of human skeletal muscle is positively correlated to the percentage of fast-twitch fibers in a given muscle (Bosco et al., 1983; Hakkinen et al., 1984).
2. Hypertrophy (increased size) of muscle fibers occurs mainly in fast-twitch fibers in response to stimulation afforded by weight training, and most especially weight training that is explosive in nature (Hakkinen et al., 1985; Thorstensson et al., 1976).
3. The ultimate potential for explosive movements is determined by the fast-twitch composition of muscles (Hakkinen et al. 1985).
4. Endurance training reduces the inherent capability of the neuromuscular system for maximum power output (Dudley & Fleck, 1987).
5. Vertical jumping ability—inherently a fast-twitch muscle function—decreases with endurance training (Bosco et al. 1983; Ono et al. 1976).
6. Strength training with weights induces little or no increase in aerobic power, but markedly improves anaerobic endurance (i.e., short-term endurance such as the type necessary in sprinting, football, etc.) (Hickson et al., 1980).
7. Strength training in conjunction with endurance training may enhance performances in endurance events where occasional explosive bouts of effort are called for (Dudley & Fleck, 1987).
8. Endurance training performed concurrently with weight training (e.g., every other day approach) interferes with optimal strength, power, and size development in muscles involved (Hickson, 1980; Dudley & Djamil, 1985).
9. Concurrent endurance training and weight training markedly

interferes with an athlete's ability to perform explosive movements, due mainly to adaptive responses in the muscle (Hickson, 1980; Dudley & Djamil, 1985; Dudley & Fleck, 1987).

10. None of the above findings result from overtraining or poor research design (Dudley & Fleck, 1987). Thus, it would appear that these findings are real, and should be considered by strength coaches and strength athletes.

11. The mechanisms by which power, size, and strength are reduced as a result of endurance training most probably are mechanical destruction of existing white (fast-twitch) fibers, their replacement by red (slow-twitch) fibers, and enzymatic and neuromuscular changes more appropriate for slow, endurance types of movements (Armstrong, 1987).

There you have it, fellow iron freaks. Now, I don't want to belabor this issue, but this is what we've been saying for quite some time now. But the scientists sure do have a nice way of saying it, don't they? Now I'd like to say it for the average athlete.

SOME PRACTICAL SPORTS APPLICATIONS

If all you've been doing is slow, continuous tension movements, reread some of the recent issues of *Muscle & Fitness* where both Jeff Everson and I speak about holistic training. In holistic training, all of the

Sprint-loading techniques, such as stadium step running, belong in the middle of the plyometric phase. Such loading is for strength, not speed. Performed too close to competition, this technique could slow you down.

clements of your cells (mitochondria, capillaries, sarcoplasm, myofibrils, and satellite cells) are stimulated in the appropriate amounts for maximum development.

You should, under any circumstances, recall the age-old principle of superspeed training (performing your reps and sets at maximum speed) as a step up the ladder of training intensity. Remember, it's the white fibers—the ones that contract fast—that will give you the greatest returns in both strength and size. So, never neglect these important fast movements.

But, perhaps as importantly, remember that all the endless hours of ergometric cycling, running the beaches, or stadium steps, and other similar endurance-type activities will ultimately rob you of your ability to achieve maximum strength, size, and power. Clearly, the answer to the next question, what to do to lose fat, is *not*—repeat—***not*** endurance training.

Your percent body fat should be within two percentage points of your competition level at all times. That means that your nutritional status, and your supplementation schedule, must be a constantly monitored aspect of your training. That includes your off-season protocol—for it's then that laziness, easy training, and poor dietary habits most often strike.

ATHLETES AND OTHER FITNESS ENTHUSIASTS

Both strength and endurance can be improved to levels far beyond the norm by combining training elements from both objectives. In fact, you can improve your endurance to maximum levels while weight training (it's not possible, as we've seen, to reach your potential in strength while endurance training).

So, for sports where maximum strength and power output are not as critical (such as soccer, basketball or middle-distance running, and swimming) but where good cardiovascular endurance is critical, then you should mix your endurance training with weight training for improved strength and power.

For strength and power athletes though, a normal oxygen uptake ability (45–55 ml/O_2 per kg of body weight per minute) is sufficient, so additional work is sure to be counterproductive to your training objectives. Instead, you should concentrate on anaerobic endurance, and the best two ways of achieving this specific kind of sports endurance are interval training using explosive running, and weight training. Football players, boxers, weight athletes, bodybuilders, and powerlifters are the kinds of athletes who fit into this category.

17

YOUR HEART AND WEIGHT TRAINING

Who was it that came to America in search of the fabled Fountain of Youth? Ponce de León? One of those bemetaled fellows. Little did he know that his quest would continue for hundreds of years, on into the era of American history that, hundreds of years from now, will be referred to as the Age of Fitness.

In case you haven't been watching what's going on around you, that's now. And if you listen to guys like Dr. Kenneth Cooper, that fountain of youth can only be approached from a dead run. But if you listen to others it's located under a pile of pig iron.

So, where is it? And can we, like the hordes of joggers believe—in their (ahem) hearts—get there at a gallop? Or are we obliged to pump iron 'til our hearts' content?

APPLES AND ORANGES

I can settle the apparent polemic right now. These guys aren't really at odds, you see. They simply dance to the beat of different drummers. It isn't really iron heads versus road warriors or anything like that. But that doesn't resolve our initial problem—where's that fountain? And what's the best way to get there?

If I may, I'd like to settle that one up front, too. You see, it doesn't make any difference because, at last reckoning, people who exercise regularly, and that means those who run as well as those who lift weights, really don't live significantly longer than the average healthy

148

person. There is no magic way of living longer. I guess you really do only go 'round once.

Quality, Not Quantity

But the benefits of fitness reside primarily in the realm of life quality. Healthier, more productive, more confident, more zestful, less depression, less anxiety—these are the well-known benefits of the fitness lifestyle.

But I still have a problem with all that. I still want to know whether I can get the same benefits for my heart as runners get if I train with weights. There seems to be a real hot debate going on within the ivory walls of the Tower of Academe on that subject.

So, let's see how the research literature stacks up. But, I'll tell you right now, you ain't gonna see me out there poundin' the ground! No indeed! I'm an ironhead through and through! So, if it appears that I'm stacking the deck for weight training as the ultimate form of exercise, you'll at least understand if not agree.

Relative Versus Absolute Endurance

Contest time! In corner one we have your typical marathon runner, weighing 154 pounds, much of which is comprised of cardiac muscle. In corner two sits a just-as-typical bodybuilder, resplendently adorned with 210 pounds of massive skeletal muscle. Their task is to see who can carry 20 100-pound kegs up to the second-floor pub the fastest. That's a real feat of endurance, if ever there was one.

Score one big one for the bodybuilder.

Task two is to see who can carry 50% of their own bodyweight up to the same pub 20 consecutive times the fastest.

Well, it'd be a tossup, I reckon, depending on who was most motivated by the prize.

So, don't tell me that runners have more endurance than weightlifters. I know better.

Of course, the former task is an example of absolute endurance, the winner of which is most often going to be the physically stronger of the contestants. The second task is an apt example of what relative endurance is all about, and in that the odds are often more equal. Even there, I'd put my beer money on the bodybuilder.

So, what kind of a test of endurance is a marathon run? After all, the runner is carrying over 50 pounds less baggage than the body-builder. For a moment, try to picture what'd happen if the marathon runner had to wear a lead-filled vest to bring his bodyweight up to that of the bodybuilder. Who would win the marathon then? Hell, who'd even finish?

You can devise all sorts of devilish means of proving your own point, depending on who you'd like to see win. The point is, you're still comparing apples and oranges.

Who Has the Strongest Heart?

Because the marathon runner puts adaptive stress on his heart for longer periods of time more frequently than the typical bodybuilder, I daresay he'd probably have a more developed heart muscle. That is to say, his heart rate will be slower because he's pumping a greater volume of blood per beat than the bodybuilder. Also, he's probably going to have a more equitable oxygen uptake because, relative to his heart's pumping strength and body weight, he has less tissue to absorb oxygenated blood.

But no one has ever looked at the problem in what I consider to be the right light. By George, the bodybuilder *still* carted those beer kegs up the stairs faster than the runner!

A CASE STUDY

In the first and only study of its kind, noted cardiologist Dr. Kenneth Lynch (himself a marathon runner) pumped 20 millicurries of technetium 99m, a radioactive tracer substance that attaches itself to red blood cells, into the veins of a fellow who had been a powerlifter for over 25 years: Me.

His plan was to study my heart via radio-angiography for the purpose of seeing what he could see. He had done many distance runners in the past, but never an ironhead. I was placed on a supine bicycle ergometer under a nuclear camera that was interfaced with an electrocardiogram and a computer. The computer converted the radioactive images picked up by the camera into visual images (on a TV monitor) of my heart as it moved through systole and diastole.

The left ventricle is the part of the heart that pushes blood throughout your body. It also happens to be the part of the heart most often associated with cardiac diseases such as myocardial infarction, atherosclerosis, and similarly bad sounding conditions. That's the part of my heart Dr. Lynch was most interested in.

What did the good doctor find? Well, of course, it didn't surprise me a bit, but the doc was flabbergasted. As the ergometer workload increased in intensity, here is how my heart responded in regard to the one parameter most often overlooked by researchers who have displayed a penchant for comparing weight trainees with runners—ejection fraction. That's the percentage of blood in the left ventricle that's pumped out with each beat.

900 kg meter/min. workload: HR = 93; EF = 79%
1,100 kg meters/min. workload: HR = 117; EF = 84%
1,300 kg meters/min. workload: HR = 133; EF = 96%

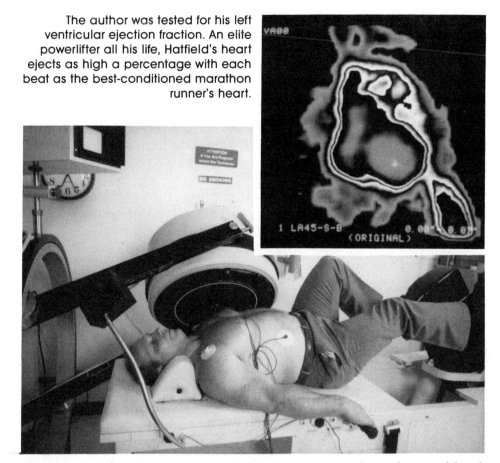

The author was tested for his left ventricular ejection fraction. An elite powerlifter all his life, Hatfield's heart ejects as high a percentage with each beat as the best-conditioned marathon runner's heart.

During the last six minutes of the stress test, when the workload equaled 1,300 kg meters/min., my heart rate varied as high as 160 beats per minute. No left ventricular wall abnormalities were found, meaning that the blood supply to my heart muscle, via the coronary arteries, was unimpeded.

A few noteworthy comments are in order. First, according to Dr. Lynch, he's never tested a marathon runner with a better ejection fraction than mine. My ventricular muscle, it appears, contracts fully enough to squeeze almost every bit of the blood out of it before it relaxes to fill up again for the next beat.

Was I relieved to hear that?

Also of note was the fact that no marathon runner alive can come close to matching the workload that I performed at, let alone keep his average heart rate at 133 beats per minute. Most marathon runners aren't physically strong enough to endure workloads of beyond 800–900 kg meters/min without incurring massive work-stopping oxygen debt.

So, how come I can't run a marathon?

The answer is in training specificity. First, I weigh 260 pounds, nearly double the weight of your average successful marathon runner. That means, of course, that my heart muscle has to supply blood to twice the tissue.

Also, and of equal importance, each of my muscle cells is adapted to explosive, single maximum contracture. I am a powerlifter. Within each of a marathon runner's muscle cells are numerous, highly developed mitochondria, the organelles that are responsible for the cell's oxidative functions. I have relatively few of them because I don't train in a manner that is conducive to their development. So, even if I could get sufficient blood to my working muscles, I couldn't use it efficiently.

The result of all this is that the marathon runner's ability to use oxygen, called his *max VO$_2$* uptake, is typically in the range of 75 ml of oxygen used by each kilogram of body weight per minute. Contrast this figure with that of the average powerlifter, whose max VO$_2$ uptake is in the range of 45–50.

CAN WEIGHT TRAINING IMPROVE CARDIOVASCULAR FUNCTION?

Max VO$_2$ uptake isn't the only indicator of cardiovascular efficiency. As I noted earlier, for example, there's also stroke volume, heart rate, and ejection fraction of the left ventricle. There's also the performance of the cardiac muscle, a related aspect of ejection fraction having to do with unimpeded circulation of blood through the cardiac muscle.

Many recent studies have shown conclusively that weight training can reduce the incidence of coronary disease by significantly reducing your low-density lipoproteins and increasing your high-density lipoproteins. HDL cholesterol in the blood prevents the buildup of LDL cholesterol on your arterial walls. One study showed that three weight training sessions per week (lasting 45–60 minutes) can produce a 10%–15% reduction in cholesterol, and up to a 30% reduction in blood-borne fat (triglycerides).

Also, not all fitness experts agree that weight training serves no useful function in regard to its ability to increase your max VO$_2$ uptake. Dr. Mike Stone, formerly head research scientist for the Auburn University based U.S. Strength Research Institute found that Olympic style weight training produced increases in max VO$_2$ uptake averaging up to three ml/kg/min in just five weeks of training. He also found significant reductions in body fat (increased muscle mass with no decrease in total body weight), yet another beneficial aspect of weight training insofar as cardiovascular function is concerned.

Researchers reporting their findings in the Journal of Pediatrics (January 1984) noted that teenagers suffering from hypertension (high blood pressure) were able to reduce their blood pressure through weight training to levels apparently lower than those obtained with ordinary endurance training. The teen subjects of this study performed six exercises for three sets of five to eight repetitions three times weekly.

One explanation for this effect is that weight training, unlike running, involves the use of most of the muscles of your body. Thus, your peripheral circulation is enhanced, as is your arteries' muscle tone and elasticity, both factors in reducing blood pressure. Of course, the typical athlete or weight training enthusiast is far more likely to be conscious of sound dietary habits that involve less saturated fats, less sodium, more complex carbohydrates, and a better protein supply.

RESOLVING THE CONFLICT

Why can Dr. Stone, using Olympic weight training techniques, show significant improvement in his subjects' max VO_2 uptake, whereas several other researchers failed to show significant improvements in cardiovascular function after strenuous weight training? To me the answer is obvious, but having no data to support my claim, I am left with only my writer's prerogative in forwarding an hypothesis that remains untested.

- Olympic weight training movements are radically dissimilar to typical weight training movements in several ways.
- Weight training raises heart rate, but restricts venous return of the blood to the heart.
- This, in turn, causes a decreased stroke volume—less blood is available to be pumped out.
- The occlusion of venous return is known to cause a "pressor response," which in turn activates certain stress chemicals (catecholamines) that increase heart rate relative to VO_2 uptake.
- Since stroke volume must be elevated in order for there to be an improvement in cardiorespiratory adaptation, the circulatory restrictiveness of weight training must be reduced if there is to be an improvement in max VO_2 uptake to be derived from weight training.
- Olympic weight training is nonrestrictive in comparison to other forms of weight training. The movements are very explosive and short in duration, with ample relaxation of all muscles involved between each repetition. Thus, there is no occlusion of blood return.
- In normal weight training, there is an inordinate increase of sustained duration in intrathoracic pressure (from holding one's breath), and forcefully grasping the bar or handgrips for a sustained period (throughout an entire set).

Thus, for ordinary weight training to be beneficial in improving max VO$_2$ uptake values, it must be nonrestrictive, rhythmic with relaxation pauses between each rep, of sufficient intensity to maintain a pulse rate of above 60%–70% of the trainee's maximum heart rate, and of greater than 30 minutes duration. Also, each repetition should be an all-out effort as well—maximum contracture against submaximum resistance, so multiple reps can be performed.

So, while weight training can definitely be tailored to benefit your heart as well as your muscles, it will never get you ready to run a marathon.

To train for a marathon, you're going to have to run, get your body weight down to a level that's small enough so your heart's pumping ability is sufficiently great to service it with oxygenated blood. Be prepared to look like a pencilneck on the beach, too.

To me, a better way to go is to stop trying to compare apples with oranges. Since fitness means different things to different people, whatever form of fitness you strive for should be the kind that's going to improve the quality of your life most.

As for increasing your chances of living longer, forget it. Be happy with warding off disease and staying healthy and, most importantly, stay happy with yourself and your body. And, for my money, for the vast majority of people out there, weight training is going to give you far more dividends than running ever could, especially if you're into looking good and, at the same time, having a reasonable level of cardiorespiratory efficiency.

18

SQUATS:
King of All Exercises

Louis Sullivan is famous for his proclamation that form follows function. He was referring to state-of-the-art architecture. His words ring as true for the human body in many regards. Your form in many exercises will determine the precise training effect you receive, and therefore the functional capacity and appearance of the affected muscles. The same holds true for squatting.

How you squat—reps, sets, speed, frequency, load, technique—will affect your legs in different but predictable ways. That the guesswork has been taken out of squatting technique isn't generally known, considering the incredible array of squatting styles and beliefs that persist around the world of iron. Even many orthopedic specialists continue to insist that squatting is bad for your knees, back, hips, or whatever. It seems that these folks have taken out the guesswork as well, albeit predicated upon gross misinformation. Their arguments are often very convincing, given the growing number of patients they see with bad knees from exercising improperly.

That's the kicker—squats, perhaps more than any other exercise, must be done properly. So much weight is used in the squat, and in such a precarious way (knees and spine are fragile) that injury often seems an inevitability of squat training. But injury need never occur if some simple rules are applied. The benefits you'll derive far outweigh the risk of injury.

In case you didn't know it, there are at least 10 different methods of squatting, each having its own unique advantages. And, in the case of

Fred "Dr. Squat" Hatfield as he squats with 1,014 pounds at a body weight of 255 pounds.

competitive powerlifting such an array of squatting styles exists that it's impossible to list them all. Each powerlifting technique is designed to maximize the user's individual strengths while minimizing his weaknesses. (See table of competitive powerlifting squatting styles.)

But, before I begin to talk about each style, let's look at the general benefits of squatting and, as importantly, some of the pitfalls that can make your training agonizingly dangerous and counterproductive, and ways of avoiding them.

Above, I stated that the nay-saying orthopods (and other folks who advise against squatting) base their concerns upon gross misinformation. You see, most of them have either never been under heavy iron, or never worked with well-trained athletes, and therefore couldn't possibly know how valuable squats can be. Their response to my foregoing statement is typically, "You don't have to jump off a bridge to be able to accurately predict what's going to happen to your body if you do." Extending their concern to squats, they point to all of the catastrophic knee, hip, and soft tissue injuries they see among weight trainees (most of whom are ignorant of sound training practice). They've apparently never looked at X rays of athletes who have squatted properly for years, or carved on cadavers of former weight trainees for signs of stress adaptation. Had they, it would have been clear that:

- Muscles are strengthened far beyond the norm, making injury far less likely, and performance improvement more likely.

- Bones are strengthened, both in density as well as improved strength of ligamentous and tendonous insertion points, making injury far less likely.
- Ligaments and tendons (connective tissue) are increased in thickness, viscoelasticity, and tensile strength, making injury far less likely.

As for those athletes who do heavy squats for the sake of great strength, notably powerlifters, but certain misdirected athletes as well, similar adaptation occurs. But because of the nature of competition—and most competitive sports are inherently dangerous, making injury omnipresent—maladaptive forces tend to negate the beneficial aspects. For example, many powerlifters suffer arthritis after their competitive careers end. Other athletes do as well, and the culprit is often excessive heavy squatting during their competitive years.

For these indomitable souls, I make no apologies or excuses—they paid the price of athletic glory. Besides arthritis, bone spurs, calcium deposits, torn cartilage, bursitis, and a host of other stress injuries often plague them long into retirement. That, unfortunately, is the nature of competitive sport, pushing your body to points beyond normal limits for the sake of a record performance. Most who suffer such post-career ailments would never have changed anything. They went into sports with open eyes, knowing the inherent dangers.

Even competitors could have avoided most of their problems, however, with some proper guidance on both technique as well as on training methods. Such post-career trauma, often of a near-crippling intensity, can often be avoided.

No, those who recommend against squatting never recognize the vast majority of bodybuilders and other weight trainees who have benefited greatly from squats. They see only those who come to their clinics with problems—the healthy people go unnoticed. Healthy athletes, you see, don't go to the doctor much.

WHY SQUAT?

With so many different types of machines on the market that tend to minimize inherent dangers associated with putting a heavy chunk of iron on your back and descending into a full squat position, it doesn't seem unreasonable to ask, "Why squat?"

Leg press machines, back squat machines, leg curl machines, leg extension machines, in/out thigh machines—the list is long—all have their place in most bodybuilders' training regimen. But none can replace the excellent intensity afforded by squats. This intensity is essential for complete development of the legs, either for athletic reasons or for bodybuilding appearance.

There must be balance between the extent that you isolate a muscle

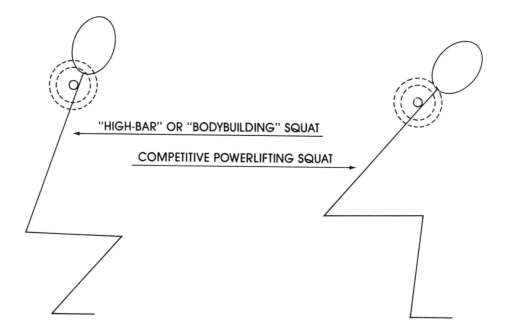

"HIGH-BAR" OR "BODYBUILDING" SQUAT

COMPETITIVE POWERLIFTING SQUAT

This comparison between the "high-bar" squat (left) and the "power" squat clearly shows differences between the two techniques. For example, the hip, knee, and ankle angles are of critical importance. At left, the glutes and hamstrings are of far less consequence in squatting than they are at right. Instead, emphasis is placed on the quadriceps at left. Note also that the bar is higher on the shoulders at left, and farther down the back at right. This affords the powerlifter greater leverage (for lifting heavier competition weight). And finally, at left the bar is centered over the middle of the base of support, whereas at right the bar is over the heels (for less quadricep and more hamstring/gluteal involvement).

and the amount of intensity applied. Too much isolation and the muscle is placed at such a leverage disadvantage that little weight—and therefore, little stress—is applied. Of course, this situation diminishes overall training effect. On the other hand, resorting to the use of exercises that involve several muscle groups often robs the target muscle of needed stress because the stress is absorbed by the other muscle groups.

Squatting properly—with upright torso, knees extending over the feet, and to a position near or below parallel—centralizes the majority of the stress in the quadriceps. The hamstrings, glutes, and erector spinae receive some stress too, but not enough to rob the quads of major effect.

There's nothing wrong with compound exercises, providing the target muscle is made to be the weakest link in the chain. You ensure this by adjusting technique accordingly. Then, being the weaker of the muscles acting in the movement, it receives overload stress, while the others receive less than overload stress and are relatively unaffected by comparison.

Squatting properly ensures that the quads will receive overload stress to an extent that no other exercise can afford.

HOW TO SQUAT

There are five reasons for squatting: rehabilitation, muscular size, strength, power, or endurance. Each requires a different approach, and an array of different squatting techniques.

Leg Size

The holistic bodybuilding approach to squatting is best applied for improved muscular size of the upper legs. Variation is the key. You should perform your squats with something close to the following approach:

1. Heavy weights (85% 1RM) for 4–6 reps, 3–4 sets
2. Moderate weights (75%–80% 1RM) for 10–15 reps, 3–4 sets
3. Light weights (50%–60% 1RM) for up to 40 reps, 3–4 sets

The heavy sets should be performed with compensatory acceleration—moving the weight out of the hole as fast as possible every inch of the way up, but "putting on the brakes" near the top of the movement to avoid throwing yourself off balance. This will ensure maximum effect upon the fast-twitch fibers, and also provide high-quality overload for every rep, every set, and for most of the movement in each rep, maximizing myofibrillar growth.

The moderate weights should be moved with both compensatory acceleration as well as with controlled, rhythmical cadence. One or two sets of each technique is recommended. This will help both red (slow-twitch) and white (fast-twitch) fibers achieve maximal myofibrillar growth as well as sarcoplasmic and mitochondrial proliferation.

The light weights should be handled with slow, continuous tension movements, never pausing at the top or bottom of the squat. The continuous tension provides improved capillarization to the muscle cells (bringing in more oxygenated blood), and maximum growth (in both size and number) of the mitochondria in the muscle cells.

Bodybuilders who try this approach consistently report to me that they've never really worked their legs before—the effect is so profound. Be prepared for the workout of your life.

Leg Strength and Power

Myofibrillar growth is the most important component in improving your leg strength, since it's the myofibrils of your muscle cells that deliver the contractile force. But for power—the ability to deliver strength with explosive speed—there needs to be more than just high-tension exercise. I've found that both can be achieved through the application of compensatory acceleration. Then, through a six-week peaking period, leg strength and power can be brought to a maximum and held for a short period (perhaps as long as one month). Your fast-twitch fibers are the central target.

1. Use heavy weights (80%–85% 1RM) for five to eight reps, four to five sets using compensatory acceleration on every rep during off-season training.
2. Follow a six-week peaking program to maximize strength and power.
3. Agility, explosiveness, and body control drills are imperative in any leg strength/power program, and should be done both off-season and preseason.

Step three is important, and can aptly be illustrated with an analogy. What's the sense of coming off the line like a shot from a cannon if the guy in front of you simply has to sidestep out of harm's way? Power isn't enough in most sports—agility and body control are also essential, and that requires something more than squats can provide.

In powerlifting, however, strength and power suffice—the weight on your back isn't going to trick you. All you have to do to excel in powerlifting is to achieve massive strength and power. Other sports aren't that accommodating.

Leg Endurance

Many sports, including rowing, cycling, and long-distance running, require high levels of muscular endurance in the legs. Bodybuilders, of course, require muscular endurance too, but more for the improved size and definition that aerobic-type exercise provides. For sheer endurance, the central cellular targets are the extensiveness of the blood supply (capillaries) and the efficiency of each cell's oxygen uptake and utilization mechanisms, the mitochondria.

1. Light weights (50%–70% 1RM) for 20–40 reps, three to four sets using slow, continuous tension.
2. Light weights (50%–70% 1RM) for 20–40 reps, three to four sets using high-speed compensatory acceleration movements.
3. Accent should be on forcing yourself past the "pain" barrier that is felt with extreme fatigue, and on maintaining a high heart rate (generally above 60% of your maximum heart rate, which is computed by subtracting your age from 220 and then multiplying that number by .6).

A FEW HELPFUL HINTS

Foot Spacing. A myth persists that wide-stance squats develop the inner thigh (vastus medialis) while close-stance squats develop the outer thigh (vastus lateralis). Well, "myth" may be a bit strong, but in all my years of training, I have never seen this happen to any noticeable degree. The quadriceps share a common tendon of insertion at the knee joint, making differential contracture from foot spacing either unlikely or miniscule in effect. My opinion is that you'll do as well with a foot position that you're comfortable with in squatting, and to apply a variety of squatting techniques to supplement your squats. Greater all-around leg development will result.

Type of Bar. For the average fitness freak or bodybuilder, the kind of bar you use for squats will make little difference, so long as it's sturdy and fitted with safety collars. However, for the behemoths among you—the bodybuilders, athletes, and powerlifters who are using tonnage only dreamed of back when Olympic weightlifting was the only game in town—you'll have to be a bit more careful about the bar you use. Your bar should not whip up and down excessively, as this can cause muscle tears or spinal injury from being thrown off balance when stepping backward with the bar. Choose a sturdy bar, preferably one measuring at least 29 millimeters in diameter, and with center knurling to prevent the bar from slipping on your shoulders. The plates should fit on the bar loosely, and the collars should not clamp the plates tightly against the inside collars. Tight-fitting plates cause the bar to absorb the kinetic energy generated by walking backward, and it whips more. With loose-fitting plates, the rattling that is caused absorbs the energy, thereby preventing dangerous whipping.

Spotters. When I walk into a gym to get in a squat workout, most of the guys know what's going to happen. "Oh, no! Hatfield's here! He's going to ask me to spot him!"

Well, that's the breaks in the game, fellow ironhead. Gym etiquette dictates it, and I'd do the same for you. I can't help it if it takes five of you. It's amazing how many "bad backs" or torn muscles show up when I ask for assistance. Be a nice guy, won't you? Help your gym partners when they need spotting assistance—it could be *you* who gets hurt from lack of adequate spotting.

Miscellaneous. You may find that wrist wraps help in holding the bar firmly on your back or shoulders. Weak wrists can cause the bar to slip. Also, heavy squatting can injure your wrists over a period of time by disrupting the carpal tunnel, the passage through the small wrist bones through which your hand's nerves pass.

Your shoes should have strong lateral support to prevent rolling outward on your feet. Old, worn sneakers or bare feet are definitely *not* recommended when squatting—they're dangerous.

Maintain a clean, litter-free area for both yourself and your spotters. It you get in trouble, you want both you and your spotters to have a clear track back to the rack.

Don't wear belts, wraps, or supersuits when squatting with under 80% of your max. Doing so robs your support muscles and legs of needed stress that will force them to adapt. Personally, I refrain from wearing any supportive garb until I'm over 85% of my max. The whole point of training is to deliver adaptive stress to your body so it'll get stronger, bigger, or more enduring. Absorbing the stress with supportive garb is counterproductive.

Once you get super heavy—and that shouldn't happen any more than one to three weeks prior to the end of a cycle—then you can don your support clothes. It's safe to do so at that point. But not before.

SQUATTING—WITH A NEW TWIST

Every once in a while, something new comes along that is revolutionary, earth-shattering. Y'know . . . sliced bread, hip pockets, sulfur matches.

Well, earth-shattering may be a bit strong, but no one can deny that these are the things that make life measurably more enjoyable. If you're into training, and I suspect most of you are, you no doubt have come across many such innovations in the gym. Arm blasters, adjustable barbells, rotating sleeves.

Hold onto your training belts, fellow iron freaks, for I am about to describe a new invention that is destined to literally revolutionize your leg training. Of such mammoth proportions is the importance of this new device, that every gym in the land will have at least three or four of them. The Soviets are bound to have warehouses full.

"Hold on, Dr. Squat!" you say. "What's wrong with squats? You have always touted squats as state-of-the-art when it came to leg training."

True, I have indeed. But always with the admonishment that squats must be done correctly. To work best—with the utmost safety and effectiveness—squats must be done with an upright torso, with knees extending over the feet in order to maximally isolate the quads, and to a position just short of rock-bottom to ensure adaptive response in the tissues comprising the knee.

Powerlifters, of course, turn to the more effective technique of spreading the stress to the hips, hams, back, and quads when it comes time to enter contests. But even the most scientific powerlifters train with the upright bodybuilding style during the off-season. And athletes of every persuasion do squats as described above.

Squats are, after all, the singlemost effective leg exercise ever conceived, whether your training goals are those of a bodybuilder, power athlete, endurance athlete, or fitness freak.

So, what's this about a new invention? Quite appropriately, and

Safety squat

perhaps for lack of a better name, its inventor calls it the *Safety Squat Bar*. Jesse Hoagland may not be a name any of you know. But those athletes who have used his bar aren't likely to forget it. Many of them with knee problems or bad backs were doomed to try competing in their sport without the benefit of squats. His new bar gave them a new lease on their respective athletic careers.

Personally, I began using the Safety Squat Bar exclusively in my training about 6 years ago. I went from an all-time best of 920 pounds to an official 970, then to a lift of 1,014 pounds in Hawaii a few months ago. I can clearly see 1,100 in the near future. I credit this amazing bar for that.

Safety Squats

Let's take it from the top. What exactly is this new bar, and what's so great about it that makes it both more effective as well as safer than the conventional straight bar?

The conventional straight bar has several inherent weaknesses or dangers:

1. The chance of leaning forward or rounding your back under heavy loads is always a problem—serious injury can result.
2. Falling off balance forward or backward also jeopardizes your safety when under heavy squatting loads.

3. Your shoulder girdle, shoulders, wrists, and elbows often take a beating holding the straight bar in place.
4. Missing a squat attempt is something that happens to all of us from time to time, often with dire consequences.
5. Discomfort to the back of the neck where the bar sits is a problem we all shrugged off as part of the game.
6. Individual anatomical peculiarities often made it extremely difficult—if not impossible—to assume the most efficient stance in order to derive maximum benefit from squats.
7. Not being able to squat because of the lack of competent spotters has been one of my personal gripes in the past.

Despite these problems, all of us have learned to put up with them and get on with the business of learning good technique, taking proper precautions, and doing what we knew was best for us. We squat no matter what, because it was best to do so. That we got by and made progress with conventional squats is due in no small measure to our belief that squats worked best, and we made them part of our program.

Now listen carefully—I am sometimes accused of making overt statements, but this time it's warranted. Read the list of problems again. *None of these problems arise with the Safety Squat Bar.*

The truly great thing about it is that because of the elimination of these inherent problems with conventional squatting, you will realize faster gains, less stress and strain on your back, knees, and other joints, fewer potentially devastating misses under heavy iron, and in general a far more enjoyable workout. The exquisite isolation the Safety Squat Bar provides for your quads will be a truly unique experience, I assure you.

Let's go over the points outlined above one by one.

The hands are not holding the bar allowing you to grasp the handles on the power rack. Because of the heavy loads involved in squatting when returning to the upright position, there is tendency to "round" the back and place unnecessary stress on your lower back. This is now avoided by exerting pressure against the power rack handles and thus maintaining a perfectly straight back throughout the entire squatting motion. The use of the hands also prevents the trainee from falling forward or backward.

During the squatting motion the resistance varies from one point of the lift to another. When you start up from the low position (thighs parallel to the floor) you need a lot of resistance. As you move out of the squat, your strength decreases, therefore you can handle less resistance. When you reach your "sticking point," the resistance must be at its lowest. When the "sticking point" is passed, your strength increases and therefore you can handle more weight.

By carefully analyzing this range of motion and resistance

changes, you immediately realize that in using the conventional squatting bar the trainee is forced to use a load that can be handled in the weakest position. This results in using an inadequate amount of weight in the strongest position of the squatting motion.

This problem is solved by use of the hands in the Safety Squat Bar. When the muscles are overloaded and the "sticking point" is reached, the hands can be used to help you through the weak points of the squatting motion. This unique feature allows you to work with heavier weights when you are strongest and gives you help when you are weakest. You are exerting near-maximum effort through the entire range of motion.

The padded yolk that the Safety Squat Bar is equipped with virtually eliminates neck discomfort. And the fact that you needn't use your hands to hold the bar on your shoulders eliminates wrist, shoulder, elbow, or shoulder girdle discomfort.

Using your hands to assist has some benefits beyond allowing greater loads to be handled. You can also regulate your position—that is, your posture under the bar can be adapted to suit your own anatomical peculiarities so that you can literally tailor your squatting style to afford maximum overload and consequently muscular development.

There is a five-inch camber at both ends of the bar. When weight is placed on the ends of the bar, the two stems of the shoulder yolk hang downward. As you approach the bar, you slip your head under the yolk stems and rotate them upward and forward. Doing this also causes the weights to rotate upward and forward.

Once on your shoulders, and standing upright, the weighted ends of the bar cause the yolk stems to press downward onto your shoulders, thereby holding the bar securely in place, and leaving your hands free to either hold the handles of the squat rack or simply hang to your sides, on your thighs, or on the ends of the yolk stems.

Most important, however, is the fact that now the weighted ends of the bar are perfectly aligned with your body's center of gravity. Conventional squatting placed the weight behind you, fully four or five inches behind your body's midline. That caused you to lean forward for balance. With the Safety Squat Bar, the weight is distributed directly in line with your body's midline, and completely eliminates the need—indeed, the ability—to lean forward.

Your back problems and knee problems are a thing of the past. Now you can squat again, safely, effectively, and quite probably with bigger weights than ever before.

And that amounts to better progress toward your training goals.

Power squats: The object in competitive powerlifting is to lift as much weight as you can. When squatting, this is done by sharing the weight being hoisted with several muscle groups so that no single muscle ends up a weak link, thereby limiting your performance. The

Power squat

body position in powerlifting squats spreads the force to four major muscle groups, the quadriceps, hamstrings, gluteals, and erector spinae. The erectors act primarily as torso stabilizers rather than important prime movers, whereas the glutes act only at the bottom of the squat, ending their function beyond the sticking point (roughly 30° flexion). The hams and quads work throughout the squat.

High-bar squats: The chief function of high-bar squats is to affect the quadriceps in a major way, with less emphasis upon the glutes, hams, and erectors. Thus, an upright torso and acute knee angle is called for.

Sissy squats: The chief advantage of sissy squats is to get almost 100% isolation on the quads. Proponents of this method claim that they're far more effective than leg extensions in providing a proper balance of isolation and intensity to the quads, although not as well as do high-bar squats. Since little stress is placed on other muscles, it's an excellent alternative to regular squats during times of back injury or other problems keeping you from squatting normally.

Jefferson squats: All but forgotten, Jefferson squats still remain a great alternative to regular squats when you have back, knee, hip, or shoulder injuries that can detract from your leg training. The key is to keep an erect torso, and alternate the forward leg on subsequent sets.

Hack squats: Like the sissy squats and Jefferson squats, hack squats are an excellent alternative to regular squats during times of injury. The great isolation provided the quads can be adjusted by foot placement (if a hack squat machine is used) or by knee/hip angles (if a barbell is used).

Front squats: Front squats are a holdover from the old days, when the Olympic weightlifters exerted their influence on training tech-

High-bar squat, with Akeem Olajouwan

Sissy squat

Jefferson squat

Hack squat

Front squat with Joe Weider, the Master Blaster

nique for bodybuilders—we're talking 1930s and 1940s. It remains an excellent quad isolator, with reasonably good intensity to boot. A conventional Olympic grip or the cross-handed grip (depicted here) can be used.

Partial squats: Partial squats require that extremely heavy weights be used because of the leverage advantage gained in the upper ranges of the squat movement. Thus, a belt is mandatory (to help stabilize the lumbar spine), and the exercise should be done inside a power rack for safety. Despite these important disadvantages, some strength coaches who are afraid of their athletes hurting their knees on deep squats still insist on partial movements. For the bodybuilder, partial squats should only be used sparingly, probably during times of glute, hip, or knee injury. For athletes, they afford little in the way of advantage, and much in the way of disadvantage owing to the inherent dangers. To make them truly effective, loads heavier than the spine can safely bear must be used. Still, they can be used, as with bodybuilders, as an alternative to regular squats during glute, hip, or knee injury and rehabilitation. Just be extremely careful!

Front lunges: When you think about it, front lunges are no different than regular squats, except that the emphasis is placed on one leg at a time—the front leg. The advantage is that groin flexibility is achieved at the same time front leg strength is being developed, and that's good. The disadvantage, however, is that explosive movements (compensatory acceleration) cannot be safely exercised because of the precariousness of the position (the groin muscles are too easily pulled with explosive movements out of a split-squat position).

Side lunges: I'm surprised that more bodybuilders and athletes don't do side lunges. It's probably due to lack of groin flexibility and

Partial squat

Front lunge

Side lunge

the fact that side lunges require a bit more care in balance than do regular squats or lunges. Notwithstanding, side lunges exercise each leg separately, a practice that offers many of the same benefits that dumbbell training has over barbell training—exercising one limb at a time allows you to exercise greater strength output by that limb than when both limbs operate at the same time. Therefore, overload is improved; training effect, too. Again, side lunges are more precarious than front lunges, and make compensatory acceleration movements extremely difficult if not dangerous. Still, overall, side lunges are more effective than front lunges because the weight is centered directly over the leg. In front lunges, the front leg is in front of the weight source, and the force in standing up is directed backward rather than straight up. This tends to minimize the adaptive stress being delivered to the quadriceps.

19

PREDICTING STRENGTH LOSS FOLLOWING MAKING WEIGHT

In coming years, athletes will find it once again imperative to turn to sound training, scientific nutrition, and, when answers to training problems aren't available, scientific research in their quest for performance excellence. There's been a lull of late in this proven approach to achieving peak athletic performance capabilities. The reliance on pharmacological aids rather than hard work, smart training, and keen desire are, in large part, responsible for the lull. At least that's my subjective appraisal of what's happening among younger power-lifters who tend to cling to the notion that some sort of "free ride" can be derived from the use of drugs.

Everywhere I go I see young athletes training the same old way as the old-timers. They seem blind to the fact that in order to beat the established records set by the old-timers whose training they're emulating, they must adopt new technology. Old technology will make them only as good, not better.

Part of the old technology involves the use of drugs.

Introducing new technology is laborious, hard to believe in, and it takes ever so long. What's a young athlete to do? Do what the old-timers did years ago! Find a way! Innovate! Think! That's one lesson I advise youth to learn from the old-timers.

In truth, it can be done.

One small but highly significant innovation is to become more scientific in your approach to contests, especially when you have to "make weight," which usually means losing a few pounds to qualify for competition in a certain weight class.

POWER CURVE TO PREDICT STRENGTH LOSS FROM MAKING WEIGHT

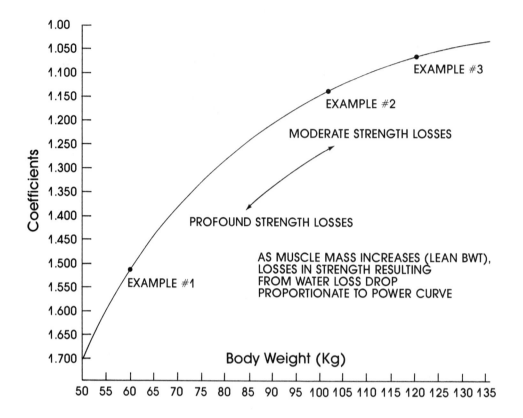

What strength losses can I expect from dropping five pounds? Twenty pounds? In which class should I be competing? How can I improve my contest efficiency?

I brought one approach to this problem back with me from Moscow. I've been playing with it for two years now, and have adapted it to powerlifting. I have found it to be so thoroughly accurate in its predictive capabilities that it far overshadows the accuracy of anything that has been used in the past. The Soviets call it the coefficient of contest efficiency.

It doesn't take a mathematics whiz to understand the concept that a smaller person will suffer more from weight losses than will a bigger one. It's simply that five pounds is a greater percentage of a smaller person's body weight than it is for a bigger person. The Soviets generated a power curve on the basis of researching hundreds of athletes who had to make weight for a contest (weightlifting), and recorded their success rates. Plotted against some simple tabulations they were able to predict with startling accuracy the exact amount of weight each athlete would lift at their respective contests. I reworked the Soviet power curve for use in powerlifting. Here's how it works.

THE CONTEST EFFICIENCY COEFFICIENT

Step one, of course, is to find out how many attempts you were successful at in your last contest. On the basis of how many you made you will know how heavy you should open with in your upcoming contest. For example, if you make one squat, then you're not paying attention to any semblance of your efficiency. If you make all three attempts, open with 94% of your max, and if you make two attempts, you should open at 96%. But how do you determine what 100% is for that particular contest?

Let's use an example to illustrate how it's done. Our man benches 170 kg in training while weighing 62 kg. He wants to compete in the 56 kg class. Since he has a history of doing 2% more during training than he does in a contest, his efficiency coefficient is only 0.98.

Using the 170 kg bench press as a starting point, determine (from the power curve values on the accompanying graph) values for his current weight (62 kg) as well as for his contest weight (56 kg) and solve the equation as follows:

$$170 \times \frac{1.494 \ (62 \ kg)}{1.646 \ (56 \ kg)} = 155 \ kg$$

Thus, his true *readiness* at a body weight of 56 kg in a contest situation is only 155 kg despite his better performance in training. Then, considering his 0.98 efficiency coefficient, he'll most likely do 2% less in *reality*. Thus, $0.98 \times 155 = 152.5$ kg is his true 100% level for the upcoming contest.

His starting attempt should be 94% (143 kg), his second attempt should be 96% (149 kg), and his final attempt should be 98% (152.5 kg)—his true capability based on his past performances and his weight-loss record. It is clear that the 18.5 kg decrease in actual contest outcome resulted from loss of weight and low contest efficiency history.

Let's compare this strength deficit with that of a big guy, weighing in at 125 kg. In training he bench pressed 300 kg weighing 6 kg over the limit (just like the 62 kg lifter who had to lose 6 kg). He too has an effectiveness coefficient of 0.98.

$$300 \times \frac{1.045 \ (131 \ kg)}{1.065 \ (125 \ kg)} = 294 \ kg$$

0.98 × 294 = 288.12 (his predicted max contest bench)

The big guy will then have to open with a bench press of 276 kg (94%), move to 282 kg (96%) for his second attempt, and finish with 288 kg (98%—his true contest efficiency).

Clearly, the big guy lost only 12 kg from his benching strength as a result of his weight loss and low contest efficiency, whereas the lighter guy lost a full 18.5 kg for the same weight loss and same contest efficiency.

Now for my own prediction: If you use this method of choosing

EXAMPLE OF HOW TO COMPUTE CONTEST READINESS

Name _____

Lifting or Competing as _____ kg bwt.

At (Contest Name)   Coefficient of
                                     Efficiency

Squat during training _____

Squat at meet   _____   _____

Bench during training _____   _____

Bench at meet   _____

Deadlift in training   _____   _____

Deadlift at meet   _____

Best Lifts During Training For

Squat _____ at bodyweight of _____

Bench _____ at bodyweight of _____

Deadlift _____ at bodyweight of _____

Readiness Coefficient:

$$\text{Best training lift} \times \frac{\text{training weight value}}{\text{competition weight value}} = \text{readiness}$$

True Readiness Coefficient:

Efficiency coefficient $\times$ readiness = true readiness
Squat:
Bench:
Deadlift:

Attempts:

% of True Readiness

	Squat	Bench Press	Deadlift
98%	_____	_____	_____
96%	_____	_____	_____
94%	_____	_____	_____

contest poundages, you will never again miss a lift from lack of strength. Most of you older fellas and gals out there won't use this technique because you're too stubborn. So, expect to have your records taken away—that's the nature of progress.

Let me end with some rather revealing statistics gathered by the Soviets. They compiled statistics for all world records set in weight-lifting during the past 20 years and came up with these findings:

- Eighty percent of all records were set by those lifters who tend to do better at contests than in training.
- The remaining 20% of all records over the past 20 years were set by lifters who tend to do about the same in contests as in training.
- Virtually no world records have been set by lifters with a contest efficiency coefficient less than 1.00.

So, your goal should be to lift more in contests than in training. How do you do that? How do you get a contest efficiency coefficient of greater than 0.98? Simply by adhering to the predictive procedures outlined for choosing your attempts when competing, and exercising care and restraint during your peaking period.

Once your contest efficiency coefficient exceeds (or, at least equals) 1.00—preferably in the 1.10 to 1.20 range—then you will be on your way to new lifting heights. Maybe even a world record or two.

20
ACCOMMODATING STRENGTH TO SKILLS

At some point in your preseason training, you have to get away from purely strength exercises—squats, bench presses, or military presses, for example—and begin doing exercises that are more compatible with your sport's skilled movements. To simplify this training concept, you go from very general strengthening exercises to very specific movements that are designed to strengthen you in the movement pattern you'll have to perform in your sport.

Listed in the next few pages are typical examples of how you can accomplish this task—called "the accommodation principle" of weight training for sports—for skills such as running, jumping, lateral agility, throwing, and swinging.

RUNNING

Running speed is dependent upon the strength and power you can generate in the muscles of the hips and legs. But to convert that strength and power to speed, some very specialized exercises must follow your early preseason squats, leg curls, and toe raises. Skill at running is not purely a genetic gift. It also entails training and skill, both of which you can improve upon for greater running speed.

Leg Kicks. This exercise is designed to improve the quickness that you need to recover after a stride. Stride frequency (the number of steps you take per second) is greatly improved by an explosively quick return of each leg so you can take another stride. The movement should be ballistically fast, and only cover about 10–12 inches of forward movement of the knee.

Glute–Ham–Gastroc Raises. Your forward movement in the stride comes from the leg extensors (hamstrings, glutes) and the foot extensors (gastrocnemius or calves). Of course, these muscles are strengthened with leg curls, squats, and toe raises, but glute–ham–gastroc raises more closely simulate the running movement of these muscles. A great benefit of this exercise is that you'll never pull a hamstring again.

Sled Pull. An example of sprint resistance training, pulling a weighted sled behind you can help improve strength in the muscles involved in running. However, because your stride frequency and stride length are altered, you should only perform this strengthening exercise on days that you are also running for form and speed.

JUMPING

Basketball, track and field events, and many other sports require great vertical jumping ability. For jumping, squats are king. No doubt about it. But for the polishing edge on jumping ability, you need some additional exercises, depending upon the nature of your sport's requirements.

Strength Shoe. Formerly called the Legg Shoe, this calf developer is the best exercise since squats were invented for improving your

Your calf muscles add greatly to starting strength in running. The Strength Shoe is the best way ever developed to improve gastrocnemius strength and size.

jumping ability. Wear them only a few minutes a day at first, gradually keeping them on longer until you can actually wear them through an entire game or practice session.

Power Snatches. Using a wide grip on the bar, rip it from the floor at maximum velocity to an overhead support position. Keep the bar within two inches of your body the whole way up. Soon the exercise will become a total body expression of upward power, teaching you to use each body part involved in a sequential, smooth upward motion. Just like jumping.

Weighted Jumps. Hold a couple of dumbbells in your hands (more than 10 pounds each, but not more than 50 pounds) and perform simple kangaroo-like bounding movements. Do them one foot at a time or with both feet together. Perform three sets of about 20 yards each, attempting to cover the distance with less and less leaps as time goes by.

AGILITY

Agility is the ability to perform a series of explosive movements in opposing directions, as quickly as possible. Agility requires a strong base of strength and power beforehand. Then, to convert that great strength and power to useful sports skills such as lateral movement, quick stops-and-starts, or changing directions, you should use lighter weights and perform movements similar to your sports skills.

One-Legged Squats. In football as well as many other sports, straight up-and-down strength from regular squats isn't enough. Try doing them one leg at a time. Take a wide stance and slowly lower your weight down onto one leg, using the other leg as merely a balancing agent. Stand and repeat to the opposite side. This movement will prepare you for lateral explosiveness.

Front Lunges. With a sturdy 6–8-inch platform about two feet in front of you, and the barbell on your shoulders, stride forward with one leg onto the platform, and lunge into a deep squat position. Keep your back leg as straight as possible, and watch your balance. Push back to a standing position and repeat on the other leg. This exercise promotes groin and hip flexibility while promoting strength. It's especially good for runners from any sport.

Weighted Box Drill. With dumbbells in hand (10–50 pounds each), leap from corner to corner on a four-foot square on the ground. Do it with feet together at first, then on each foot separately. Gradually, you can add a half-twist to your leaps. Do three sets of five trips around the square, emphasizing speed.

THROWING

Whether it's a football, baseball, or shot put, you want your strength training to result in a faster movement of the arm so your implement will go faster, straighter, or farther. This conversion from pure strength to speed requires some rather specific exercise techniques that go beyond conventional iron pumping. Because of the ballistic nature of throwing, muscle injury is omnipresent. Here are three techniques for improving your throwing ability as well as improving your chances of avoiding ballistics-induced injury.

Rotator Cuff Plyometrics. With a 3–6 pound *Versa-Ball*, and a partner to throw it to you, lie on a flat bench with your arm bent at 90°. Catch the Versa-Ball and throw it back to your partner, ensuring that the catch and the throw are performed with your elbow unmoved. Rotation for the throw takes place in the shoulder joint, and the impetus for the catch and throw takes place in the rotator cuff muscles. This is a great way to avoid rotator cuff injury as is so often the case with pitchers.

Mid-Height Pulley Rotations. Much of the impetus for a hard throw comes from the oblique muscles of the sides. Twisting explosively against the resistance of a weight stack and pulley arrangement (found in most gyms), you can improve the strength of your throwing motion dramatically. To avoid having the weights bang against the top or fly farther than the movement, try "dampening" the weight stack with a length of surgical tubing.

Shot Put Presses. Again, the ever-present pulley system found in all gyms proves useful. First dampen the weight stack with a length of surgical tubing. Then using the same body rotation and sequential body segment movement as the shot put, drive the pulley handle upward for six to eight reps.

SWINGING

Baseball bats, tennis racquets, and hockey sticks all have one thing in common: They're designed to impart maximum force to a ball or puck. But you're the one who has to generate that force, and you're the one who has to absorb the impact of the implement with the ball without getting hurt. Tennis elbow, for example, is known to result from the arm absorbing the force of impact. Skill is obviously essential in maximizing the force needed to swing hard, but so is great power and strength, especially in contributing to great ballistic speed of the implement.

Mid-Height Pulley Rotations. This exericse differs slightly from the one used for improving your throwing ability. Note that for throwing the torso twists around-and-down, whereas for hitting it twists around evenly. This seemingly slight difference is important in maximizing the effectiveness of your throw or swing. You may even want to use the actual bat, tennis racquet, or hockey stick that you use and attach it to the pulley as a handle.

Versa-Ball Throws. Throwing an 8–16 pound Versa-Ball back and forth between partners helps to stimulate specific strength and power for improved hitting. Plyometric drills such as this one are best reserved for preseason training (the last four to six weeks) because they're very taxing and require good levels of strength beforehand.

Isokinetic Swings. A special apparatus designed to control the speed of movement so maximum effort can be applied throughout the entire range of movement (called an isokinetic device) can be a useful adjunct to improving the power in your swing. Simply simulate the actual swing against the resistance of the machine. The speed can be set anywhere from slow to fast.

21
PUMPING WATER

I don't know too many people who don't enjoy the water. Water soothes, cools, caresses, and massages. It's a source of fun and frolic, a great way to end a workout, and tastes great on a hot summer's day. It's the home of trillions of fish. Two-thirds of the Earth's surface is covered with it.

However, I don't know too many people who make it their training place. Sure, there are plenty of swimmers and fitness freaks who love to do laps. But aside from them, water worshippers approach the beach, the pool, the Jacuzzi, or the lake with one thing in mind—rest and relaxation.

This amazes me. When you consider some of the benefits that water affords, it's hard to imagine that someone hasn't capitalized on its therapeutic use, its use as a source of training resistance, and the buoyancy it provides. Oh sure, some enterprising folks have attempted to do so, but the public resisted their efforts because they view water as a source of fun, not work—a means of relaxing the body, not stressing it. As a result, there's a graveyard of would-be exercise devices out there somewhere, far from any body of water, and far from any body desiring to use them.

Until now.

Until now, all the contraptions I've ever seen were just that. They failed to make use of water's benefits in such a way that any real benefits were forthcoming. They were unwieldy, relatively ineffective, and too limited in their application.

WATER BENEFITS

I'll tell you about a great way to exercise in the water in a moment. First, let me set the record straight on what the benefits of water really are. They're everything I said they were, and more.

- Water training is the lowest impact form of training there is, next to outer space.
- Water training affords almost complete elimination of injurious ballistic stress on your joints, connective tissues, and muscles.
- Water affords you with almost perfectly smooth resistance that is isokinetic in nature. Its natural resistance slows your movement speed so there's time to apply maximum force.
- At the same time, as little force as you wish can be applied, a great benefit for rehabilitative therapy.
- You can simulate almost perfectly any sports skill there is, whether it's an explosive type of skill such as swinging a tennis racquet, shot putting, or a bodybuilding movement such as curls or deltoid raises.
- Water training can be totally anaerobic—quick, powerful movements—or aerobic, with all the attendant cardiovascular benefits of running or aerobics classes but without the same debilitating stresses.

In short, water provides a training medium that rivals any other form in its versatility, effectiveness, and availability. That includes pumping iron.

"Whoa! That's heresy, Dr. Squat! Iron is in our blood. You can't convince us to give up our dumbbells for water wings. Our snatches, curls, squats, and low rows for what? Pumping water?"

Not on your life. I love iron. I love to move it—lots of it. Water can't replace weight training. It's not my intention to convince you of anything of the sort. But water can provide you with some extremely beneficial alternatives in times of staleness, overtraining, and injury. You need never miss a day of training again because of a pulled muscle, mental or physical burnout, or joint soreness.

If that seems like a pretty heavy promise, let me assure you that I was very impressed with the effects I experienced the first time I trained with *Hydro Tone* water bells and water boots. The guys who developed these water training devices are iron pumpers themselves, and know very well that bodybuilders will never be convinced to relinquish their gym memberships to join the local swim club for their training. What they have done is given us a new way to blitz stubborn body parts, to overcome sticking points in our training for power or size, and—more by design than accident—given a broad spectrum of the population of fitness enthusiasts an opportunity to

Hydro Tone Exercise Equipment, Inc. is located at 3535 N.W. 58th Street, Suite 1000, Oklahoma City, OK 73112. Equipment depicted and described in this article was supplied by *Hydro Tone.*

experience some rather remarkable gains in strength, size, and cardiovascular efficiency. You can get all of this in the privacy of your backyard pool. Or at the beach. Or wherever chest-deep water is available.

WHAT ARE WATER BELLS AND WATER BOOTS?

In the past, water training devices attempted to make use of water's natural resistive quality, but most missed the mark by designing their contraptions in a one-dimensional plane. The water bells, held and used exactly like regular iron dumbbells, afford great resistance through all planes of movement because they're multi-dimensional in design. The boots, which fit onto your feet exactly like ski boots, offer the same form of multi-dimensional resistance advantage as the hand-held bells.

Now, here's the kicker. Visualize any movement pattern whatsoever. If your body is designed to accomplish that movement, then the bells or boots can be used to afford you with almost limitless resistance while you simulate that movement in the water. The ease of use of these two devices, and their multi-dimensional design, make them perfect for:

- Therapy during times of injury
- Muscle reeducation following long periods of limb immobility
- Stress-free aerobic training, with practically zero-impact stress, ballistic stress, or weight-bearing stress
- Near-perfect isolation of muscles because of the water's natural buoyancy, eliminating the critical need for synergists and stabilizers in any given movement
- Any exercise than can be performed with weights, plus literally scores of other exercises that are not possible with weights or weight machines
- Older folks and youngsters alike, who would otherwise need assistance training in a weightlifting gym or therapy center. The water bells and boots are totally safe—you can't injure yourself
- The most rugged, positively stressful training session your muscles have ever experienced

HOW DO THE BELLS AND BOOTS WORK?

Most athletes have tried training with various forms of isokinetic devices before. As you pull or push on such a device it affords resistance equal to the force you exert. A mechanism in the device controls the speed with which you are able to move the handles, so whether you exert 5 pounds of force or 500 pounds of force, the speed remains relatively constant.

This form of training affords you with a means of recruiting a maximum number of muscle fibers providing your speed is slow. Over time, by adjusting the machine to move faster, you can actually "teach" yourself to recruit maximum numbers of muscle cells in a shorter period of time, thereby improving your explosiveness.

Water, while not a perfect source of isokinetic resistance, still allows the same advantages with a couple more thrown in for good measure. You can adjust your movement patterns and movement speed to a degree where there are no ballistic forces, or to where the ballistic forces approximate those experienced in any given sports movement.

Minimizing ballistic forces has advantages for anyone wishing to optimize muscle activity without trauma to joints or connective tissue for such reasons as injury, soreness, or recuperation. However, for otherwise healthy individuals, ballistic movements can be very beneficial if controlled. Ballistic training is critically important in preparing your body for sports competition, and water is the perfect way to control it.

In order to achieve maximum muscle size you have to apply a variety of different forms of stress on your muscles: heavy weights with explosive movements for muscle density and myofibrillar growth; slow, continuous tension movements for increasing your muscle's mitochondrial mass and blood supply; and moderate-speed pumping movements for increasing the muscle's sarcoplasm content (storage protein) and satellite cells. Training with the water bells and boots is an ideal means of achieving this level of diversity in your training stresses. And you have a built-in means of performing antagonistic supersets in the process.

Supersetting affords you with a means of achieving balanced development between two opposing muscles. For example, when you perform a set of bicep curls, you go straight on to a set of tricep extensions. Then you repeat this alternating process until both muscle groups are sufficiently stressed. With the water bells and boots, you are able to do one curl followed by one tricep extension, another curl, and so forth. This kind of supersetting—the purest form of supersetting there is—gives your arms a truly great workout that I'm sure will greatly impress you. The same advantage is gained with virtually any exercise you can conceive.

You're going to be hearing a lot more about *Hydro Tone* in the future. I believe that the effectiveness of these two water training devices is going to make a big splash (pardon the pun) in the fitness marketplace. And, as for hard-core athletes, well, I for one intend to use them as an adjunct to my training. I'm convinced that they afford much, and I already have enough iron in my diet. Gains will have to come from somewhere else. Why not from water?

PART III
YOUR BODY'S PROCESSES

22
FATIGUE FACTORS

Gut-busting, burning, gasping for air, last rep max: You've been there. Inspired by images of greatness, you enter the torture zone, willingly accepting pain as if it were signaling ecstasy. You push on. There's no turning back until total fatigue virtually shuts you down.

Lactic acid strikes again.

It's good, though. This sort of fatigue is what the uneducated gurus of the fitness world call "the good hurt." It's one of the factors that are necessary in forcing an adaptive process to take place in your muscles. Nature overcompensates for this sort of fatigue by making you less susceptible to its limiting effects. You're getting in shape.

There are many forms of fatigue, however, and fitness enthusiasts as well as competing athletes need to recognize both their presence and their significance. Their presence will, I assure you, not go unnoticed.

But knowing what's happening and why will lend clues as to how you can make fatigue work for you rather than against you. It will give you the methods you'll need to combat it in the future. In a very pragmatic sense, your tolerance to fatigue is the most important sign of whether you're in shape.

THEORIES OF FATIGUE

Dr. Christian Zauner from the University of Florida categorized the research on fatigue into five distinct (but overlapping) groups:

- Fatigue of the circulatory/respiratory systems
- Fatigue stemming from body temperature fluctuations
- Fatigue resulting from dehydration
- Fatigue stemming from depletion or blockage of energy sources
- Fatigue arising from psychological manifestations

These factors of fatigue overlap in the sense that you may experience more than one at a time. For example, when running long distances, your body temperature increases, your heart is taxed, your energy systems are depleted, and your mental anxiety from the pain all take their respective toll. Problems arise when you try to compute which of these phenomena is responsible for your falling prostrate on the ground—quitting, as it were—instead of finishing the race.

Exercise scientists are quick to respond. One very popular theory has it that circulation and respiration failure may be the culprit. From the outset of exercise, there's plenty of oxygen in the blood to support continued training. However, as time goes by, the heart and lungs have more difficulty supplying the working muscles with needed oxygen.

Why else would athletes have greater oxygen-consumption capabilities, better cardiac output, and more blood than their lazy counterparts? The theory seems to hold water, until you realize that even in an exhausted state there's plenty of oxygen coursing through working muscles.

If there's plenty of oxygen, we have to assume that the exhaustion came from something else. Maybe the lactic acid that's accumulating in the working muscles? Lactic wastes accumulate faster than the blood can carry it away, so perhaps fatigue is still a result of cardio-respiratory inadequacy.

Again, however, there's a hole in the theory. Lactate concentrations vary from individual to individual in a fatigued state, and training appears to drastically improve your tolerance of lactic acid. To highlight the inadequacy of the lactic acid theory of fatigue, consider people like Jack La Lanne, who can do pushups all day, or pull a barge from Alcatraz by his teeth and with his hands tied behind his back.

Body temperature theories that explain fatigue seem to be more adequate. At around 40°C (approximately 104°F) fatigued athletes consistently fail. Perhaps some temperature-sensing mechanism in the body shuts down activity in order to maintain life functions. While you may be able to delay the onset of your body's core temperature reaching the shut-down point, there appears to be little you can do to alter the shut-down point itself.

Still, fatigue isn't fully explained with this theory either. All you have to do is remember the last time you performed a set of curls to failure. Your biceps may have been fatigued to a point of failure, but your body temperature certainly wasn't even approaching 40° C.

Mr. Universe, Tom Platz, knows the meaning of the word *fatigue*.

This same objection can be raised in the case of theories centering on dehydration as the cause of fatigue. Certainly, if you were to exercise to a state of dehydration, your blood would be diverted to the skin to cool your core temperature. But the muscles would then be deprived of oxygenated blood because it's all getting cooled down near the surface of the skin. Exercise stops from lack of oxygen, mounting core temperatures, or both.

But simple muscle fatigue certainly can't be explained by dehydration any more than it can be explained by cardiorespiratory inadequacy.

Some scientists have postulated that fatigue is the result of impaired, inadequate, or depleted energy sources. Researchers have identified three sources for muscular energy: muscle glycogen, blood glucose, and blood-borne FFAs (free fatty acids). Even in severely fatigued states, however, there is ample glycogen, glucose, and FFAs present to sustain work in your muscles. *Blockage* of these energy sources may cause work to stop. If glucose reaches a certain point of depletion, for example, your neural transmissions may be somewhat impaired, resulting in your muscles never being signaled to contract. And if your blood's free-fatty acids reach a certain point of depletion concurrently with a rise in lactate concentrations, you will not be able to mobilize more energy-giving FFAs from fat stores.

None of these energy related explanations of fatigue hold up, because at any given time—even in highly fatigued states—you have plenty of one or the other (or all) of the energy substrate.

Maybe fatigue is all in the mind. Some people can push themselves to the point of collapse—even death (as was the case with the now-famous Phidippides of ancient Greece)—while others among us cave in with naught but mild discomfort. This phenomenon is very interesting, and bears a bit of discussion. In laboratory tests, sedentary people have been exercised to total fatigue. According to Dr. Zauner, the following observations are typical:

- Lack of perspiration at fatigue
- Pallor, syanosis, and other signs of poor peripheral circulation
- Heart rates of less than 150 beats per minute
- No signs of acute respiratory distress
- Bodys' core temperatures approaching the critical 40° C
- Low blood volume, which is required by working muscles (leaving skin circulation shut down and unable to dissipate body heat)

Now compare these findings with those of trained athletes pushed to failure due to fatigue:

- Drenched with perspiration
- Heart rates typically exceeding 200 beats per minute
- Exchange of over 100 liters of air per minute (plenty of oxygen)
- Peripheral circulat excellent (keeping core temperatures down and muscle circulation up to par)

Clearly, fatigue becomes a personal value judgment. Athletes and sedentary people alike appear to have their own peculiar shut-off point, beyond which the pros and cons are weighed as to whether it's worth it to continue. World champions are far more likely to put up with pain and continue. Great athletes, but not good enough to be world champions, stop sooner than their more successful counterparts, and sedentary folks stop at the drop of a hat.

Dr. William Morgan, sports psychologist and expert on sports hypnosis, from the University of Wisconsin-Madison has spent years researching the concept of perceived exertion and fatigue among peak-performing athletes. On one occasion, Dr. Morgan hypnotized a football player who, under normal circumstances, could perform about 40–50 reps in the seated military press with half his body weight. Under hypnosis, this subject actually was able to perform several hundred reps. Dr. Morgan ceased the experiment before the subject was willing to stop, presumably a prudent decision.

There are other examples such as this one that clearly imply that fatigue is, after all, in the mind—at least for highly trained football players.

AN INTEGRATED THEORY OF FATIGUE

While the reason for ever wanting to formulate an integrated theory about fatigue escapes me at present, Dr. Zauner has elaborated on the need for one:

> When blood sugar drops, the nervous system is deprived of its only energy source. Work stops so that the nervous system may continue its other important integrative activities, such as regulation of circulation and respiration. Of course, psychological considerations can intervene at any of these stages and cause cessation of work.
>
> In the untrained subject, perhaps the psyche interferes at the second or third phase. The athlete probably has no significant psychological intervention until he is quite near to 'physiological fatigue.' Furthermore, central body temperature might become a factor in some individuals prior to significant reduction of blood glucose. In particular, an untrained individual may be stopped by elevated temperature because he is unable to expose blood to the cooling functions of the skin.

Admittedly, this simple explanation of fatigue does not clarify why you have to stop when you're experiencing those gut-wrenching, burning, gasping-for-air, last reps in your set. Just as obvious is the fact that highly trained athletes have a far greater tolerance, both physical and mental, to fatigue than do nonathletes. Indeed, training stands out as the best method of arming yourself with such a tolerance. But there are a few other things that you may want to try—at least they'll help you get that armor a bit more expeditiously:

- Inosine helps delay the onset of short-term fatigue (anaerobic).
- L-carnitine helps delay the onset of aerobic shutdown.
- A good hypnotherapist can help you tolerate greater levels of fatigue before quitting.
- Four or five square meals per day will assist greatly in keeping energy levels soaring. Keep the calories per meal down to avoid getting fat.
- A high-quality multivitamin/mineral pack taken each day will, if consistently practiced over time, aid in keeping energy optimal.
- Learning to cope with stresses associated with everyday living can dramatically improve your energy levels, your outlook, and your tolerance to training-induced fatigue states.
- Keep an open mind on new methods of training and nutritional supplementation (e.g., gama oryzanol, trimethylglycine, amino acids, etc.), for many hold much promise for improving your state of mind, your tolerance to fatigue, pain, and discomfort, and your overall health.

But most of all, the way to fend off fatigue is to get in shape!

23
RECOVERY TIME

Have you ever wondered what the split system of training accomplished? The double split? If you've been around ironhead gyms long enough, you will no doubt respond, "Why, to maximize recovery time, and to maintain high intensity in all exercises."

The state of the art of weight training has, for several years now, dictated these split systems for advanced training. But friends, science stands still for no one, and remains ever vigilant for new techniques and information to improve your overall training capabilities. Until now, the double split system of arranging exercises was state of the art for maximizing training intensity. The new system herein described can take you to the next intensity plateau. It's called the *variable split system*, and is based on the following factors, which collectively determine each muscle's requirements for recovery time.

Typical splits may involve doing chest, shoulders, and arms on Monday, Wednesday, and Friday, for example, and legs, back, and midsection on Tuesdays, Thursdays, and Saturdays. Or, another typical split would be to pull-push alternately. The double splits, a bit more complicated, involves two workouts per day instead of one, with unrelated body parts being worked on the same day.

In the new, more advanced system, the variable split, an accounting is made of the 12 factors above, and an attempt is made to train each muscle when it is ready to be trained—never sooner, and never later. Within the bounds of time and dedication, it is far more effective than any system ever devised because it completely eliminates losses in

TABLE 23-1

VARIABLES AFFECTING RECOVERY TIME

1. Larger muscles take longer to recover than do smaller muscles.
2. Predominantly white (fast) fiber muscles take longer to recover than do red (slow) fiber muscles (white fiber muscles are suited to power, whereas red fiber muscles are suited to endurance).
3. High-intensity exercise with weights exceeding the 80%-85% maximum level requires greater recuperation time than do high rep (under 75% maximum intensity) exercises.
4. Full-range movements typically cause greater amounts of connective tissue damage, and necessitate greater recovery time than do partial movement exercises.
5. Older trainees (35-40 years) require more recuperation time than do younger trainees.
6. Recovery rate can be improved as a result of properly conceived aerobic weight training programs, or retarded with generally little or no aerobic efficiency training.
7. Bigger muscle groups take longer to recover than do smaller muscle groups.
8. Nutritionally sound eating and supplementation habits can significantly shorten recuperation time, while poor dietary and supplementation practices can prolong it.
9. Drugs and other substances that are anabolic agents reduce recovery time, whereas most types of recreational drugs (e.g., alcohol) can markedly increase recovery time requirements.
10. Eccentric (negative) muscle contraction causes increased recovery time requirements.
11. States of overtraining, whether biological or psychological in origin, increase recovery time requirements. So does undertraining.
12. A generally healthy body recovers faster than an unhealthy one.

development resulting from losses in time from either overtraining or undertraining individual muscles.

The variable split can only be constructed after careful evaluation of each muscle's recuperative capabilities. This evaluation is done through the use of a simple grid table (see Table 23-2). Each muscle is evaluated on the basis of the 12 criteria in Table 23-1, and then given a final score. The score is then evaluated on the basis of your own experience regarding how each exercise you do is performed. That is, do you do sets of five? Explosive? Slow, continuous tension? High reps? Do you do a variety of movement speeds and do you do more than one exercise per muscle? These kinds of considerations, of course, influence your recovery rate.

Let's take each of the example exercises and muscle groups in Table 23-2 one at a time—you will see how the grid works in establishing each muscle's recovery requirement. First, however, we can save a lot of time and printing space by eliminating factors 5 through 12 from discussion right off the bat. These factors are constants—they remain essentially the same for you regardless of the exercise you are engaged in. Really, the nitty gritty of the entire process of determining recovery requirements can be boiled down to factors 1 through 4:

TABLE 23-2

EXAMPLES OF HOW RECOVERY REQUIREMENTS CAN BE CHARTED FOR EFFECTIVE INCLUSION IN A VARIABLE SPLIT SYSTEM

Muscle	Factors from Table 21-1												Average Score
	1	2	3	4	5	6	7	8	9	10	11	12	
Quadriceps (Squats)	5	4	5	4	3	5	3	1	1	5	1	1	39 ÷ 12 = 3.25
Biceps (Curls)	1	4	3	4	3	5	3	1	1	5	1	1	32 ÷ 12 = 2.67
Pectorals (Bench Press)	3	4	4	3	3	5	3	1	1	5	1	1	34 ÷ 12 = 2.83
Calves (Standing Calf Raises)	2	1	3	4	3	5	3	1	1	5	1	1	30 ÷ 12 = 2.50

muscle size, red versus white fiber ratio within the muscle, the intensity of your workout, and the extent of stretch and contracture the muscle undergoes. In certain instances, factor 10—the extent of eccentric contracture involved in an exercise—may vary from exercise to exercise, but generally all exercises have around 50% of the total movement eccentric in nature. That is, you raise the weight, and you put it back down.

Recalculating our results from Table 23–2 strictly on the basis of the first four factors, then, gives us a much clearer picture of what's going on.

Muscle	Average Score
Quadricep	4.50
Biceps	3.00
Pectorals	3.50
Calves	0.83

The average scores in the recomputed table above are ballpark figures for how recovery requirements for each muscle varies from one another. In this case, you can see that calves can be worked five times for every time the quadriceps are worked. Their size is smaller, they have far greater endurance because of the preponderance of red muscle fiber in the calves, not nearly as much weight is used, and the reps are generally higher for calf work. All these factors add up to much quicker recovery for the calves.

Factors that would tend to alter the recovery rate, as I said before, include training practices stemming from instinctive training and muscle priority training. These factors generally dictate the number of reps, sets, intensity, and exercises-per-body-part factors. For example, if you have opted to do four different exercises for the chest, your

THE VARIABLE SPLIT SYSTEM

	1	2	3	4	5	6	7	8	9	10	11	12	13	14	15	16	17	18	19	20	21	22	23	24	25	26	27	28	29	30
Upper Back	x			x			x			x			x			x			x			x			x			x		
Lower Back	x					x					x					x					x					x				
Thighs			x					x					x					x					x					x		
Lower Leg	x	x	x	x	x	x	x	x	x	x	x	x	x	x	x	x	x	x	x	x	x	x	x	x	x	x	x	x	x	x
Mid-section	x		x		x		x		x		x		x		x		x		x		x		x		x		x		x	
Shoulders		x			x			x			x			x			x			x			x			x			x	
Upper Arms			x			x			x			x			x			x			x			x			x			x
Forearms	x	x	x	x	x	x	x	x	x	x	x	x	x	x	x	x	x	x	x	x	x	x	x	x	x	x	x	x	x	x
Chest		x				x				x				x				x				x				x				x

You may want to switch days or move to a 2-a-day workout schedule if one exercise interferes with another. This may be advisable if your training intensity on one exercise is diminished because of a previous exercise using similar muscles.

Your body part workout frequency is based *entirely* upon your recuperative abilities. Each body part responds differently, and each has its own recovery rate. This table works for a majority of athletes, but you may want to rearrange the number of days you spend on recovery for each body part. This table will get you started.

recovery time will be greater than if you only did two exercises, but certainly not by a factor of twice the time. Other factors in the list will modify the recovery requirement downward because you are dealing with averages.

In the example above, the modified table scores are my own. I have found that I can effectively recover from my squat workout in 4.5 days on average. Bench press workouts require 3.5 days on average, and so forth. These figures are not writ on stone—they are meant to give you a guide in establishing a prioritization of exercises on a day-to-day basis.

To complicate the entire concept, let's say that you performed bent rows, an upper back exercise that requires on average, three days' recovery time. On the next day you are scheduled to do stiff-legged deadlifts for your back, as the computed recovery time dictated. However, your bent rows also stressed the lower back, and you find that you can't do the stiff-legged deadlifts effectively because you're still sore from the previous day's training. This is one of the many scheduling problems that may confront you when establishing a viable training program based on the variable split.

You should not assume that because of these kinds of difficulties the variable split is too complicated or too difficult to adopt. The answer is simple. All you have to do is wait an extra day for the stiff-legged deadlifts! It's better to lose a single day on one exercise than it is to lose the same amount of time on all of your exercises!

Simply put, the variable split is the most effective means there is in maximizing training time efficiency. Less overall time, muscle for muscle, is lost with the variable split than any other system yet devised. It may not be the easiest system to incorporate, but no one ever promised that it would be easy. Still, it's workable enough for even the greenest beginner to use, yet efficient enough for the most advanced superstar to benefit from.

24

RESTORATION

Roaming the globe, as I often do, in quest of superior training wisdon, I get bored out of my skull. There just ain't too much of it around. The most fertile ground, if you dig deep enough, has been the Soviet Union.

"Yeah, yeah! I know! The Ruskies beat us all the time!" you may often lament. "I'm gettin' tired of hearing how great they are and how puny and sorry our athletes are!"

Sorry about that, but swallow your ethnocentric pride for one moment of objective reflection on the facts. The fact is, to get to the top, I'll take help from wherever I can find it. Much can be learned from the Soviets when it comes to peak performance in sports.

One area woefully neglected in this country, and carefully studied in the Soviet sports system, is the science of restoration. Recuperating fully and swiftly between workouts as well as during workouts, so you can train harder more often is both a science and an art. At worst, practicing restorative techniques will make you a better athlete or bodybuilder virtually overnight. At best, it will make the difference between third runner-up and champion. At worst it'll keep you healthy. At best it will prove so productive that you'll no longer find a need for steroids.

So, what does restorative therapy entail? Here's a partial listing that Dr. Mike Yessis published in his recent book, *Secrets of Soviet Sports and Fitness Training,* all of which are currently in use by Soviet athletes:

- Massage
- Hydrotherapy
- Electrical muscle stimulation
- Rest
- Nutritional substances
- Trigger point massage
- Reflexology
- Psychological techniques
- Light therapy
- Color therapy
- Electrosleep
- Electrophoresis
- Ultrasound
- Hyperbaric chambers
- Electrosonics
- Ultraviolet irradiation
- Air ionization
- Magnetic field therapy
- Laser beam therapy
- Herbology
- Sauna
- Cycle training techniques
- Physiological monitoring
- Emphasis on quality training

Your initial response please.

OK, some of them are old hat. Others are too esoteric to even consider. Still others are either too expensive or too difficult to incorporate into your routine on any sort of regular basis. Nobody promised you a rose garden. Besides, how many of the above listed methods of restoration do you already practice? Even rest and nutrition, the two cornerstones of modern bodybuilding and sports training, aren't incorporated into your daily regimen on any super-scientific basis, I'll wager.

They not only should be, they **must** be. Ditto for several other above-average mentioned techniques. That is, if you sincerely aspire to maximize your true potential, instead of just talk about it.

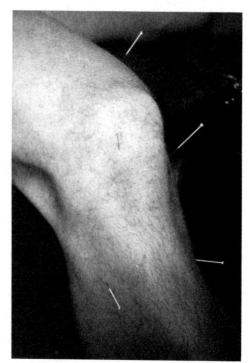

Acupuncture has been around for 5,000 years because of its success rate. Period. The patient being treated in this photo has patellar tendinitis.

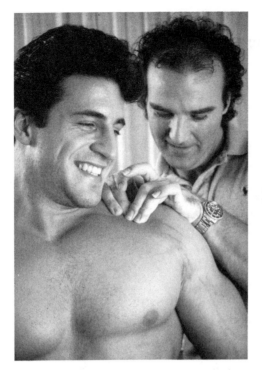

After training and jacuzzi, deep cross-fiber massage hastens recovery markedly.

In the rest of Part III, I shall endeavor to unlock the true stories behind each of these substances and techniques and how each relates to your training, your lifestyle, and most efficacious methods of use. I believe as do the Soviets that restorative therapy holds the key to truly maximizing performance.

In the meantime, let me give you a brief, easy-to-use system of restoration that you can easily incorporate into your training right now. It involves several items from the above list, but in a way that is maximally beneficial for your bodybuilding efforts.

1. *Nutrition.* Eat 4–5 small meals about four hours apart, spacing your workouts 1–2 hours before one or two of the meals. Be sure to get about 25–30 grams of complete protein at each meal, and supplement with the appropriate vitamins/minerals early in the day.
2. *Inosine.* Before each workout for rapid ATP regeneration during heavy sets, use inosine in its free form (do *not* use inosinic acid). And, after workout use inosine for more rapid recovery and improved protein synthesis.
3. *Jacuzzi or Shower.* Immediately after a workout, run a stream of warm water (about 96° F) on the muscles you just finished training for about six minutes. This assists in rapid removal of metabolic wastes from the muscles and infusion of oxygen-rich blood.
4. *Deep Fiber Massage.* Practice on your training partner, and let

him practice on you. About 10 minutes of deep, rapid, cross-fiber massage of the affected muscles will not only assist in removal of lactic waste and provide blood circulation to the muscles, but also helps prevent the formation of adhesions occuring among muscle cells. Such adhesions, over time, can limit your mobility, predispose you to injury, and make it more difficult to add muscular size becase of the "binding" effect the scarring or adhesions have on the muscle as a whole.

5. *Visualize Success.* Right after your Jacuzzi and massage, lie quietly in a secluded place with your eyes closed. Conjure images of your recently trained muscles performing each rep and set at levels you only dare dream about. Make yourself visualize success! Feel each muscle movement. The neuronal stimulation each of your muscles receives during such visualization is very relaxing and also restorative. Each visualization session should last for about 15 minutes.

6. *Before-Bedtime Supplements.* If you've been having any trouble falling asleep or if your sleep is less than thoroughly sound, use tryptophan on an empty stomach right before bed. It'll help your sleep by stimulating serotonin release. However, if your sleep is perfect, then use ornithine (2–3 grams) and/or arginine (about 3–5 grams) to induce a greater-than-normal release of growth hormone during the first hour or two of sleep.

These are some simple things you can do. Depending on your resources, many other methods of improving your restorative powers can be used.

25

YOUR BODY'S STRUCTURAL PROTEINS:
How They Work to Provide Energy, Recovery, and Development

One of the most elementary bits of information all athletes learn from the first day they lift a weight is that they need more protein in their diet. Work hard, eat a lot of protein, and get big, that's the ticket, right? Not necessarily.

During intense exercise, as well as afterward, proteins are mobilized in much the same fashion as a well-trained corps of troopers, providing energy for muscular contraction, speeding the recovery process, and building more contractile muscle tissue for ever-increasing strength and size.

The process of protein mobilization is infinitely complex, but nonetheless warrants our close scrutiny for the array of rather important (and, in some cases, startling) information we need for scientific nutritional application. After all, isn't this the age of scientific training? Aren't we *expected* to exceed the great feats of our predecessors? Of course, but this won't happen without some rather specialized knowledge of how our bodies work to grow stronger and more massive.

Picture yourself inside an athlete's body. I mean *really* inside, where the protein molecules are—in the blood, liver, and muscles. In much the same backdrop as was used in the movie classic, *Fantastic Voyage*, your presence there will be rewarded tenfold when you emerge with a more profound understanding of what you'll have to do to make your training pay off. So, buckle your seatbelt, for the journey is beginning right now.

THE MOBILIZATION OF STRUCTURAL PROTEINS

Heavy, intense weight training forces your body to do three things in order to defend itself from the stress: gear up for the stress by providing more energy, rebuild the tissue that was destroyed by the stress, and rebuild even stronger tissue to withstand subsequent stresses. All three of these processes are implemented by the rapid mobilization of your body's structural proteins.

Think of structural proteins as big bundles of bricks. Each bundle can be quickly disassembled into individual bricks—the amino acids—for use anywhere they're needed to perform one of the three processes described.

The stress of training causes the activation of three bodily mechanisms, which are responsible for mobilizing these structural proteins:

1. During intense training. protein synthesis is suppressed. The energy requirements for muscle contraction are so great that it causes an energy shortage for protein synthesis. A huge reserve of free amino acids is thereby created inside the muscles.
2. Tissue degradation (resulting from a destructive process that heavy, intense training causes inside the muscle) also results in an increase of the free amino acid pool.
3. There is an outflow of deposited and unused free amino acids, in addition to the amino acids liberated in protein degradation, from some tissues to be used by other tissues.

Some of this free amino acid pool is used later in protein synthesis, but the bulk of it is used during exercise for energy necessary to augment the functioning of various body organs. This energy production process is accomplished in two ways: through the glucose-alanine cycle, and through the oxidation of the branched-chain amino acids inside muscle tissue.

Wait a second! Let's take a breather! "What does all of this mean to me?" you are no doubt asking. "How can I benefit from this mumbo-jumbo?" Let me boil it down for you into a simple statement.

Exercise creates a large pool of free amino acids, most of which are used for energy. Alanine and the three so-called branched-chain amino acids (BCAAs) are in abundant supply in your muscles, comprising a large percentage of the muscle's protein. The remaining free aminos are kicked around until you're done training, and then used in the rebuilding and supercompensation processes.

What does this mean to you as an athlete? You'd better have your fair share of alanine and the BCAAs, for one thing. For another, keep your training sessions short and intense. Long-term, submaximal intensity training has no such suppressive effect on protein synthesis.

MUSCLE DEGRADATION DURING TRAINING

Scientists know that there's a destructive process going on during intense exercise because they can measure the effects of it. Uric acid, a by-product of muscle catabolism, appears in your sweat, urine, and blood. But the question is whether protein degradation takes place in the contracting myofibrils or within the free amino acid pool.

By measuring the amount of urea excreted and that found in blood plasma, scientists have determined that a protein breakdown rate of 13.7% per hour takes place in cabohydrate-depleted trainees, whereas only 5.8% of protein is lost if one has carbo-loaded. The fact that the available free amino acid pool isn't large enough to sustain this enormous protein loss signifies that much of the protein breakdown is occurring in the muscle tissue.

These data suggest that you should have an adequate amount of muscle glycogen stored in order to reduce the amount of muscle breakdown that takes place. And just carbo-loading won't necessarily ensure this. Scientists also found that in fed subjects, exercise still increased the rate of breakdown, but there was only a small decrease in protein synthesis. Fasting trainees, however, experienced a more profound decrease in protein synthesis during training.

Besides proper pretraining nutrition, testosterone has a significant impact on reducing muscle catabolism during training. Your body manufactures testosterone, and its rate of synthesis can be augmented nutritionally.

Adrenaline also has an inhibitory influence on protein catabolism, as does a substance endogenously produced called cyclic AMP. Of far greater significance to the practicing athlete—especially muscle-hungry bodybuilders—is the protein metabolism that follows intense exercise.

PROTEIN METABOLISM DURING POSTEXERCISE RECOVERY

You'd think that after the exhaustive stress of exercise, your muscles would cease their breaking down process and begin building. In other words, a shift from the catabolic effects of stress to the anabolic process seems logical. It isn't. In fact, there is a simultaneous augmentation of both the catabolic and the anabolic processes during the first several hours following exercise.

Take heart, though—all is not destruction and mayhem. The results you achieve from your training should tell you that much. Scientists compared the various metabolites and excretions during and after exercise and found several significant differences in the catabolic processes causing the destructive protein breakdown. Stress destroys myofibrils during training, but enzymatic changes caused a rapid turnover—a changing of the guard, if you will—of the protein molecules comprising the myofibrils.

Training causes a physical exhaustion of the structural elements of your muscle cells. To ensure that improvement in their contractile qualities takes place, they are destroyed enzymatically and rebuilt bigger and stonger than ever. So, there's both a protein molecule turnover as well as a supercompensation process taking place.

While the turnover process is technically referred to as a catabolic process, take heart in the fact that your muscles are coming out of it for the better, so you shouldn't try to interfere with this worthwhile destruction. It's sort of like tearing down a slum and rebuilding better buildings in its place.

What can be improved upon, however, is the anabolic process—the rebuilding. The supercompensation process, which makes your muscle cells stronger and bigger than before, is augmented by the presence of testosterone.

There's that word again—testosterone. We all know the word. Usually it's spoken in hushed tones and behind closed doors. After all, its use is illegal, isn't it?

If you're an avid reader of *Muscle & Fitness* magazine, you no doubt have a large index of the ways in which you can coax your body into making its own testosterone in greater abundance, so I won't get into that subject any deeper than to say that it's possible. Of greater significance, I believe, is how you view and approach the whole picture of nutrition before, during, and after exercise. Here are a few guidelines by way of summary:

1. Ensure adequate preworkout stores of muscle glycogen.
2. Be sure that you avoid foods that cause a rapid rise and fall of your blood sugar both before and after exercise.
3. Supplementing your preworkout meal with the BCAAs and alanine may assist in your energy production and postexercise recovery.
4. Improve on your postexercise anabolism by ensuring adequate and scientific use of the various anabolic substances that aid in testosterone production and hGH release.
5. Keep your workouts about an hour long, and keep them intense to ensure an adequate free amino acid pool for energy, recovery, and growth.
6. Be aware that protein turnover—rejuvenation—takes place for days following intense exercise. Your need for adequate nutrition and supplements is therefore constant. Of greatest importance is your need for adequate (not excessive) protein at set intervals throughout the day. Four to six meals per day is recommended, each of which contains adequate supplies of complete proteins and amino acids.

26

THE NERVOUS SYSTEM

The human is a purposeful being, and the study of mechanical principles alone will reveal only a fraction of the entire spectrum of his
movements—perhaps the fraction of least significance.—Phillip J.
Rasch, Ph.D. and Roger K. Burke, Ph.D.

Rasch and Burke—two cool dudes who wrote the book on human
movement—were, in their own inimitable style, trying to point out
that the nervous system is utterly complex. In fact, so complex that
man's nervous system is not even remotely capable of a detailed
rational understanding of its own complexity. Conditioning, learning,
remembering, forgetting, relearning, personality, motivation, meaning, significance, even raw consciousness, are beyond the limit of
human understanding. These are the functions of your nervous
system while acting in an integrated manner with other body systems. Yet, there are some bits of near-understandable information
that even feeble man can use to modulate his lifestyle a bit. Perhaps
even athletes.

Let's take a quick look at how the nervous system is arranged, and
then see what we can glean in terms of improving on our efforts in
the gym.

THE MIND/BODY LINK

Your nervous system is made up of two major parts. The *central
nervous system* (CNS) is comprised of your brain and spinal column.

You should think of them as being one organ and not separate. The CNS receives messages and after interpreting them it sends instructions back to the body. The *peripheral nervous system* (PNS) does two things: it relays messages from CNS to the body (the *efferent system*), and it relays messages from the body to the CNS (the *afferent system*).

Pretty simple so far—no more complex than turning your light switch on and off. But it gets hairy. For example, your efferent system, the system designed to cause action, is divided into two distinct and important parts: the *somatic system*, which is responsible for voluntary action, and the *autonomic system*, which processes and activates involuntary action.

Your afferent system, the part of the PNS that sends messages to the CNS, receives messages through three different classes of receptors: *proprioceptors* (located in joints, muscles tendons, and the inner ear) are responsible for picking up messages such as body position and movement (kinesthesia), *exteroceptors* (located near the surface of your skin) receive information from outside your body such as sight, touch, pressure, heat or cold, and *enteroceptors* (located in your blood vessels and viscera) report inner body sensations such as hunger, thirst, pain, pressure, fatigue, or nausea.

Let's simplify the whole nervous system and put it all in a nutshell. Actually the nervous system does three things for you:

1. It senses changes inside and outside your body.
2. It interprets those changes.
3. It responds to the interpretations by initiating action in the form of muscular contractions or glandular secretions.

Obviously, then, all the articles and rhetoric you've been exposed to over the years regarding the crucial link between your mind and your body all boil down to this one fact: that link is your nervous system— the CNS and the PNS. Let's explore some of the implications of this mind/body link for athletes.

CAN YOU MODIFY YOUR NERVOUS SYSTEM TO YOUR ADVANTAGE?

That's the big question. What good is it to know all about how the nervous system works unless you can gain some sort of tangible payback? And, if you can expect some sort of physical reward for working hard to understand your mind/body link, will the reward be of sufficient magnitude to warrant giving it the attention and time to extract payment?

The answer to that last question is a resounding YES! Not only can you modify certain aspects of your nervous system function, but the rewards in terms of sports success can indeed be significant. Some of the most apparent areas of concern to athletes are improved strength output, better mental concentration, greater training intensity, pain management, and glandular secretions. All of these areas are modifiable to at least a measurable degree, and can therefore improve your efforts in the gym. All are inextricably related to and controlled by your nervous system.

Improving Your Strength

Strength is ultimately controlled by the mind. The strength of your muscle contracture is modified by both internal and external stimuli that the CNS interprets on the basis of both built-in defense mechanisms (e.g., your muscle spindles and Golgi tendon organs) as well as past experience. Strength output then is a voluntary movement, the stimulus for which originates in your various receptors, interpreted by the brain, and called into action by efferent motor neurons leading from the CNS to your muscles.

What part of this process can be modified to produce greater strength? It's probably true that the excitation threshold of individual motor units inside your contracting muscles can be altered somewhat, as can that of the Golgi tendon organs. Heavy training, explosiveness training, and full-amplitude movements appear to modify these elements to a measurable degree, thereby improving strength output.

But the greatest source of modification lies in the mind. How you perceive the weight, how you approach your training, how you view its importance on the rest of your life, how strongly you cherish your goals—all have a degree of influence on how much you can lift.

Skill at Sports

All motor movement, sports related or otherwise, must be learned. The simple act of walking really isn't so simple when you view it from a temporal perspective—it took each of us months to learn how to do it. Highly complex gymnastics movements often take as long or longer to master. And, for you right-handed folks reading this article, have you ever tried doing a precision layup in basketball left-handed?

Such skills require time-consuming reintegration of nervous function. You have to learn exactly when to "turn on" certain muscles, "shut off" others, how much chemoelectrical charge to send to the muscles, the precise timing involved in literally dozens of sequentially simulated muscles, and so forth. It doesn't happen by accident. The learning process is called *practice*, and the end result is called *coordination*.

Skill at Producing Strength

Applying great strength in any given movement also requires this kind of practice and coordination. Your workouts aren't simply a means of improving upon the number of contracting elements in each muscle cell, or getting your muscles bigger so they can handle more stress. That's only a small part of strength training.

You have to learn how to coordinate your movements—the dozens of muscles involved as prime mover, synergists, and stabilizers—so that maximum usable force is applied to the resistance, and minimum negative forces are generated. It takes practice to learn such a skill. Sometimes, for a few of us, it can take years to learn strength coordination.

There is also a process that some (few) wise strength trainees build into their training techniques. It's called *deinhibition training*. It is a process of pushing back the threshold at which some of your proprioceptors (e.g., the Golgi tendon organ and the muscle spindles) are stimulated to send an inhibitory message to the CNS. Of course, the CNS is "conditioned" through learning to shut the muscles down when stress becomes too great. The result is a premature shutdown in your strength levels.

This shutdown mechanism is of course one of your body's important defense mechanisms, designed to keep you from ripping yourself apart by the strength of your own muscles. Experience and research tell us that the shutdown levels are typically very conservatively placed. That is, there is ample room most often to push the threshold back a bit to allow for greater than normal strength output.

Doing so requires a special form of training that can be extremely dangerous. This deinhibitory training requires high-amplitude movements so that the muscles and tendons are stretched fully with each rep, explosive movements of a high magnitude so that the initial kinetic energy far surpasses the normal level of the muscle's contracture strength, and a careful monitoring of training progress to ensure that overtraining does not occur. Amplitude training and explosiveness training take their toll quickly, so careful cycling of your training is mandatory. Only a few weeks of such intense methods can be endured before your body begins to respond negatively.

It's important to remember that nerve injury can result from such training. Overtraining is one thing, but you certainly don't want to rupture tissue because of overzealous amplitude (overstretching) or explosiveness (kinetic stress) training. In weight training and bodybuilding, tissue injuries are directly caused by overtraining (cumulative microtrauma), overstressing tissue from exaggerated amplitude, and initially overstressful explosive application of muscle effort (kinetic force). So, again, a word to the wise: Be careful. Your efforts will pay very handsomely, but only if you train wisely.

THE STRENGTH OF CONVICTION

Often, strength is most limited by barriers you have set up in your mind. Such barriers appear because of such influences as your momma telling you to "Be careful, it's heavy" or "Girls shouldn't do those kinds of things." Maybe you hurt yourself once as a result of improper training or overexertion. This kind of traumatic episode can erect an impregnable barrier in your mind, preventing you from ever exerting yourself enough to cause such an injury again.

These kinds of mental barriers are learned, and they can be unlearned. Indeed they *must* be unlearned if you are ever to progress to levels of performance required to achieve Olympian status.

Most typically, dedication, singleness of purpose, a keen desire to excel, and other such admirable athletic qualities are what it takes to confront these mental barriers and to break them down for easy passage. Some of us are blessed with this kind of mental toughness. Others require the assistance of a trained psychologist, notably a hypnotherapist.

As with skill training, which requires a reintegration of nervous circuitry, mental training requires a reintegration of memories, fears, anxieties, and supportive data stored in your conscious and subconscious mind. A single experience, if strong enough, can either set up barriers to performance or they can be shattered. More often, however, building up or tearing down such barriers is a process that often takes weeks, months, or (for some of us slow learners) years.

EPILOGUE

I had a friend who raced sports cars in the SCCA. He spent thousands of dollars making his ride lighter, stronger, and more roadworthy. He, on the other hand, was 250 pounds of overweight slovenliness. Upon realizing that fact, he lost fifty pounds of excess baggage and began winning races.

What good is it to pop vitamin pills, spend hours in the gym, give up partying, quit your job, and not tend to the one aspect of championship training that makes the most difference? How strikingly foolish my friend seemed to himself once he realized that it was he, and not his car, that prevented success. And, how satisfying it was when he finally achieved it.

Tend to that mind-body link of yours. Look at your training efforts, and incorporate some of the techniques that will bring out the greatness in you. Dig deep into your own mind, and identify barriers to success, and take the necessary steps to remove them.

27
NERVE INJURIES

When you say "nervous system" to most people, and follow it with some form of scientific explanation—or pseudo-scientific, as the case may be—they're turned off. "This stuff's too complicated for me to understand it," is the self-admitted reason. It isn't complicated at all. And, it's important to know.

Example: Bang a hammer down onto an electrical wire and you crush it. It may still conduct electricity, but not as efficiently as it once did.

Example: Pass an electrical wire through a small hole and then close the hole to make the wire immobile. Again, it'll conduct electricity but when you begin moving it, the flow will be disrupted.

Final example: Hook a lot of appliances to either of the two wires mentioned above, and turn on the juice. Depending upon the nature of each appliance, some amount of dysfunction is bound to occur.

That's the way it is with injuries to your body's nerves. Nerves emanate from your spinal column and go to all of your body's organs, including your muscles. When you injure any one of them, either pain or dysfunction occurs, or both.

If you haven't had a nerve injury of one kind or another over your years training in the gym, you're one of the fortunate few. If you have, you appreciate how debilitating such an injury can be. And disruptive of your training! When it happens, you ask yourself three questions:

1. What can I do now to heal this problem?

2. How can I train if the problem is permanent?
3. How can I avoid having this ever happen again?

Without belaboring the three examples listed above, the answers are really quite simple. Don't bang 'em with a hammer and don't crimp the hole. *Prevention* is the key, both in treating such injuries as well as in avoiding them in the first place.

DIAGNOSING NERVE INJURIES

When it comes to injuries, I've been down the road! It seems like every time I go to a doctor to get looked at, a new kind of diagnostic technique is used to uncover the nature of the injury. Here are a few you can expect:

Magnetic Resonance Imaging(MRI). An enormous electromagnet that looks like a four-foot doughnut outfitted with dials, tubes, and gadgets is filled with liquid helium and nitrogen to bring the magnet's temperature down to improve conductivity. The athlete sticks his arm or leg through the hole in the magnet and exercises while the machine measures chemical changes inside the appendage. By measuring the magnetic nature of the nuclei of the atoms comprising the athlete's tissues, the machine is able to "reconstruct" a picture of what's going on inside.

Electromyography (EMG). Tiny needles are inserted into the muscle to electrically stimulate the nerves. The EMG records the impulses. Differential speed of conduction between nerves of the left and right arm can, for example, indicate a nerve problem in the arm with the slower conduction speed. Aside from documenting precise problems with EMG, the doctor can usually pinpoint the precise location of any nerve compression.

Hands-on Manipulation. For a majority of nerve-related injuries, an experienced physician (M.D., D.O., D.C.) or therapist can usually isolate the problem and the location of the damaged nerve tissue by simply having the athlete perform a series of specific movements and noting responses. Palpation can often reveal "trigger" points indicating myofacial pain syndrome, for example. Or, tingling sensations in the extremities may give the physician a clear indication of the problem's origin.

SOME COMMON NERVE INJURIES IN SPORTS

By far the most common of all nerve-related injuries among athletes (including bodybuilders) occurs in the upper extremities. For example, researchers Y. Hirasawa and K. Sakakida studied the sports-related nerve injuries coming through their Japan-based clinic for over 18 years. They reported that fully 40% of all such cases involved the brachial plexus and the radial nerve (see Figures 27–1 to 27–3). Compression of brachial nerves, radial nerves, posterior interosseous nerves, and suprascapular nerves during typical sports training can result from:

- Heavy squats: The bar sits on the area of the cervical spine where the brachial nerves emanate.
- Heavy benches: severe stretching (as with so-called full-range dumbbell benches) of the brachial plexus or the suprascapular nerve occurs.
- Elbow hyperflexion: All exercises requiring severe hyperflexion of the elbow (e.g., squats, overhead presses, certain curls such as Scott curls, close-grip bench presses, tricep extensions) can cause compression of the radial nerve (entrapment) or the posterior interosseous nerve.

The scenario is simple to understand when you study the illustrations accompanying this chapter. They show how the nerves pass through some pretty tight spaces. Look at how the suprascapular nerve passes through the shoulder, for example. Observe that any kind of jamming or overhead movement has the capability of impinging that nerve. Take a look at the elbow joint. There, the brachial nerve and the posterior interosseous nerve pass through some spaces that are constantly pinched or crimped, especially during extreme elbow flexion movements.

To me, it's a wonder that more nerve-related problems don't exist among iron pumpers.

A CASE STUDY: MYSELF

Several years ago, I had rotator cuff surgery to repair the torn supraspinatus, infraspinatus, and teres muscles. Later, after rehabilitation was completed, I developed a grip problem while deadlifting. Simply put, my grip strength was reduced in my right hand. After years of diagnoses from several different physicians (ranging from Eastern to medical, from osteopathic to chiropractic) the following suspicions were recorded:

- Carpal tunnel syndrome (see Figure 27-3)
- Nerve entrapment resulting from the surgery
- Brachial plexus syndrome
- Posterior interosseous nerve syndrome (located at the arcade of Frohse—see illustration)
- Radial tunnel syndrome (located inside the supinator muscle)
- Myofacial "trigger" points impinging nerve tissue

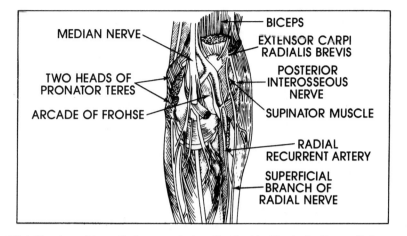

Figure 27-1. The brachioradialis muscle is reflected to illustrate the radial nerve as it divides into the superficial and posterior interosseous branches. Adapted from Grant's Atlas, ed 5. Baltimore, Williams & Wilkins Co, 1962, plate 46.

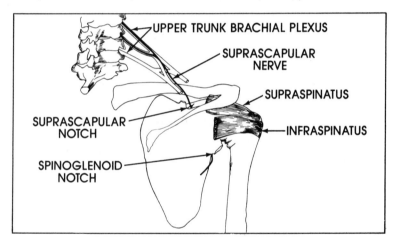

Figure 27-2. The suprascapular nerve and upper trunk brachial plexus may be involved in a neck and shoulder stretch injury. Adapted from Haymaker and Woodhall.

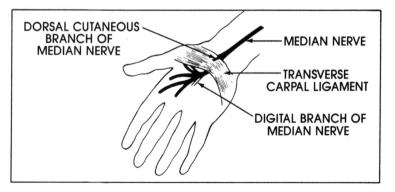

Figure 27-3. In carpal tunnel syndrome, the median nerve may be compressed within the carpal tunnel under the transverse carpal ligament. Adapted from Haymaker and Woodhall.

I've been down each road in my quest to rid myself of the problem. Nothing seems to work, and it's either because (1) none of the diagnoses were accurate, (2) all or many of them were accurate (which would require multiple treatments, or (3) surgery is indicated, a suggestion I have avoided considering.

LOW BACK INJURIES IN SPORTS

Pain radiating throughout the low back area, buttocks, and thighs may indicate an extrusion of some kind of the intervertebral disc(s) of the lumbar vertebrae. A "slipped" disc will frequently cause an impingement of the nerves passing through the tiny central hole, so will worn or "flattened" discs.

Sports movements requiring severe hyperflexion and hyperextension of the lumbar spine are the most frequent culprits in causing this kind of problem. Exercises such as heavy squats and overhead presses cause such hyperflexion and hyperextension, respectively.

But the biggest culprit in low back problems comes from improperly performed abdominal exercises.

For years now, it has been common knowledge that situps were bad for the back, and that crunchers should be done instead. In doing so, you eliminate the inordinate pull of the iliopsoas muscle, which originates on the anterior surface of the lumbar spine. This is the muscle that causes you to sit up, and it does so by pulling you upward by the lumbar spine! Over time (but not very much time) your discs are irretrievably translocated anteriorly, and you have a fully blown case of sciatica or some other manifestation of nerve impingement.

Not too many athletes do situps anymore.

But in every gym I go to I see thick-headed athletes still doing Roman Chair situps, leg raises, and other such abdominal exercises which, like situps, cause your iliopsoas muscle to do the work. Sure, you're getting some ab work in, but you're also doing some irreversible damage to your low back!

THE BOTTOM LINE: PREVENTION!

Here's a simple list of dos and don'ts to avoid all of the nerve-related problems listed in this chapter:

- Avoid heavy lifting of all forms unless you've established a solid foundation in all superstructural and synergistic muscles first! You can't shoot a cannon from a canoe!
- Avoid severely flexing or hyperextending any joint in your body, especially your shoulders, low back, neck, elbows, and wrists. These are the most vulnerable to nerve impingement.
- Be careful not to overtax any movement in phases of your train-

ing cycle when either heavy lifting or ballistic movements are necessary.

- Use spotters when a precarious movement or a heavy lift is being attempted.
- Periodic deep massage and chiropractic care are advised.
- Learn early signals of nerve compression and get symptoms checked out by a competent sports physician.

28

MUSCLE SYNERGY

When you began lifting, what was the first thing you learned about proper technique? Chances are, it was to *isolate* your muscles each time you did an exercise. You probably learned that you could *shape* that muscle by getting strict isolation. And you were *cheating* if you did anything less. And what was it you were told about the best way to do an exercise? *Through the full range of motion.*

Hogwash!

Not only is it totally impossible to achieve true isolation of any muscle in your body, but it's also not the most fruitful practice to perform certain exercises through a full joint range. Furthermore, you've heard me say this before, you can't shape an individual muscle. Only the good Lord can do that.

The ingrained dogma relating to the concepts of isolation, shaping, and full range of movement are hard to eradicate. Secret techniques of the stars are credited for their success in the realm of perfect proportion, giving understandable credence to these old notions. After all, who knows better than they?

Well, fellow iron freaks, after you finish this chapter, *you* will!

ISOLATION

Each of your body's muscles gets help from its neighbors. This is called *muscle synergy*—a cooperative action of several muscles to provide maximum force, and to control movement patterns.

216

Let's look at a few notable examples.

When you do front dumbbell raises, what's your objective? To isolate the anterior deltoids, right? But have you ever considered the fact that it's impossible to perform this movement without strong assistive action coming from the clavicular (upper) pectoralis? And, did you know that the short head of the bicep as well as the coracobrachialis were also targeted.

The most simple of all exercises—bicep curls—provides a classic example of synergism. No less than eight different muscles act in this exercise, with a score more acting as stabilizers of the shoulder girdle, trunk, and lower body. The eight "movers" that act synergistically are:

1. Biceps brachii
2. Brachialis
3. Brachioradialis
4. Pronator teres
5. Flexor carpi longus
6. Flexor carpi ulnaris
7. Palmaris longus
8. Flexor digitorum superficialis

Now, I don't mean to dissuade you from your belief that it's possible to shape a *body part*. The portion of the upper arm we conventionally refer to as the bicep can indeed be shaped to a noticeable degree. But get it out of your head that you're shaping the individual muscles that comprise this body part. It can't be done. Lay to rest the notion that you can isolate any one of the eight muscles that contribute to elbow flexion. It's simply impossible.

Let me give you another example of a commonly used exercise that's traditionally believed to allow isolation of a target muscle. Squats done with the bar resting high on the trapezius, the torso erect, and the knees allowed to project outward during the movement are said to isolate the quadriceps. During the performance of a single squat (upward movement), your knee extends, your hip joint extends, and most of the rest of your muscles are involved in stabilizing the body. Hip extension requires strong action from:

1. Gluteus maximus
2. Biceps femoris
3. Semitendinosis
4. Semimembranosis

. . . and synergistic action from:

1. Gluteus medius
2. Gluteus minimus
3. Adductor magnus

Knee extension requires primary force from:

1. Rectus femoris
2. Vastus lateralis
3. Vastus intermedius
4. Vastus medialis

So, squats don't isolate the quads any more than front dumbbell raises isolate the anterior deltoids or curls isolate the biceps.

What's the big deal? Isolation is not only impossible, it is not desirable. Synergistic action from surrounding muscles gives you the opportunity for greater overload, fewer injuries, more controlled movement, fuller body part development, and greater overall size and strength.

When a portion of a body part seems, in the mirror, to be lagging behind in development, you may want to try and minimize synergy in favor of more careful and direct stressing of the target muscle. But this practice is most typically nothing more than a pipe dream—it's possible only in a few exercises.

FULL-RANGE MOVEMENTS

Sometimes full-range movements are desirable. Full-range movements often maximize the time over which stress is applied to a muscle, thereby improving the quality of overload. An example of this principle is doing curls or dumbbell flyes.

But there are many instances where full-range movements are not desirable. Sometimes the full-range movement is nonproductive, and sometimes it can actually be counterproductive.

Seated dumbbell presses, for example, do not require full-range movement. In fact, you shouldn't do full-range presses. The lower half of the movement (until your upper arm is perpendicular to your body) is a deltoid exercise. The upper half of the movement is performed by the serratus anterior and triceps. If you're inclined backward a bit, the clavicular pectorals are also involved.

It's probably more desirable to use heavy dumbbells in the lower range—performing partial presses for the deltoids, and (as yet an exercise foreign to most athletes, but common among weightlifters) "topside" presses for the serratus muscles. In the upper half of a pressing movement, the deltoids are statically contracted, acting only as stabilizers. They do not contribute to the movement at all. So, why do full presses? The answer is, you shouldn't.

Why shouldn't you? If you're using a weight light enough to press all the way overhead, you aren't stressing the deltoids enough to force an adaptive process to occur. Haven't you ever noticed that when a weight is barely too heavy to press, your sticking point is when the

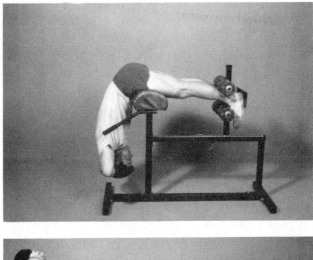

The GHG exercise takes its start from a hyperextension but continues upward for a full-range flex of glutes, hamstrings, and gastrocnemius.

arms are perpendicular to your body—right where the deltoids stop working? The deltoids are significantly stronger than are the serratus or triceps. Here is a case where it is appropriate to strive for greater isolation—at least in the sense that performing unnecessary movement detracts from the overall effectiveness of the exercise.

A NEW APPROACH TO SOME OLD EXERCISES

With a bit more knowledge about isolation, synergy, and full-range exercise movements, it's fun to play with some of the exercises you've always taken for granted. Take leg curls, for example. Primarily for the hamstrings, right? Does the exercise yield maximum isolation, overload, and movement range capabilities? Nope.

Try this instead. Dr. Mike Yessis' adaptation of a Russian sprinter's exercise improves the range of motion of traditional hamstring curls, and in the process, improves the fullness and strength of the leg biceps. He calls it the GHG exercise (glutes, hamstrings, and gastrocnemius). Lying over an apparatus similar in appearance to a hyperextension bench (but with the feet secured), do a hyperextension but continue upward by continuing to flex the hamstrings at the knee joint. *That's* full range! (See illustration on page 219.)

Here's another one. Unfortunately training technology hasn't progressed sufficiently to provide this kind of movement capability in most gyms, but if you're inventive, you'll find a way to jerryrig some pulley systems. Perform a fly movement from a position of extreme pectoral stretch. With a conventional pulley system, overload is lost halfway through the movement, but with a double-cable system—one for the first half of the fly and one slightly higher for the second half—you can maximize the stress throughout the entire range of possible movement.

There are many ways you can improve the overload quality of your exercises, but remember that the isolation principle, the full-range principle, and the so-called shaping exercises are neither hard and fast laws nor always possible in bodybuilding practice. On paper they may sound great, but in the gym, where sweat, effort, and determination reign supreme, they're only tools that often need considerable overhauling to make them work for you. As for synergism, don't neglect it. You couldn't if you wanted to, so make it work for you.

PART IV
NUTRITION AND SUPPLEMENTATION

29

DIET AND NUTRITION

Perhaps the most controversial topic in all of sportdom is diet and nutrition. This is not surprising, since most athletes are, by nature, taken to excesses in most of the things they do. Too, the study of nutrition is an infant science, and the few facts that have emerged over the years have come so infrequently that the whole picture has never been observed by nutritionists because the whole picture was never there to be observed. It still isn't.

Athletes have been told that since their muscles are comprised largely of protein, they need more protein than the average person, presumedly because they have bigger muscles and use them more often and to a greater extent. This belief has led to all sorts of misconceived dietary practices, most of which are actually counter-productive. More will be said on that later. First of all, let's take a look at calories—what they are, how they're used, how many are needed, and where they should come from.

A calorie is a measure of heat. The amount of heat that is required to raise the temperature of one gram of water 1°C equals one calorie. The caloric content of food is measured by how much heat that food can produce when burned. The food we eat is ultimately converted to glycogen and stored in the muscle to be burned during activity. The enzymes located in the muscle, primarily in the tiny organelles called mitochondria, are what effects this metabolism of calories.

The specific speed at which calories are utilized by a person at rest (e.g., lying in bed) is called basal metabolic rate (BMR). It is determined by age, sex, body size in area, body weight, and endocrine function. The average BMR for a 20-year-old man is approximately equal to 1 calorie per kilogram of body weight for a 24-hour period. For the average 20-year-old woman, it is approximately .9 calories per kilogram of body weight for the same period of time.

Athletes older than 30 will, due to a relatively lower BMR, use fewer calories per day, but the differences are probably minimal if we can assume that most athletes are relatively similar in daily activity levels. If such is not the case, then adjustments must be made accordingly in one's computations.

Many charts and graphs have been generated in recent years that illustrate how many calories are burned when engaging in various types of sports or activities. The average person has come to believe that the significance of these tables is in the choice of activities, assuming that engaging in more strenuous activities requiring more calories is the best thing to do. The true significance is in the computation of one's caloric requirement per day, rather than using the table as a guide to activity. The table presented below is designed specifically for weight-training athletes.

TABLE 29-1

APPROXIMATE KCALORIES PER MINUTE EXPENDED PER BODY WEIGHT AND HEART RATE FOR MEN AND WOMEN

Body Weight (lbs.) & Sex	Heart Rate			
	100	125	150	175
100 M	2.75	5.75	8.75	11.75
F	2.48	5.18	7.88	10.58
114 M	3.75	6.75	9.75	12.75
F	3.38	6.08	8.78	11.48
123 M	4.0	7.0	10.0	13.0
F	3.6	6.3	9.0	11.7
132 M	4.5	7.5	10.5	13.5
F	4.1	6.75	9.45	12.15
148 M	5.0	8.0	11.0	14.0
F	4.5	7.2	9.9	12.6
165 M	5.5	8.5	11.5	14.5
F	5.0	7.65	10.35	13.05
181 M	6.0	9.0	12.0	15.0
F	5.4	8.1	10.8	13.5
198 M	6.5	9.5	12.5	15.5
F	5.9	8.55	11.25	13.95
220 M	7.25	10.25	13.25	16.25
242 M	8.0	11.0	14.0	17.0
275 M	9.0	12.0	15.0	18.0
300 M	10.0	13.0	16.0	19.0
325 M	11.0	14.0	17.0	20.0

*These approximations were extrapolated from other sources.

FORMULAS FOR DETERMINING BASAL METABOLIC RATE (BMR)

Men's Basal Metabolic Rate (BMR) = 1 × Body Weight kg × 24
Women's BMR = .09 × Body Weight kg × 24

To understand the significance of the caloric expenditure table, let's look at an example. A lifter weighing 181 pounds will, in a normal workout consisting of 5 sets of 8 reps with rest periods of about 5 minutes between sets, approximate the following calorie expenditure during the course of his workout:

Time per set	2 minutes
Average Heart Rate (HR) during set	150 BPM
Average HR during recovery	
1st minute	125 BPM
2nd minute	110 BPM
3rd minute	100 BPM
4th minute	98 BPM
5th minute	96 BPM
Average for 7-minute period × 118.43 BPM	
Average HR for entire hour of workout × 118.43	

By simple interpolation procedures, we can determine the approximate number of calories expended during the hour workout:

Calories burned during set	24.00
Calories burned during recovery	
1st minute	9.00
2nd minute	6.83
3rd minute	6.00
4th minute	5.80
5th minute	5.60
Average caloric requirement for 7-minute period × 57.23 BPM	
Average caloric requirement for 1-hour workout × 490.54	

Compare this figure to the number of calories expended during the course of an hour of running at a pace of one mile every seven minutes. The same 181-pound lifter will burn in the vicinity of 1,000 calories.

If we can assume that our example athlete is relatively sedentary other than during workouts, he will burn about 1,980 calories at a basal activity level, and an average of an additional 500 calories just walking around, studying, or other light activities during the day:

Basal requirement	1980
Workout requirement	490
Normal activity requirement	500
Total caloric requirement for a 24 hour period	2970

Reference to the table on page 227 will assist you in deriving a more accurate caloric requirement for your supplemental activities during the day.

The estimated energy requirements are based on a 154-pound man. You must add or subtract 10 KCal per hour per activity for each 5 pounds that your own body weight deviates from the 154-pound baseline. Remember that due to differences in age, sex, body area, and weight, one's KCal count is only an estimate.

Determining your approximate daily caloric requirement will assist you in establishing a sound dietary regimen, particularly when you wish to gain or lose weight.

WEIGHT CONTROL

Fats, carbohydrates, and protein are the chief sources of calories in our diet. The calories one derives from these three sources are burned differentially. The energy to burn one gram of fat is 9.45 KCal, carbohydrate is 4.10 KCal, and protein is 5.65 KCal.

It becomes immediately obvious that fat constitutes a very concentrated form of energy, with carbohydrates being the lowest. It takes about 3,500 calories to make one pound of adipose tissue, with ingested fat being required in lesser amounts than protein or carbohydrates, respectively (by actual weight).

Gaining Weight

The human organism cannot biosynthesize muscle tissue any faster than about one half to one pound per week, with the lighter weight individual nearer the one-half pound figure, and the heavier individual nearer the one-pound figure. This gives us a clue as to how rapidly we can expect to gain muscle weight.

By computing your normal caloric requirement per day, and adding between 250 and 500 calories per day to your diet, thereby creating a positive caloric balance, it is possible to gain weight at the specified rate. However, there is virtually no way under the sun to ensure that the additional calories will be used in the manufacture of muscle tissue except through weight training. Weight training must accompany the increased caloric intake, or the result will surely be that fat (in the form of adipose tissue) is added to the body. The obvious moral of that story is that, in no case, should a bodybuilder strive to gain muscle weight faster than one pound per week.

ESTIMATED ENERGY REQUIREMENTS OF SELECTED PHYSICAL ACTIVITIES*

Physical Activity	Estimated Kcal/Hour
Sleeping	70
Lying quietly (awake)	80
Bull Session	90
Sitting in class	90
Studying/Reading	105
Playing cards	140
Driving a car	180
Walking (normal pace)	180
Cleaning	185
Calisthenics	200
Bowling	215
Billiards	235
Cycling (easy pace)	300
Walking up stairs	300
Golf	340
Badminton	400
Disco	450
Swimming (steady pace)	500
Basketball	560
Racquet Sports	870
Running (7-minute mile)	950

*Adapted from: Krotee, M. and Hatfield, F. "The Theory and Practice of Physical Activity", Kendall/Hunt Pub.: Dubuque, 1979.

If our 181-pound lifter wishes to progress to 198 pounds, without sacrificing hardness, he must gain 17 pounds of muscle. This will take 17–34 weeks to accomplish, with the best guess being closer to a 30-week period since only the big men of our sport can gain muscle at the maximal rate, owing to their greater size. The table on page 228 is a guide for athletes wishing to gain weight. It is assumed that you are on a very efficient training program and a nutritionally sound diet.

Should you gain weight at a faster rate than what the table specifies, beware that the increase is not coming in the form of body fat. The table figures appear not to apply to women because of the difference between the sexes in their capacity to metabolize muscle mass. The male hormone testosterone is the key here, and the average woman's testosterone level is considerably lower than the average man's. The female athlete is well advised to constantly monitor her percentage of body fat during periods of positive caloric balance, to ensure that muscle is being laid down rather than fat. In fact, this is a good idea for men as well.

THE RECOMMENDED NUMBER OF WEEKS REQUIRED TO GAIN MUSCLE WEIGHT

PRESENT LEAN BODY WEIGHT (IN POUNDS)						
100	10	20	30	40	50	60
120	9.5	19	28.5	38	47.5	57
140	9	18	27	36	45	54
160	8.5	17	25.5	34	42.5	51
180	8	16	24	32	40	48
200	7.5	15	22.5	30	37.5	45
220	7	14	21	28	35	42
240	6.5	13	19.5	26	32.5	39
260	6	12	18	24	30	36
280	5.5	11	16.5	22	27.5	33
300	5	10	15	20	25	30
	5	10	15	20	25	30

INCREASE IN POUNDS DESIRED

Losing Weight

Losing weight presents different problems than gaining weight. A negative caloric balance must be achieved in order to lose weight. That is, one must take in fewer calories each day than the number being burned. However, the problem is not so simplistic as counting calories. As with gaining weight, weight training is the real key to ensuring that the weight lost is not from the muscle mass, but rather from the fat.

For example, studies indicate that during the course of a fasting diet, 65% of the weight lost in the first 10 days was lost from muscle breakdown, and only 35% from fat. It is necessary to maintain the integrity of muscle mass during the weight-loss period. The only way known to science to accomplish this is to train with weights during the period of negative caloric balance. The weight training program most desirable is a bodybuilder's regimen, and daily exercise is essential to ensure that a minimal amount of muscle is lost.

Again, as in gaining weight, the range of 250–500 calories per day is appropriately applied to this process. One should not attempt to lose more than half to one pound of fat per week. To attempt to lose weight at a faster rate exposes the lifter to the danger of losing lean body mass as well.

PERCENT BODY FAT

I have talked quite a bit on the subject of percentage of body fat. The question must have entered your mind as to what constitutes an appropriate level of body fat. The answer is that it varies from

Body Fat	Classification
1% – 10%	athletes – men
9% – 14%	athletes – women
10% – 14%	fit adult male
14% – 18%	fit adult female
20%	average men
20%	average women
20% – 22%	clinical obesity – men
25% – 28%	clinical obesity – women
28% – 30%	chronic obesity – men
35% – 38%	chronic obesity – women

These classifications are the recommended levels of body fat for the clinical interpretation of one's percentage of body fat. Chronic obesity is the point at which clinicians refer to the condition as a "disease."

individual to individual, depending on factors such as one's yearly climate, activities engaged in, hereditary factors, and others. However, for any athlete, there is rarely any sound reason for percentage of body fat to exceed 10%.

Clinicians recommend that adult men stay within the 10%–14% range, and women between 14%–18%. However, these figures are recommended as "good," and in no way apply to the serious athlete.

Some fat is needed by the body. Fat acts in the insulation of nervous tissue, padding between the joints, lubrication for the space between skin and muscle, and padding for some of the vital organs. No one can live without some fat. However, far less is needed than the normal person generally carries.

Over the past 15 years, I have measured every college student entering my weight training classes, and have found that the averages are at the clinical obesity levels for both men and women at the beginning of the semester. By the end of the semester, the averages dropped to 15% and 21% for men and women respectively.

These fat losses are probably attributable to a number of factors—weight training, altered activity levels, changes in BMR, changes in diet, and changes in caloric intake.

Altering Basal Metabolic Rate

Earlier in this chapter, the notion was put forth that one's BMR controlled the speed with which calories were utilized. On numerous occasions, I have been approached by athletes who claimed that they couldn't gain weight (or lose weight) because their metabolic rate was too fast (or slow). We've all heard the same story. "I eat like a horse! Why can't I gain weight?" Or, "I'm only eating one meal a day and stay away from all carbohydrates and fats! Why can't I lose weight?" Two

RECOMMENDED HEART RATES DURING EXERCISE DESIGNED TO ALTER BMR*

Age	Maximum Heart Rate	80-85 Heart Rate for Athletes
20	200	160–170
22	198	158–168
24	196	157–167
26	194	155–165
28	192	154–163
30	190	152–162
32	189	151–161
34	187	150–159
36	186	149–158
38	184	147–156
40	182	146–155
45	179	143–152
50	175	140–149
55	171	137–145
60	160	128–136
65	150	120–128

These heart rates are based on an average resting heart rate of 72 for men and 80 for women. To find your true maximum heart rate, use the rule of thumb of subtracting your age from 220.

*Adapted from: Bailey, C. "Fit or Fat?" Houghton Mifflin, 1978, pg. 24.

problems manifest themselves in each of these examples. One problem is that the person is not eating in the right manner; that will be addressed in the next section of this chapter. The other involves the person's BMR. It can be altered, either up or down.

If one's goal is to gain weight, a reduction in BMR is called for, but only if there is a "problem" with gaining muscle weight. Under normal conditions (comprising the vast majority of cases), athletes wishing to gain weight can do so simply by following the guidelines in the previous section of this chapter. This method includes: increasing caloric intake by 250–500 calories per day, eating nutritionally sound meals, and training appropriately. With the "problem" gainer, the additional method of lowering BMR may be the step that'll make all the difference. It involves simply being lazy. The only calories being burned each day, other than those burned at workout, should be burned at the basal level. Engage in no other activity requiring increased caloric expenditure.

In Part I, I presented the mechanisms involved in strength, along with the functions of each. It was learned that the mitochondria are responsible for the oxidative functions of the body cell, and also contained a majority of the enzymes that collectively were associated with energy production. As it happens, increasing mitochondrial mass is the most efficient method of increasing one's BMR. Any method—be it running, swimming, cycling, or weight training—that

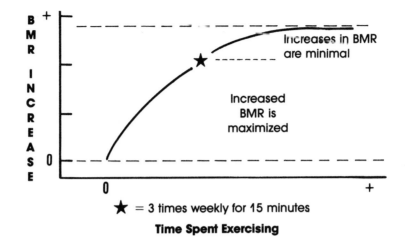

★ = 3 times weekly for 15 minutes

Time Spent Exercising

increases one's heart rate to 80%–85% of one's maximum heart rate for about 15 minutes three times weekly is sufficient stress to force this adaptive process to occur. With the application of such stress, the enzymes responsible for metabolizing calories increase in concentrations, and the mitochondria increase in size and number. The result is that, whereas one's BMR may have been such that 1,900 calories were burned each day at a basal level, as many as 2,400 calories can now be burned!

The recommended method of achieving this BMR change for strength athletes is *not* running. Running tends to be traumatic to the joints, especially the hips, knees, and lower spine. Weightlifters suffer enough trauma under the iron! I recommend swimming, or, if a pool isn't available, try stepping up and down from a bench for the 15-minute period—far less trauma to the joints results from this method than from running, since the full weight of the body is not constantly hammering away at the joints. Cycling is also a good method.

Exercising in this manner more than the recommended three times weekly for 15 minutes each time is not recommended. First, it'll rob you of normal training time and energy, and second, the gains will not be worth the effort. The chart above is a graphic example of the kinds of gains one can expect by exercising more or less than the recommended amount.

One can clearly see that beyond three times weekly the returns rapidly diminish, and become less and less with time. The trauma of the training will, at these higher levels, become counterproductive, and should only be engaged in by endurance athletes.

How to Eat

How one eats plays a vital role in whether fat is deposited, food is utilized maximally, and whether digestion is completed. Research dealing with rats (and later verified with human subjects) yielded some startling results. Rats were put on a diet consisting of fewer calories than they needed each day. Group one ate their calories in one big meal, and group two ate as they pleased all day. Both groups had the same number of calories given them daily. Thus, both groups lost weight. However, when returned to normal diets, the "one big meal" rats gained more weight than the rats that ate a little all day. Studies were made of the enzymes associated with the deposition of adipose tissue in both groups of rats, and it was discovered that the "one big meal" rats had ten times the concentration of these enzymes than did the other rats. The result was that they had "adapted" to the stress of famine by gearing their bodies to store fat. The same happens to humans who eat only one meal per day. In their efforts to lose weight, they are actually making themselves more prone to put on fat!

The human body interprets famine (fasting) as stress, even if the fast is only 23 hours long. It adapts to this type of stress by increasing the fat-storing enzymes. However, there's another reason that is more mechanical in nature. The body cannot accept all of the calories taken in in one big meal, and consequently must eliminate them or store them. The enzymes then take over in the storing process.

Eating four or five smaller meals (consisting of the same total number of calories per day as the large meal) will allow full assimilation of the calories, and therefore full utilization—no fat will be stored. This concept is important for all athletes, including those wishing to gain weight, lose weight, or stay the same but get harder.

Another problem with how one eats is common in our society. That is the habit of snacking. Research tells us that complete digestion and assimilation of one meal takes roughly three to four hours. The digestive process involves a stepwise procedure of various enzymes and gastric juices being introduced as they are needed. As one completes its job, the next comes as the first is dissipated. And so forth until digestion is complete enough for assimilation to occur. However, if one snacks during this process, the original digestive enzymes are forced to enter, thereby negating the effectiveness of the ones already there. Digestion stops for the original food, and it often sits in the stomach for up to 72 hours before ever getting digested enough for assimilation! This kind of problem definitely interferes with one's attempt at gaining weight, since much of the food never gets into the system when it's needed. Further, it interferes with losing weight since much is stored in fat.

For athletes then, or anyone else for that matter, the appropriate method of eating appears to be to eat three meals minimum per day (preferably four or five). Each meal should be of equal size, calorie-wise, and spaced about three or four hours apart. No snacking is the general rule. If you count calories, this method of eating is by far the most efficient method of gaining muscle weight, losing fat weight, or remaining the same weight while increasing muscle mass.

WHAT TO EAT

So far in this chapter, I have explored some of the factors involved in how much to eat and how to eat. I have also discussed a few ideas as to how to increase caloric expenditure. I will now direct my discussion to the problem of *what* to eat. As noted previously, one's chief sources of calories are fats, carbohydrates, and protein. These sources for calories are derived from the food we eat. Foods are subdivided into groups as follows:

- Meat and egg group
- Bread, whole grain, and cereal group
- Vegetable and fruit group
- Dairy group

Each of these food groups has fats, carbohydrates, and proteins in it to varying degrees. It, therefore, is advisable to include all of the food groups in each meal you eat. Further, this mixing of food groups happens to be the only method of ensuring that you are deriving the proper balance of vitamins, nutrients, and minerals from each meal. More will be said on this subject later.

Fats

One of the gravest injustices performed by the self-proclaimed "experts" on nutrition has been the rap that fat is bad, and should be avoided like the plague. In fact, fat is a vital part of sound nutrition. Fats are the richest sources of vitamins A, D, E, and K. The three so-called essential fatty acids, arachidonic acid, linoleic acid, and linolenic acid are essential to life itself. They cannot be manufactured by the body, and therefore must be derived from other sources. Most of the best protein sources are high in fat content, so it is extremely difficult, if not impossible, to derive one's daily ration of protein without also getting plenty of fat.

The average American will consume in the neighborhood of 45% of his or her daily calories in the form of fat. It is an exceptionally concentrated source of calories, requiring roughly 9.45 Kcal of energy to burn one gram of it, in comparison to the 5.65 Kcal and 4.1 Kcal for proteins and carbohydrates.

Fat comes in two forms, saturated and unsaturated. The American Medical Association informs us that about 23% of our daily calories should be derived from fats. This, presumably, is due to the fact that much of the fat Americans consume comes in the form of saturated fats, which are not as desirable as are the unsaturated fats. The reduction from the common 45% to the recommended 23% should come from the saturated fats—the highest source of which is animal fats (meats, cheese, milk, and eggs). However, recent research emanating from Harvard University informs us that ingesting skim milk, for example, actually reduces the amount of cholesterol in the blood by as much as 17%. In fact, eggs, a high source of cholesterol, were once said to be bad for us in excessive amounts due to the cholesterol level. Eggs also have much lecithin, which, like cholesterol, is a "cousin" to the fatty acid family. Normally occurring lecithin aids in the breakdown of cholesterol so that it can be taken up by the cell and used as energy, rather than deposited on the arterial walls in the form of plaques.

It appears that, if one's diet consists of fats derived from natural sources (unrefined and untampered with), the body will accept and use them without problem. This is especially true if one's diet excludes sugar as much as possible.

The best sources of fats are vegetables (unrefined, fresh oils), fish, nuts and seeds, dairy products, and eggs. Animal flesh is marbled with much saturated fat, and should be only a limited source of fats.

Since the weight training athlete rarely ventures into the aerobic pathway for energy, less fat is needed in his or her diet than might be the case for the average person or an athlete engaged in long-distance training. It is therefore recommended that you limit your fat intake to roughly 10% of the daily calories taken in.

Carbohydrates

Carbohydrates are formed by various combinations of carbon, hydrogen, and oxygen molecules. The three basic classifications of carbohydrates are monosaccharides (simple sugars, or glucose), disaccharides (sucrose), and polysaccharides (starches).

Carbohydrates comprise the major portion of any nutritionally sound diet, with the recommended allowance for athletes being in the vicinity of 60% of his or her daily caloric requirement. The major source for muscular contraction during anaerobic activity (such as lifting) are carbohydrates. There has been much contradictory advice coming from our soothsayers and self-proclaimed experts on nutrition about carbohydrates. Closer scrutiny of the differences in the forms of carbohydrates is the answer.

There are, as indicated, three types of carbohydrates. There is a great deal of difference between these types of carbohydrates. While all types ultimately become glucose, a simple sugar, they do so at different rates. The complex carbohydrates become blood glucose very slowly, while the simple sugars like table sugar, milk lactose, and maltose, become blood glucose very rapidly. The simple sugars are actually a form of "predigested" sugar, and cause too rapid a change in blood sugar levels. All forms of horrors have been associated with the consumption of simple sugar, ranging from inability to utilize cholesterol to hypertension and even propagation of criminal tendencies! The FDA, a very conservative organization normally, was quoted as saying that if they knew 50 years ago what they now know about sugar, it would have been banned from the grocery shelves.

Suffice it to say that it is the complex carbohydrates—in the form of vegetables, fruits, whole grains, and nuts—which are most desirable in one's diet, for they not only form the major source of energy, but also have many of the nutrients everyone needs. The so-called "starch" foods, like potatoes, corn, pasta, and the like are unduly scorned also. Sources such as these are also high in many nutrients, and both are good sources of fiber, which aids in the digestive process and in bowel regularity.

To illustrate the extent of differences between types of carbohydrates, let's look at a single kernel of corn. In England, nutrition experts used actual enzymes from a human digestive tract to break a corn kernel down into its component parts. It was found that 12% of the kernel was indigestible, being comprised of cellulose, hemicellulose, and lignin. Most people have noticed that kernels appear in feces; it is the outer layer of the corn, the roughage, that they see. The remainder of the corn's inside portion is composed of sugars such as glucose, fructose, and sucrose, and also of starches. Taken as a whole, corn is much like all other cereal grains in that it is a relatively complete source of carbohydrates. Some of the benefits of deriving one's carbohydrates through such a source are:

- The roughage tends to reduce caloric value of the food.
- The roughage gives some protection to the digestive tract.
- The hard-to-chew roughage tends to discourage overeating.
- Necessary vitamins and minerals are derived as nature intended—together.
- The simple sugars in the whole grains add some taste to the food, but are delayed from entering the bloodstream too quickly.

If the average American athlete was to limit his carbohydrate intake to complex forms of the food source, rather than eating so much refined sugar and sweets, the ingestion of carbohydrates would present no problems at all. Nutritionists and exercise physiologists recommend that people derive about 70% of their daily calories from carbohydrate sources. However, in light of new research indicating athletes' need for more protein, athletes should limit carbohydrate intake to roughly 60% of the daily calorie allowance.

Protein

Americans have been bombarded with slogans that fats and carbohydrates are fattening. Protein represents the only other calorie source. So, it is a natural conclusion that we should eat more protein, and less of the other two. This is, as has been pointed out already, totally erroneous. Calories are calories! And the body needs all three sources. The generally accepted level of protein intake is about 15%–20% of one's daily calories. However, what kind of protein?

Protein comes in an array of assimilability levels. Eggs are roughly 96% assimilable because they have a very equitable balance of the *essential amino acids* available. Eggs, then, are the standard by which all protein sources are judged. Milk is next highest, with an assimilability ratio of about 60%. Next comes the meats, ranging near 40%. Vegetables vary up to about 15% at best.

The assimilability ratio describes the extent of available amino acids that have been labeled "essential." They are called such because they cannot be biosynthesized in the body. No source of protein is worthwhile to eat, except for the calories, vitamins, and minerals derived from them, unless they have all of the essential amino acids. The protein content is literally wasted otherwise. Mixing foods often will ensure that all of the essential amino acids are derived in one meal.

So, when the FDA recommends that the average person consume 15% of one's daily calories from protein sources, you should ask, "Which sources?" If 15% of your daily calories are derived from *incomplete* protein sources, this will normally necessitate consuming many more grams of protein than 15%. For example, if one's sources of protein are in the form of milk and meat, the complement of these incomplete sources will generally tend to increase the assimilability ratio to something well above that of either when taken separately.

It is said that the average strength athlete should take in about one gram of protein per kilogram of body weight. This seems reasonable, but again, be sure that your protein is *complete*. This rule of thumb will generally average out to roughly 30% of your caloric intake being derived from protein sources, with a considerably smaller amount of those proteins being totally usable.

To summarize, the following ratios of calorie sources are recommended for the lifter in heavy training:

Fats—10%
Carbohydrates—60%
Protein—30%

Endurance athletes are well-advised to ingest a higher percentage of carbohydrates, as they are a more efficient calorie source. The same may be said of fats. Athletes need slightly more protein for muscle reparation and muscle growth, but certainly not in the excessive quantities advocated by our resident soothsayers.

Eating more protein causes formation of a highly toxic ammonia in one's system called urea. This urea must be excreted, and subsequently places a strain on the liver and kidneys.

Vitamins and Minerals

There are virtually hundreds of guidebooks on the market that describe the various known and speculated values of each of the vitamins and minerals essential to humans. I will not delve into this area, partly because so much is already written, and also because I have not seen any research that is conclusive in its findings concerning the tremendously complex interactive nature of these nutrients. Many of the vitamins and minerals are coenzymatic, and many interact in unknown ways. To elaborate further would prompt speculation, and there's already an overabundance of that.

I will simply quote the Food and Nutrition Board of the National Academy of Sciences on the recommended daily allowances of vitamins and minerals, and leave the matter of deciding on their applicability to lifting and sports in general to the nutritional experts, subject to their research efforts and compare them to Bill Starr's recommendations, as cited in his 1976 book, *The Strongest Shall Survive.*

It becomes immediately clear that there are many discrepancies between the Academy's recommendations and Starr's. Some recommended dosages are more with the Academy's than with Starr's, and vice versa. In fact, Starr lists some that the Academy does not. The National Vitamin Foundation has recommended yet another listing of allowances. All three lists are shown on page 238.

Naturally, the National Vitamin Foundation, being interested in vitamins, has not generated a list of recommendations for the minerals. The Academy presents a very scientific approach to vitamin requirements, including the interactive nature of many of them, and also the changes in requirements as they may vary according to body weight, intestinal flora activity, the amount of unsaturated fatty acids in the diet, and other considerations. I have yet to observe a more detailed and scientific approach to determining recommended allowances than the National Academy of Sciences' listing.

SUPPLEMENTING

Most athletes hold dear the notion that, since they are "mega-people," they need megadoses of everything in their diet. It is well known that one's vitamin requirement is directly related to one's activity, age, present state of health, and many other factors. It is apparently safe to assume that if one's diet is sound and one's health is reasonably sound, the additional requirements can be derived from an increase of calories generally, and need not be supplemented by pills or injections. Again, a very big "if."

RECOMMENDED DAILY DIETARY ALLOWANCES OF THE FOOD AND NUTRITION BOARD OF THE NATIONAL ACADEMY OF SCIENCES

Fat-Soluble Vitamins

Vitamin A............................5,000 I.U.
Vitamin D.............................400 I.U.
Vitamin E...............................15 I.U.

Water-Soluble Vitamins

Ascorbic Acid (C)......................45 mgs
Folacin..........................400–800 mcg
Niacin.................................20 mgs
Riboflavin............................1.8 mgs
Thiamine..............................1.5 mgs

Vitamin B_6.........................2.0–2.5 mgs
Vitamin B_{12}......................3–4 mcgs

Minerals

Calcium..............................1,200 mgs
Phosphorus...........................1,200 mgs
Iodine...............................150 mcgs
Iron...................................18 mgs
Magnesium........................350–450 mgs
Zinc...............................15–25 mgs

BILL STARR'S DAILY DIETARY RECOMMENDATIONS

Vitamins

Vitamin A..........................25,000 units
Thiamine B_1.........................100 mgs
Riboflavin, B_2.......................60 mgs
Niacin, B_3.........................100 mgs
Pyridoxine, B_6.........1 gram per gram of protein
Pantothenic Acid......................100 mgs
Folic Acid..............................5 mgs
Biotin...............................100 mcgs
Vitamin B_{12}.......................500 mcgs
PABA..................................100 mgs
Inositol..............................500 mgs
Choline...............................500 mgs
Vitamin C............................4,000 mgs
Vitamin D...........................5,000 units
Vitamin E...........................1200 I.U.

Minerals

Calcium...............................2.0 grams
Phosphorous...........................4.0 grams
Magnesium.............................1.0 grams
Potassium............................10.0 grams
Sodium...............................10.0 grams
Chlorine.............................10.0 grams
Copper................................5.0 mgs
Zinc..................................1.0 mgs
Cobalt................................5.0 mgs
Iron.................................15.0 mgs
Iodine...............................0.15 mgs
Manganese............................10.0 mgs

*Source: *Strongest Shall Survive*, pg. 146.

NATIONAL VITAMIN FOUNDATION'S RECOMMENDED DAILY ALLOWANCES

Vitamin A.....................3,000–5,000 I.U.
Vitamin B_1 (Thiamine).......4 mgs per 1000 cal.
Vitamin B_2 (Riboflavin).....6 mgs per 1000 cal.
Vitamin B_6.........................2.0 mgs
Vitamin B_{12} (Cobalamin)..............5.0 mcgs
Folic acid (Pteroylglutamic Acid)..0.1 mgs. (free)

Pantothenic Acid.......................10 mgs
Niacin (Niacinamide)................to 10 mgs
Biotin.............................Unknown
Vitamin C (Ascorbic Acid)...............70 mgs
Vitamin D (Including D_2 and D...........400 I.U.
Vitamin E (Tocopherols)................to 30 I.U.
Vitamin K.............................0.5 mgs

Most athletes are *not* healthy—from the standpoint of total fitness and being free from any stress or microtrauma. There is considerable evidence that supports the notion that, under extreme duress or physical stress, a person's need for certain vitamins and minerals increases.

I believe that in light of the best available evidence the average athlete need supplement only to the extent of dietary deficiencies. As an insurance policy, however, I don't believe it hurts anything to indulge in a good brand of multivitamin/minerals each day. Poor diet should not be used as an excuse for megadosing. Try to derive sound nutrition from natural foods, and by all scientific reasoning, you'll be better off.

During recuperative periods (e.g., after surgery and perhaps before as well, or recovering from an injury), many nutritionists (such as Adelle Davis) recommend increased doses of certain vitamins and minerals to aid the recuperative capacity of the organism.

The best advice I can give is to buy yourself a good calorie counter (with foods, portions, calories, vitamins, minerals, protein, fats, and carbohydrates all tabled), and build as sound a dietary regimen as you can, and stick to it. It's a hassle at first, but your efforts will pay dividends.

One possible exception to the supplementing guidelines mentioned above has to do with international trips, where you don't know what kind of food you're going to be forced to eat. In such instances, try to limit your food intake to those foods with which you are thoroughly familiar and used to. Also, bring an array of vitamins and mineral supplements to be sure that extended visits in a foreign country (and consequently prolonged dietary abnormalities) aren't going to take a toll.

THE PRECONTEST DIET

Athletes traditionally rationalize when they lose a meet, with excuses ranging from poor coaching, to poor peaking methods, to injury or illness. It is usually clear to them why they lost. The reverse is seldom true. Athletes rarely are able to pinpoint reasons for winning, and are apt to offer generalities like, "I felt good today," or "I was on." This inability to articulate reasons for winning has given rise to all sorts of strange and ritualistic practices by athletes, not the least of which is their precontest eating habits.

Football players are famous for their "need" for a thick steak and all the trimmings before games. Other athletes will eat only salads, assuming that they will lose weight that way. Still others consume large quantities of pasta or sweets before contests. What accounts for this tremendous array of eating habits? Especially in light of the fact that many of these same athletes go on to break world or national records, or have exceptionally good games despite their strange eating habits.

There are, to be sure, many individual differences that must be accounted for in choosing the appropriate diet before contests. One of the most pervasive issues is nervous tension. Nervous tension often results in finicky stomachs, and a decided decrease in the blood flow to the stomach and small intestines, where absorption occurs. Athletes with psychological aversions toward some kinds of food are affected by those foods in a detrimental way despite the fact that it's only psychological. The precontest meal should be planned according to these general guidelines:

1. Energy intake should be adequate enough to ward off hunger or weakness occurring through the entire contest.
2. The diet plan should be carried out early enough to ensure complete emptying of the stomach and upper gastrointestinal tract at the time of weigh-in and during the contest.
3. Fluid intake should be sufficient (both before and during competition) to ensure sufficient fluid replacement from sweating or dropping weight for weigh-in.
4. Indulge in foods that will allow comfort to the gastrointestinal tract. Avoid foods that are irritants (i.e., spicy foods).
5. The meal should consist of foods that the athlete is familiar with, and likes. Avoid eating foods that you rarely or never eat elsewhere.
6. Never miss meals. Even athletes with a weight problem should eat a little to avoid extreme hunger and depression from lack of sufficient calories.
7. Avoid massive intakes of food prior to competition and during competition, and make sure that all foods you consume are of the low glycemic index variety.

The simple fact is that the fewer deviations from your normal eating habits, the better. However, there are some additional considerations that the wise athlete should consider in his or her precontest eating habits, and perhaps incorporate into the general precontest routine to avoid "shocking" the gastrointestinal tract with surprises. To quote from the *Journal of the American Medical Association* (Nathan Smith, M.D.):

Limit salty foods such as:

table salt	salty and smoky meats and fish
monosodium glutamate	mustard
sauerkraut	relish and pickles
potato chips	soy sauce
pretzels and other salty snacks	Worcestershire sauce

sausage   dry cereals
sardines   catsup
cheese   bouillon cubes
canned soups   peanut butter
instant cocoa mix

Limit high fiber foods such as:
raw fruits and vegetables, salads
dried fruits: raisins, apricots
nuts
whole grain cereals, breads and granola or bran, berry and fruit
    pies
Limit milk and cheese severely (one or two servings per day, and
    none within 24 hours of competition).
A few other considerations that should be accounted for on an
individual basis are as follows:

1. Two hours (minimum) should elapse between meal and competition to allow digestion and assimilation to take place.
2. Protein foods stimulate gastric secretions which yield organic
   acids. These will be retained rather than excreted when renal
   blood flow and filtration are reduced through exercise; so, limit
   protein intake for the last 12 hours before competition.
3. It is recommended that bland, nongreasy, easily digested and
   absorbed foods be eaten before competition. They should be
   higher than normal in carbohydrates (especially low glycemic
   index carbohydrates) and can include the liquid meal on the
   market, pancakes, waffles, or toast.
4. Avoid high intakes of simple carbohydrates such as table sugar,
   honey, cake, and other sweets, as these will cause a hyperglycemic state if ingested more than a half hour before competition.
   Sugar also delays fluid absorption to a marked extent, and is
   therefore quite dangerous for the dehydrated athlete who just
   had to make weight. Also, on particularly hot and humid days,
   sugar is worse than poison, since it robs the body's cooling
   mechanisms of needed fluid.

SUMMARY

Throughout this chapter, I have taken the middle-of-the-road approach to sound nutrition. I have avoided the faddist approaches, the
megadose approach, and the quackery emanating from our nutrition-
ist soothsayers. Sound nutrition should stem from sound eating; but is
this possible? Gaining and losing weight should be accomplished with
a minimum of fat added and a maximum of muscle mass kept,

attesting to the great importance of exercise along with a sound diet. When preparing for a meet, and special dieting is necessary, or when water loss is called for, exercise all due caution that the practice will not detract from meet performance. I have become thoroughly convinced that appropriate dieting is one of the keystones of the champions, but far more research is needed to be totally specific.

30
PERFORMANCE NUTRITION

Startling though it may be, athletes and sports nutritionists the nation over doggedly cling to Momma's recipe for growing up to be big and strong like Daddy. Well-known admonishments from our childhood, like "eat your veggies" or "no dessert until you've eaten it all" cling like a sweaty nylon T-shirt in an age of supersophisticated sports training.

Well, hold onto your hats, fellow fitness freaks. You too, Momma. By today's standards of excellence, Daddy was a wimp. And, it just may be that his eating habits were to blame. There's a whole lot more to maximizing your performance through sound nutritional practice than eating all of your rabbit food or pasta.

When it comes to your body's biochemistry, you can't leave things to chance by simply shotgunning food down your throat. If your intention is to achieve peak athletic performance capabilities, you also have to know how often to eat, what to eat at each sitting, how to eat, how much to eat, and what supplements to use.

A DAY IN THE LIFE OF A PEAK PERFORMER

The long-term commitment to sports excellence requires that a basic question be asked when planning your next meal. "What am I going to be doing over the next three and a half hours?" It takes about that long for your meal to be digested and assimilated, and then it's time to eat again. Your body needs a continual supply of calories. Eating once every three to four hours provides those calories far more efficiently than more or less frequently. If you take in too many calories at once, your body will store them as fat, whereas eating less frequently results in a caloric deficit that forces your body to cannibalize lean tissue.

Excess body fat, as you know, is the mortal enemy of a peak-performing athlete. But taking in fewer calories than needed to get you to your next meal is a more insidious foe, for you've worked hard in the gym to gain your muscle tissue. Your fat stores aren't tapped first for needed energy (as most believe), your muscles are. Muscle is precious.

But let's look at a slightly broader picture than just a single meal. Looking at a day's worth of eating will help you to schedule your meals and their contents in a more integrated and effective manner.

First, it's clear that in order to preserve muscle and prevent fat deposits, you must eat four or five meals a day (most competing bodybuilders eat six meals per day to maintain their fat-free massive appearance). That's not as difficult as it may seem. Brown paper bags have been around for a long time. Use them.

There's a simple way of deciding how many calories you need at each meal throughout the day:

1. Trying to gain muscle mass? Add 100 calories to each meal beyond what's required to maintain present body weight.
2. Trying to lose weight (especially fat)? Reduce each meal's caloric value by 100 calories.
3. Have a workout scheduled within the next three hours? Borrow 100 calories from each of your other daily meals and add them to your preworkout meal.
4. Taking a nap or planning to sit quietly over the next three or four hours? Reduce this meal's caloric intake to no more than 300–400 calories.

In case the significance of this calorie-shuffling exercise has escaped you, remember: too many calories and you'll put on fat, too few calories and you'll lose muscle. Your body doesn't apportion your caloric intake on the basis of days or weeks. It works on a hand-to-mouth system. Now is now, and the damage, though insignificant in the course of a day's poor eating, is cumulative and can make the difference between maximum training gains and poor progress over weeks.

There are a couple of other benefits to this sort of eating program. Over the course of a month, you will actually become biochemically incapable of putting on fat. Supplying your system with the exact number of calories it requires—no more or less—suppresses the manufacture of the enzymes responsible for depositing fat. They're simply not needed.

One important benefit is realized in regard to your need for protein. I know, I know! The AMA and FDA insist that we're getting too much protein already! I'm not convinced. If you're Joe Average, you have a doughnut for breakfast, a greaseburger for lunch, and a massive steak for dinner. Chances are, you're getting less protein than you need, but I won't quibble over the small stuff. What's more important to the peak performer is that he or she gets protein in small doses throughout the day instead of all (or most) of it at one sitting, like Joe Average does.

Your body cannot use all that protein at once, so even if you are ingesting more protein than you need, you can't use it all. Joe Average is actually protein-starved most of the day.

Glycemic Index: The area under the blood glucose response curve for each food expressed as a percentage of the area after taking the same amount of carbohydrate as glucose**

100%	60%-69%	40%-49%	20%-29%
Glucose	Bread (white)	Spaghetti (whole wheat)	Kidney beans
80%-90%	Rice (brown)	Oatmeal	Lentils
	Muesli	Potato (sweet)	Fructose
Corn flakes	Shredded Wheat	Beans (canned navy)	**10%-19%**
Carrots**	Ryvita	Peas (dried)	
Parsnips**	Water biscuits	Oranges	Soy beans
Potato (instant mashed)	Beetroot	Orange juice	Soy beans (canned)
Maltose	Bananas	**30%-39%**	Peanuts
Honey	Raisins		
70%-79%	Mars bar	Butter beans	
	50%-59%	Haricot beans	
Bread (whole wheat)	Buckwheat	Blackeye peas	
Millet	Spaghetti (white)	Chick-peas	
Rice (white)	Sweet corn	Apples (Golden Delicious)	
Weetabix	All-Bran	Ice cream	
Broad beans (fresh)**	Digestive biscuits	Milk (skim)	
Potato (new)	Oatmeal biscuits	Milk (whole)	
Swede**	Rich Tea biscuits	Yogurt	
	Peas (frozen)	Tomato soup	
	Yam		
	Sucrose		
	Potato chips		

From Jenkins, D.J.A.: Lente carbohydrate: A newer approach to the dietary management of diabetes. *Diabetes Care* 5:634. 1982 (reference 3)
*Data from normal individuals (after Jenkins et al. (13)).
**25-gm carbohydrate portions listed.
*See the Diabetes Care and Education Practice Group's companion bibliography, *Fiber and the Patient with Diabetes Mellitus: A Summary and Annotated Bibliography*, 2nd ed. Chicago: American Diabetes Association, 1983.

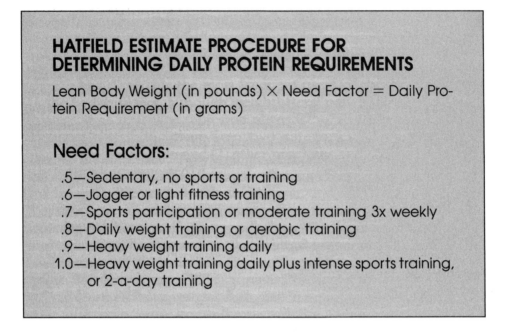

HATFIELD ESTIMATE PROCEDURE FOR DETERMINING DAILY PROTEIN REQUIREMENTS

Lean Body Weight (in pounds) × Need Factor = Daily Protein Requirement (in grams)

Need Factors:

.5—Sedentary, no sports or training
.6—Jogger or light fitness training
.7—Sports participation or moderate training 3x weekly
.8—Daily weight training or aerobic training
.9—Heavy weight training daily
1.0—Heavy weight training daily plus intense sports training, or 2-a-day training

It's impossible to tell exactly how much protein you need, but if you'll refer to the accompanying table, you'll see that several factors must be considered. The important thing to remember is to spread your protein need over the four or five meals you eat each day. That way, you'll find it much easier to gain muscle mass and strength from your training. Typically used guidelines such as one gram of protein per kilogram of body weight or 15% of your daily caloric intake simply aren't adequate for serious athletes or fitness enthusiasts wishing to maximize the effectiveness of their training and sports performance efforts.

The remainder of each meal's calories, of course, must come from fat and carbohydrates. Assuming that you'll try to minimize your fat intake—keep it at about 10% of your total caloric intake—the chief source of energy should be your carbohydrates. But all carbohydrates are not the same.

Make sure that your preworkout meal's carbs are of the low glycemic index variety. That is, the kind of carbs that do not cause a rapid rise and fall in your blood sugar, but instead a gradual rise and sustained energy until your next meal. Refer to the table showing the glycemic indexes of selected foods, and you'll see that many foods typically consumed before training simply aren't advisable if peak training efficiency is your aim. Your preworkout meal should consist of carbohydrate sources with a glycemic index under 50. Fruits (except bananas and raisins) and most varieties of beans are excellent preworkout energy sources.

Like Sasquatch or the abominable snowman, the average American is a mythical being. You are unique, and your eating habits must be

YOUR PROTEIN REQUIREMENT IN GRAMS PER DAY

LBW (lbs)*	Need Factor					
	.5	.6	.7	.8	.9	1.0
90	45	54	63	72	81	90
100	50	60	70	80	90	100
110	55	66	77	88	99	110
120	60	72	84	96	108	120
130	65	78	91	104	117	130
140	70	84	98	112	126	140
150	75	90	105	120	135	150
160	80	96	112	128	144	160
170	85	102	119	136	153	170
180	90	108	126	144	162	180
190	95	114	133	152	171	190
200	100	120	140	160	180	200
210	105	126	147	168	189	210
220	110	132	154	176	198	220
230	115	138	161	184	207	230
240	120	144	168	192	216	240

*LBW—your fat-free weight—can be estimated using any one of several anthropometric, ultrasound, electrical impedance, or underwater weighing techniques. Average man is 20% fat, and average woman is 28% fat.

reflective of your energy, growth, and rejuvenation needs. No doubt they are significantly beyond what agencies recommend for the mythical creature. That is, if you aspire to achieve peak performance status.

31

INTEGRATING NUTRITION WITH TRAINING

Supplement manufacturers want you to believe that you need all of their products all the time. Consider these obvious points:

1. You don't have room in your belly for all of them.
2. You don't have enough money to buy all of them.
3. Most of them don't do what they claim to do.
4. Of those remaining, you don't need all of them all the time.
5. Even if you did need them, you don't know how to take them (or when in your training cycle) in order for them to do the most good.

What's a poor athlete to do? Most of you are guilty of simply shotgunning pills down your throat indiscriminately, hoping against hope that the manufacturer isn't steering you wrong.

He is. Bet on it.

I offer the following alternative in the hope that you will regain possession of your senses, and your athletic career, and supplement wisely.

What's wise? Let's figure it out. Look at Figure 31–1. You'll note that the 16-week preparation cycle is divided into quarters. Are your training objectives the same in each one of these quarters? Of course not.

In the first quarter, your training objectives may be to lose fat, put on muscle mass, and improve limit strength levels in all muscles.

FIGURE 31.1

TRAINING CYCLE BREAKDOWN FOR MOST POWER SPORTS

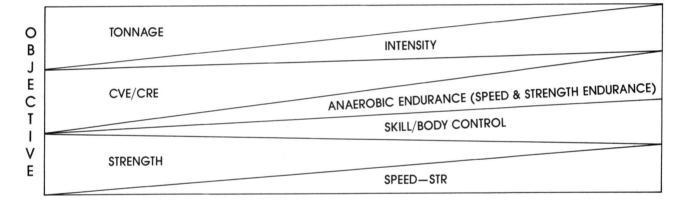

	Cycle One (3-4 weeks long)	Cycle Two	Cycle Three	Cycle Four
I	FOUNDATION TRAINING (OVERCOMING WEAKNESSES) (LIMIT STR.)			
II		FUNCTIONAL STRENGTH (SPORT RELATED) (LIMIT STR)		
III			C.A. TRAINING (EXPLOSIVENESS & BALLISTIC TRAINING (STARTING)	
IV			PLYOMETRICS	
		JUMPING/HOPPING	WEIGHTED	SHOCK
V				OVERSPEED

O B J E C T I V E	TONNAGE	INTENSITY
	CVE/CRE	ANAEROBIC ENDURANCE (SPEED & STRENGTH ENDURANCE)
		SKILL/BODY CONTROL
	STRENGTH	SPEED—STR

For the second quarter you want to get body fat to competition levels, maximize limit strength in primary (sport-related) muscles and musculoskeletal movement patterns, and improve recuperative capabilities (owing to greater levels of stress you're inflicting on your muscles and connective tissues).

The third quarter: Maximize recuperative capabilities because you've begun doing a lot of (damaging) ballistic training and improve pretraining energy stores for more intense training.

During the final quarter and the in-season period—you concentrate on how to maximize recuperative capabilities, both for healing microtraumatized tissue and for better energy levels from workout to workout.

Sure, there's overlap, but each partner has its own peculiar requirements. So, why on earth would you ever consider taking the same types of nutritional supplements throughout the entire training cycle? You shouldn't. It's not the best way to excel.

THE 10 REASONS FOR SUPPLEMENTING AN ATHLETE'S DIET

1. For improved strength
2. For greater muscle mass
3. To reduce body fat
4. For anaerobic (short-term) endurance
5. For aerobic (long-term) endurance
6. For improved recovery between workouts
7. For improved recuperation from injury, trauma, and illness
8. To reduce pain
9. For better mental concentration
10. To improve health and general metabolic processes

FIGURE 31-2

DIET/SUPPLEMENTATION FOR AVERAGE TRAINING

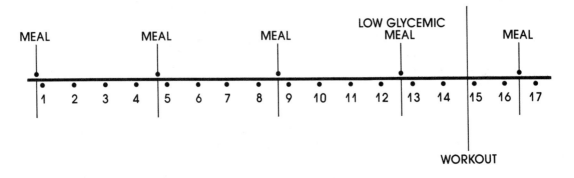

RULES OF THUMB

1. Low glycemic index foods before training
2. Ratio of fats/proteins/carbs for strength athletes is 1:2:3 (calories per meal).
3. Meal preceding training should be higher in calories than other meals.
4. On rest days or on low-volume training days eat fewer calories than on high-volume days.
5. Mixed aminos (L-form) with meals (if body weight on target) 8–10 grams each time
6. Inosine 20 minutes before workout (3 grams)
7. Ten grams arginine or 5 grams ornithine immediately before bed
8. Supplement your preworkout meal with BCAAs (6–8 grams) with L-alanine (2–3 grams).
9. One gram L-carnitine immediately after training for recovery
10. Five meals are essential because of protein needs and for caloric control. (Too many calories causes fat deposition and too few causes muscle cannibalization.)
11. Take a good quality, complete vitamin/mineral supplement daily, preferably with your morning meal.

FIGURE 31-3

DIET/SUPPLEMENTATION FOR TWO-A-DAY TRAINING

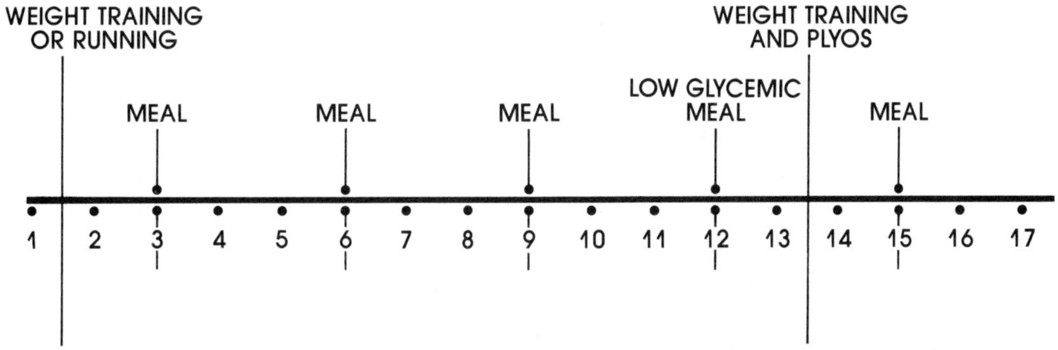

RULES OF THUMB
1. Low glycemic index foods before training
2. Ratio of fats/proteins/carbs for runners is 1:2:4 (calories per meal).
3. Meal preceding training should be higher in calories than others.
4. On rest days or on low-volume training days, eat fewer calories than high-volume training days.
5. L-carnitine 2-3 times daily between meals (empty stomach)—2-3 grams each time (max)*
6. Inosine before workouts (running and weights)—3 grams (20-30 minutes prior)
7. L-arginine or L-ornithine immediately before bed—10 grams arginine or 5 grams ornithine
8. Five meals are essential because of protein needs and for caloric control (too many calories causes fat deposition and too few causes muscle cannibalization).
9. Take a good quality, complete vitamin/mineral supplement daily, preferably with your morning meal.
*For workout recovery, take 1 gram immediately after training

The answer, or at least the best answer available to power athletes at this point in time, is to tailor your eating and supplementing habits according to your specific training needs.

The general approach illustrated on page 253 is so simple in its philosophy that I'm afraid it has been overlooked thoroughly over the years. The simple truth is that if you pick the best supplements, take them only when your training calls for them, and engage in a sensible training schedule (described in the preceding tables), you will achieve your goals.

In my experience, this kind of approach will render the use of anabolic steroids obsolete. The fact is that if you are doing everything right in your training, and support those efforts with state-of-the-art dieting techniques and nutritional supplements that have the power to make a difference, you will be able to achieve the same goals and

FIGURE 31-5

EFFICACY RATINGS OF COMMON SUPPLEMENTS

★—Highly effective
1—Effective
2—Possibly effective
3—Probably not effective
4—Not effective

	Protein/Aminos	Vitamins/Minerals	BCAAs	Inosine	L-Carnitine	Gamma Oryzanol	TMG	Caffeine	Ma Huang	Mumie	Aspirin	Boron	Growth Hormone Releasers	Glucose Polymer Drinks	Musco MXT	Eleutherococcus	DLPA	Glandulars	Beta Sitosterol	Smilax Officinalis	Brewer's Yeast	Royal Jelly	Wheat Germ	Oxygen (ingested)	Oxygen (breathed)
STRENGTH	1	1	2	2	3	2/1	3	2	2	4	4	2	1	4	4	2	4	2	3	2	3	3	3	2	3
FAT LOSS	3	3	3	2	1	2	3	2	4	4	4	4	1	2	4	3	4	4	4	4	4	4	4	4	4
SIZE	1	1	2	2	3	2/1	3	4	4	4	4	2	1	3	4	3	4	2	3	3	3	3	3	3	4
PAIN	4	4	4	4	4	4	4	3	4	4	★	4	1	4	4	4	2	4	4	4	4	4	4	4	4
MENTAL CONCENTRATION	4	4	3	4	4	4	4	★	★	1	4	4	4	3	4	2	4	4	4	4	4	3	4	2	3
ANAEROBIC ENERGY	3	3	1	★	2	4	1	2	4	4	4	4	4	★	4	3	4	3	3	4	3	2	3	1	2
AEROBIC ENERGY	3	3	1	2	2	3	1	1	4	4	4	4	4	★	4	3	4	3	4	4	3	2	3	1	2
WORKOUT RECOVERY	2	2	★	2	2	3	2	3	4	★	★	2	1	2	4	1	3	2	3	2	3	4	3	1	2
TISSUE REPAIR	2	2	2	2	2	2	2	3	4	★	★	2	1	3	4	1	3	2	3	2	3	4	3	3	4
GENERAL HEALTH	1	1	3	2	2	2	1	4	4	1	★	2	2	2	4	1	3	3	2	4	2	3	2	4	4

Slash (/) is used to indicate applicability to male/female ratings.

GUIDELINES FOR THE PEAK PERFORMER'S DAILY FARE

1. Ensure adequate preworkout stores of muscle glycogen.
2. Avoid foods that cause a rapid rise in blood sugar levels—they fall precipitously thereafter—before training.
3. Supplement your preworkout meal with the branched-chain amino acids (BCAAs) and L-alanine (another amino acid). They are elemental in providing energy for intense training and the rejuvenation process that follows.
4. Substances such as growth hormone releasers (L-ornithine and L-arginine are the best) can aid in the anabolic (musclebuilding) process significantly.
5. Keep your workouts under an hour long, and keep them intense. This practice ensures an adequate free amino acid pool from which to draw for energy, recovery, and growth.
6. Remember that protein turnover—the rejuvenation process—takes place over days following intense exercise. This requires a careful scheduling of intense training to ensure that overtraining or staleness does not occur. It also punctuates your need for careful supplementing and meal scheduling.

beyond what you may have been able to achieve with steroid use.

The question is, however, what are the best supplements? No one knows for sure because very little solid research has ever been done on many of them. Yet, some research does exist, and I have calculated (what I believe to be) each of the most prevalently used supplements according to their efficacy.

PART 5
DRUGS IN SPORTS

32

THE DRUG SCENE:
Cobwebbed Corners

In the deep recesses of the steroid user's mind, where half-forgotten and oftentimes regretted experiences lurk, there exists the thought that maybe, just maybe, drugs aren't the answer. Not so coincidentally, such thoughts remain semi-buried in his subconscious. Until, that is, he finds the guts to ask "Why?"

There are a lot of "whys" in the life of the athlete on steroids. Why use such high doses of steroids, when the risks outweigh the benefits? Why use drugs when there's no intention of competing? Why blithely continue to take the advice of guys in the gym with little in the way of scientific understanding about drugs? Why not seek the advice or guidance of a competent sports physician when using drugs? And, why continue to use drugs in instances where there are safer alternatives?

Why indeed!

PSYCHOLOGICAL ADDICTION

Hypothetically, you have decided to use drugs to enhance your chances at winning in your sport. It was an important decision to you, not one that was taken lightly. You're young, you're eager, and you're convinced that your future lies in winning at sports. That you love your chosen sport is self-evident. That winning will require sacrifice on your part is a point that you have accepted gladly.

Beware of the mentality to agree to sacrifice when such is not needed! "But, to make it to the top in sports don't I need to take steroids?"

Are you that anxious to win?

"Oh, yes! Indeed I am!"

Would you sell your soul as quickly?

"Whatever it takes."

So then—what we have here is an example of how youngsters and experienced athletes alike fall prey to the demon most call "win-at-all-costs." An irrational decision has been made based on fallacious reasoning and inadequate information.

Psychological addiction comes later.

Two years later, for example: So, how's your sports career going?

"Not so good—I ain't winning yet."

Good attitude at least. Keep on working hard—you'll get there.

"Maybe my drug program isn't up to snuff. Got any new drugs or cycling methods I can try?"

Sure pal! Why not try an off-cycle for awhile?

"Gimme a break! I'd lose size and strength—I can't go off now!"

Have you ever been off?

"I tried going off a couple times. But it was too humiliating for me because I got small! I couldn't handle that, so I went back on."

Whoa! Slow down! Do you mean to tell me that you're hooked on steroids?

"I guess I am in a way—I don't like the downer of being smaller and weaker than I can be when I use steroids. So by staying on them, I can stay big."

This aspiring athlete has made a long-term commitment. He has made a career decision to use drugs. The chances are, he'll stay on drugs until he dies (no pun intended).

He is, in a classical sense, addicted to anabolic steroids. Furthermore, a subtle switch has taken place—a switch that is disturbingly characteristic of most such athletes who have made similar career commitments. The super-keen desire to be a champion is now secondary to the desire to be big.

A COMMON MISCONCEPTION

Many steroid users argue that drugs can be good if they're not misused or abused. Many claim that steroids have had nothing but positive effects on both their bodies as well as their lives. The strength, stamina, or size they achieved was quite probably aided by their use of steroids. But only a fool would claim that steroids were the *major* contributory factor.

We've all heard this line, haven't we? A guy lifts a lot of weight, a bodybuilder gets ripped to shreds, a woman breaks a sprint record—whatever—and people say, "Yeah, but he/she's on steroids."

How much *do* steroids help? The answer to this question is both complex and speculative. However, it needs to be addressed. The common misconception that steroids are the deciding factor in sports of all description has all but changed the very face of sport history. People (athletes included) have forgotten that what makes a champion is hard work, dedication, and an absolute commitment to excellence.

Dog Tracks in the Snow

I have used this phrase before. It posits that only a fool would deny the existence of a dog after having seen its tracks in the fresh snow. Likewise, only a blind fool would deny the fact that anabolic steroids can, when used appropriately, assist in developing strength, size, or stamina. They are far, far from being the winning edge, however.

In one of our many lively discussions at the editorial offices of *Muscle & Fitness*, Rick Wayne listened patiently to my story about dog tracks in the snow. After I made my point, Rick observed, "It's all right to follow the tracks in the snow, but one must beware that they don't lead you to a pack of wolves." To be led astray by steroid misinformation and misconceptions may indeed be akin to walking into the open jaws of a wolf. To become psychologically dependent upon steroids definitely is analogous.

Remember the first time you used steroids? (Or, if you've never used them, remember the first time a fellow lifter did?) "Wow! At this rate of progress, I'll be champion inside the next year!" A typical response. Strength and muscular gains fairly fly forward at first—generally tapering off or halting altogether after about a 10% initial surge.

For you, getting hooked was perhaps a sacrifice—one of the multitude of sacrifices you knew you'd have to make to get to the top. But, maybe it was no sacrifice at all. Maybe you just wanted to put on some size and opted to approach the problem scientifically through the use of drugs. Whatever the case, gains came less and less, and soon, the gains were no more frequent than you'd have noted even without the use of drugs. At that point, you'd probably have benefited by discontinuing their use.

But you (or your friend) stuck with the drugs because you had made that crucial career commitment. You wanted to get big and that was it! So you got big—now what?

Getting Off Steroids

"I could quit anytime!" say the smoker and alcoholic. Tch, tch—even they know better! The DTs are a piece of cake next to the wretchedness of getting small, though! Once you've been monstrously big you will never again be happy being less. That is, if you're a bit loco, and hooked.

What does one do after discontinuing steroids? Does one really shrivel up like a prune? Like the aging athlete slowly riding off into the sunset? Like a shaved Sampson? It can be demoralizing—no, devastating—to actually observe your own flesh and muscle dissipating. I believe, however, that it is the *expectation of getting small* (or weak) after discontinuance that is the real culprit. I also believe too that *negative nitrogen balance* plays a great part in the lasting psychological trauma caused by discontinuance.

Slowly tapering your final dosages will generally take care of the problems stemming from, or leading to, negative nitrogen balance in your muscle tissue. However, nothing short of intensive psychiatric care is going to cure you of your paranoia over once again being of normal proportions.

THE PRODUCT-PROCESS PARADOX

Getting big or strong is a process. Becoming a champion is also a process. Being big and being a champion are products stemming from what? Drugs?

The addicted athlete views the process as more important. He views bigness as more holy than winning championships, and opts to regard drugs as the catalyst between the process and bigness. It is a means that justifies an end, and the means becomes of paramount importance.

Such extremism is a vice. Somebody of note once said that extremism in *any* form is a vice—an addiction. If there's anything unhealthy about steroids, it is this addictive quality.

Steroids, and other drugs, are a reality in sports. To ignore this fundamental fact is akin to becoming an ostrich. I, for one, don't like to eat dirt (from burying my head in the sand) any more than I like to see athletes eating drugs (or shooting them).

The following sections expose a few of the more common substances abused by athletes in their quest for supremacy. The information is presented in the spirit of getting your collective heads out of the sand—they are not presented as any kind of "user's guide."

ANABOLIC STEROIDS

To understand what anabolic steroids actually are, a few terms must be defined first. The word *metabolism* refers to all bodily functions involving the production of, maintenance of, or destruction of tissue and energy. The building processes (or *myotropic* processes) are referred to as *anabolism*, while the breaking-down processes are referred to as *catabolism*. Thus, *anabolic* effects, insofar as steroids are concerned, are those effects involving the synthesis of protein for muscle growth and reparation.

There are many different hormones in the body. Collectively, *hormones* are regulatory chemicals produced by various organs, glands, or tissues, whose purpose is to coordinate such bodily functions as growth, tissue repair, reproductive cycles, and other aspects of physical and mental processes. The male hormone *testosterone* has two primary functions. The first is to stimulate the development and maintenance of male secondary sex characteristics (such as facial hair, deep voice, the distribution and amount of body fat, and other characteristics associated with masculine features). This is referred to as the *androgenic* function of testosterone. The *anabolic* functions of testosterone include the development and maintenance of the characteristically larger musculature of males.

Thus, we can now define the term *anabolic steroids*. They are synthetically derived chemical compounds that mimic the anabolic effects of testosterone while, at the same time, minimizing the androgenic effects. This minimizing of anabolic effects was accomplished by manipulating the structure of the basic hydrocarbon molecule of testosterone in various ways. The extent to which the anabolic-androgenic ratio has been altered is referred to as the *therapeutic index*.

Therapeutic Indexes of Anabolic Steroids

The traditional methods used for establishing a therapeutic index for a synthetic anabolic steroid is to compare the growth of a rat's *levator ani* muscle with that of his *seminal vesicles*. The growth of the muscle is said to represent the anabolic effect of the test drug, while the growth of the seminal vesicles are representative of the androgenic effect. The standard against which the test steroid's effects are compared is the extent of growth stimulated by testosterone. Thus, if the levator ani muscle growth is twice that of the standard, and the seminal vesicle growth is only half that of the standard, the therapeutic index is determined as follows:

$$2 \div \tfrac{1}{2} \times 4 \text{ (TI)}$$

However, problems arise with regard to the usefulness of such an index. For example, if the test drug had four times the anabolic effect of the standard, and the same androgenic effect, the therapeutic index would be the same.

$$4 \div 1 \times 4 \text{ (TI)}$$

Needless to say, test drug number one would be useful in cases where the androgenic effects needed to be minimal, whereas if the androgenicity of the drug wasn't a factor (and it almost always is), then test drug number two would be the choice since the anabolic effects are superior.

Additionally, there is little in the way of solid research evidence to indicate that therapeutic indexes of drugs calculated by animal studies are applicable to humans, be they patients, normal individuals, or athletes. And, lastly, even if there existed a table of therapeutic indexes derived from studies on humans, factors such as diet, training, variable drug doses, variable administration schedules, and (perhaps most importantly) inter- and intraindividual variability of drug response all but nullifies the usefulness of such indexes.

But they're all we have in the way of research findings. Most athletes tend to weigh the personal experience factor more heavily when choosing an anabolic steroid. The usefulness of the therapeutic index is, at this point, relatively meaningless for use by athletes using anabolic steroids. It should not be used as the sole determiner in steroid selection.

Steroid Protein Activity Index of Anabolic Steroids

One of the most important attributes of anabolic steroids is their ability to stimulate protein synthesis. This is accomplished partly by the fact that the body tends to "save" nitrogen (the primary constituent of proteins) when anabolic steroids are used. The extent to which a particular anabolic steroid causes nitrogen retention is known to be a reasonably good index of the protein metabolism capacity of the steroid. In other words, a good estimate can be derived as to a steroid's efficiency in promoting protein metabolism through the use of the SPAI (steroid protein activity index). It is computed as follows:

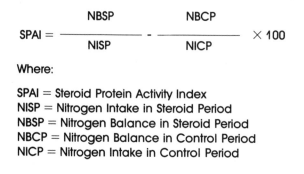

$$SPAI = \frac{NBSP}{NISP} - \frac{NBCP}{NICP} \times 100$$

Where:

SPAI = Steroid Protein Activity Index
NISP = Nitrogen Intake in Steroid Period
NBSP = Nitrogen Balance in Steroid Period
NBCP = Nitrogen Balance in Control Period
NICP = Nitrogen Intake in Control Period

Thus, the rate or extent of nitrogen retention during the time steroids are being used is compared to the extent of nitrogen retention during the period when no steroids are being used.

How Steroids Work

Once into the bloodstream via oral, pellet implant, sublingual, or injected routes, anabolic steroids find their way to individual muscle cells where they exert their activating influence on the genes responsible for protein synthesis. In much the same way that naturally occurring testosterone works, they physically attach themselves to

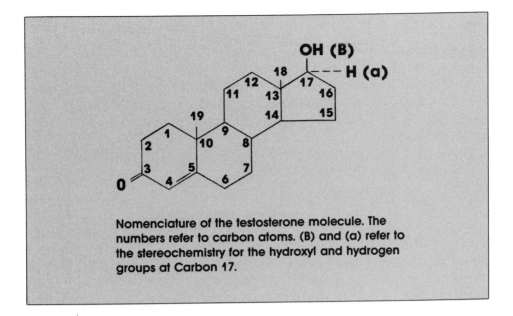

Nomenclature of the testosterone molecule. The numbers refer to carbon atoms. (B) and (a) refer to the stereochemistry for the hydroxyl and hydrogen groups at Carbon 17.

specific receptor sites within the cell, and stimulate the DNA to direct the cell's ribosomes to manufacture greater amounts of protein.

Concurrent with the administration of anabolic steroids, however, there must be sufficient vitamins and minerals available via food intake or supplements. Many vitamins are thought to be synergistic with anabolic steroids (i.e., they "help" or "facilitate" the steroid in effecting protein synthesis). Too, there appears to be reason to believe that a *need* must be present in the organism before protein synthesis will occur. The need is apparent in clinical use of steroids in cases such as anemia or malnutrition for greater protein synthesis. But in healthy athletes the need is *created* through extremely heavy training. Let me restate this point—anabolic steroids will be nigh unto useless in promoting increased strength or muscle size without proper nutrition, sufficient amino acids (protein), and extremely heavy, regular bouts of weight training. These points will be discussed again later.

Not all of the anabolic steroid molecules reach the cell receptor sites, however. Most float around in the bloodstream until they are broken down in 17-ketosteroids by the liver (hydralized), or broken down while in the bloodstream (changed to estrogens or aromatized). These by-products are believed to be responsible for many of the side effects of anabolic steroids, although in unknown ways. At any rate, to slow the rapid inactivation of the anabolic steroids by the liver, scientists soon discovered that the addition of an alkyl substituent at the 17th carbon position (see figure above) of the steroid molecule greatly increased the life of the molecule. However, again, this alteration is also believed to be responsible for a number of the unwanted side effects often accompanying steroid use.

REPORTED SIDE EFFECTS FROM ANABOLIC STEROID USE

By now, most athletes who have used steroids have heard of the side effects associated with the drug. Gym talk and steroid package inserts seem to be the chief source for such information, or—quite possibly more commonly—personal experience over years of self-administering the drug has attuned the user to the more personally unwanted effects.

Some of these hazards of steroid use are listed here, although in no particular order of import or severity.

Liver Function Alterations

Carbohydrate metabolism, protein metabolism, lipid (fat) metabolism, and the elimination, detoxification, or inactivation of substances such as urea, bacteria, hormones (e.g., anabolic steroids), and other noxious materials, are all functions of the liver. Lab tests to detect disruption of these functions will be discussed later in this manual. Among athletes using steroids, the long-term effects of such liver function disruptions are unknown; the short-term effects have proven to be minimal and reversible upon cessation of steroid use. However, toxic hepatitis can be brought about by the continued use of steroids and diuretics (amacide).

Cardiovascular System Impairment

Blood clotting factors are sometimes disrupted. The metabolism of glucose, triglycerides, and cholosterolis is impaired, potentially leading to atherosclerosis (plaque buildup in the arteries). Also, resting blood glucose levels and glucose tolerance can be reduced (dangerous for diabetics and prediabetics). Increased insulin secretion can contribute to atherosclerosis as well.

Another potentiating factor for atherosclerosis is the increased cortisol levels. Oral steroids appear to render the liver relatively incapable of breaking cortisol down, thereby increasing the concentrations of cortisol in the blood. An interesting hypothesis related to this increased cortisol level is that, since cortisol is the body's major stress hormone, athletes are able to train harder. This may be the edge athletes report oral steroids to have over injectable steroids, enabling them to train harder and possibly make better gains in strength and size with oral compounds.

While blood readings on these factors return to normal following discontinuance of steroid use, the long-term effects of such changes remain unclear. In as much as cardiovascular disease is by far the leading cause of death in the United States, the effects that anabolic steroids have (directly and indirectly) on the cardiovascular system is seen by many to be the most serious and potentially hazardous of all the reported side effects.

Hypertension (High Blood Pressure)

Elevated blood pressure over a prolonged period is known to create a potential for a host of cardiovascular diseases. Anabolic steroid use is quite frequently accompanied by considerable increases in blood pressure. Fluid/electrolyte balance is thought to be related to hypertension. Many athletes (perhaps a majority) report mild to severe edema (water retention) when on steroids. The exact nature of this side effect is not known, although it is speculated to be a result of the steroid's effect on the adrenal cortex.

Hormones secreted from the adrenal cortex play an important role in maintaining an equitable electrolyte balance in the body. As with blood and liver function, blood pressure readings usually return to normal upon discontinuance of steroid use, but the use of anabolic steroids over a long period of time remain a question. It may be that the increased body size causes the heart to work harder. Steroids are known to increase both potassium and nitrogen levels, which may increase blood pressure.

Reproductive Process Alterations

When steroids are administered via oral or injected routes, normally secreted testosterone is no longer needed in the same amounts. FSH (follicle stimulating hormone), which is secreted by the pituitary gland, is reduced when sufficient testosterone is present. The result is testicular atrophy and sperm count reduction.

In animals, prolonged FSH and ICSH reduction has been known to cause disruption in the ability of the pituitary gland to produce these gonadotropins. In any event, this effect, as well as the shrinkage of the testes and reduction in testosterone and sperm production, are reversible upon discontinuance of steroid use.

Libido (sex drive—the ability to achieve an erection, to be more specific) appears to be altered variably or not at all. Libido changes (increases or decreases) appear more frequently with larger doses of anabolic steroids. Normalcy is achieved with discontinuance of the drug.

Increased Aggressiveness

An extremely common effect of steroid use (particularly steroids with a relatively high androgenic component) is increased aggressiveness. Testosterone is known to be a major contributing factor in the higher level of aggressiveness in men than women. Also, studies show that prisoners who were convicted of violent crimes had significantly higher levels of testosterone than those convicted of nonviolent crimes. Steroid users have been known to become highly violent and aggressive when on high doses of steroids, particularly those whose androgenicity is high and also just before contests when steroid use is unusually high.

The social and psychological ramifications of such behavior changes have been known to be severe indeed—broken families, broken friendships, and a host of other socially deplorable circumstances have arisen in these instances of steroid abuse. The heightened aggression problem is seen to be one of the most dangerous side effects associated with steroid misuse. While aggression levels return to normal upon discontinuance of the drug, the residual effects all too often linger on if only in the memories of the user's loved ones and associates.

Development of Breast Tissue in Males

Called *gynecomastia*, breast tissue under the nipple is often accompanied by tenderness (soreness) to the touch. There appears to be a varied response in this regard, with certain steroids causing it and others not. Most commonly the syndrome arises with high doses of steroids, particularly those with a high androgenic component. The nipples return to normal upon discontinuance of the particular drug causing the problem. However, nodules sometimes appear, which may need to be surgically removed.

Virilizing Effects

The androgenic effects of steroids (or "virilizing" effects) include such functions as growth of seminal vesicals, penis and prostate, thickening of the vocal chords (deeper voice), increased amounts of body and genital area hair, oily skin (causing acne), and increased (or initial kindling of) sexual drive, and are generally increased by the use of steroids in adolescents. So too is another possible side effect— that of premature ossification of the long bones (possibly resulting in slightly stunted growth in height).

Women (particularly younger women) can experience similar symptoms, including clitoral enlargement and interrupted or irregular menstrual flow. While menstruation returns to normal after discontinuance of the drug, the other virilizing effects remain—*they are not reversible.*

Some athletes have reported an increase in chest hair growth and even claim that loss of scalp hair diminished or stopped upon usage of steroids. A thickening of facial hair has also been empirically observed by male steroid users.

Susceptibility to Connective Tissue Damage

While not shown in any controlled scientific studies, experience seems to show that if steroids are used by beginners in the weight training world, their strength and muscle size increases far more rapidly than the attendant tendons and connective tissues. This is believed to be due to the relatively poor blood supply in such connective tissue as compared with that of muscle tissue. With the vastly increased strength of the muscle, extreme exertion (as is often the case in many sports—particularly in powerlifting) can and often does cause connective tissue to rupture.

Degeneration of Tissue

Many old-time users of anabolic steroids (especially testosterone) who have begun to experience more than the average numbers of injuries have speculated that their increased susceptibility to injury is due to their prolonged use of testosterone. The Soviets believe that this increased susceptibility is due to a decreased viscoelasticity in the muscle, although no scientific data are available to substantiate this claim. Whatever the cause for such increased propensity for severe muscle tears may be, it is nonetheless a fact—it may be the result of prolonged steroid use or it may not be.

Some electromyographic studies indicate that steroid-produced size increases result in "abnormal" tissue. It may be that such tissue is weaker structurally.

Increased Susceptibility to Infection, Weight Loss, and Strength Loss Following Discontinuance

This syndrome is suggested to be the result of what scientists call negative nitrogen balance. After getting off the drug, the body is not yet back to normal in testosterone or gonad otropin secretion, and more than normal nitrogen is lost, particularly if one persists in heavy training during this time. With a negative nitrogen balance, sufficient protein cannot be synthesized to affect recovery. As suggested earlier, tapering off steroid use can alleviate drastic changes.

Joint Soreness and Stiffness

Upon discontinuance of anabolic steroids, severe joint pain and stiffness are often experienced. The cause of this problem is not known, but it is suggested by some that it is caused by excessive training during the negative nitrogen balance period (which can last as long as three months).

Other Side Effects

Many other possible side effects have been reported both in literature (particularly James Wright's *Anabolic Steroids and Sports*) as well as by word of mouth (case histories). While most are either rare or as yet unobserved in healthy athletes, they bear mention: Hepatitis (dirty needle), cramps, cancer, headaches, nausea and gastrointestinal upset, tendancy for nosebleeds, drowsiness, feeling of well-being, disrupted thyroid function, loss of appetite, increased appetite, intestinal irritation (blood in stool), dizziness, and, in some cases, reduction in lean body mass (loss of muscle—possibly due to poor nutrition while dropping weight for a contest).

Of all the potential side effects from using anabolic steroids, the two that appear most frequently, from the standpoint of both scientific reason as well as practical experience, seem to be: the potential for steroids to disrupt cardiovascular function, particularly in the long run, and the often acute levels of aggression displayed by the drug abusers. There seems to be conclusive evidence that high-density lipoproteins are markedly decreased when using some anabolic steroids, a significant factor in the increased risk of coronary problems.

Anabolic steroid manufacturers list the following contraindications: pregnancy, nephrosis of the kidney, biliary obstruction, liver damage, and prostate or breast cancer. Extreme caution is advised by the pharmaceutical houses for those with a history of coronary or heart disease, diabetics, and those with renal or hepatic problems (i.e., kidney or liver problems).

It is certain that the clandestine and backward way in which steroids are typically misused is perhaps the most prevalent reason for any side effects to present themselves as health threats. Open and frank discussion on the matter of anabolic steroid use is seen by many to be the single most potent, combative technique in alleviating the potential hazards.

THE BENEFICIAL EFFECTS FROM ANABOLIC STEROID USE

In therapeutic cases anabolic steroids have been used to combat anemia and as replacement therapy for patients whose hormone level is subnormal or who are unable to adequately digest proteins, are underweight, or have protein deficient states associated with various infections (gastritis, colitis, or enteritis). They have also been used to assist in the formulating of bone matrix among patients suffering from osteoporosis.

In some cases anabolic steroids have been used to combat certain aftereffects of radiation therapy. They have also been used by physicians to improve appetite, improve psychological disposition, and promote healing (administered before or after surgery). In certain cases, anabolic steroids have been administered to adolescents to stimulate growth. Relatively high doses have been administered to women suffering from breast cancer (up to 300 mg per week)

Therapeutic doses have ranged from as low as 2 mg per day for a few weeks to as high as 2 mg per kg body weight each day for as long as several years! While many factors are generally considered by physicians in determining appropriate dosages, the risk-to-benefit rule of thumb prevails. The side effects from steroid use are weighed against the severity of the disease and a decision is made regarding dosage and time (with other factors also considered).

But normal and healthy athletes have adapted the uses to which anabolic steroids have been put in therapeutic settings to facilitate sports performance. After a quarter century of experimenting, generally handed down by word of mouth, a few athletes have learned the best administration and dosage schedules to follow in order to maximize their performance while minimizing the risks associated with such use. In some quarters of the athletic world, anabolic steroid use has become highly sophisticated—a blend of scientific application and many years of self-experimentation (often bordering on drug abuse) have yielded to these athletes a knowledge of the drug (in a practical sense) that far transcends that of most physicians.

Still, a vast majority of athletes using anabolic steroids have very little (if any) comprehension as to how to go about maximizing the benefits while minimizing the risks. The vast majority of athletes are guilty of misuse and/or abuse because of ignorance. Their ignorance is understandable, since very little information has been given them, and most athletes "in the know" won't talk! All these athletes see are the "dog tracks in the snow." They know anabolic steroids work, so they take them.

Some of the most prevalent uses to which anabolic steroids have been put by athletes are as follows.

Increased Strength

The contractile elements of a muscle cell (called myofibrils) are increased in number through heavy training and appropriate dietary regimen. Anabolic steroids, owing to their primary function of stimulating protein synthesis, assist in this regard since the myofibrillar elements are comprised of protein (actin and myosin). Some strength can be gained through tissue leverage resulting from increases in cellular fluid (sarcoplasm) and general edema (water retention). This strength is temporary, however, particularly if body weight must be lost to make weight for a contest.

Increased Muscle Size

The myofibrillar growth and increased sarcoplasmic content (spoken of earlier) are the chief factors responsible for muscular size increases. The same preconditions prevail, however, to maximize size increases—heavy training and adequate nutrition must be present.

Reduction in Pain from Arthritis/Tendinitis

Such use was (and is) one of the clinical uses of anabolic steroids. Many athletes claim relief of pain from tendinitis while on steroid therapy.

Reduction in Percentage of Body Fat

While diet and training appear to be the primary factors in reduced levels of body fat, there also appears to be some body fat reduction over and above what normally might be expected when using anabolic steroids. It is speculated that increased respiratory quotients is the cause for faster than normal losses of body fat.

Increased Respiratory Rate (and Endurance)

There is evidence to suggest that mitochondria (the organelles within muscle cells responsible for various oxidative functions, among other things) are increased in number. This would have the net effect of increasing the cell's capability of utilizing oxygen during heavy training, thereby improving endurance. Possibly more explanatory, however, is the fact that cortisol levels in the blood are increased, thereby giving greater endurance. Cortisol is a stress hormone produced in the adrenal gland.

Increased Vascularity

It is not clear what causes this, but it does occur. It is suggested that the increased blood pressure that often accompanies steroid use is the main factor. Vascularity is one of the much sought-after attributes of top caliber bodybuilders.

Improved Recovery Time after Injury or Training

The fact that anabolic steroids promote synthesis and/or retard nitrogen excretion explains why improvements in recovery time following injury or surgery and particularly following heavy training, is observed. This, of course, relates to less training time lost.

Increased Capability to Do
More and Heavier Reps and Sets

This increased capacity is thought by some to be the result of an increased capacity to resynthesize creatinine phosphate (CP), an important, fast-energy substrate in the muscles. Without sufficient CP, the muscle very rapidly fatigues (lactic acid concentrations become intolerable). There is substantial scientific evidence supporting this contention, and it appears that CP synthesis is a side benefit of alkylation of (oral) steroid molecules. The increased cortisol levels in the blood are probably more responsible for increased endurance than is the CP theory, however.

Increased Aggressiveness

Increased aggressiveness/hostility was listed as a dangerous side effect, but many bodybuilders regard it as a beneficial effect. It is believed that increased aggressiveness causes one to work out harder and to put more effort into moving the heavy weights. While this may be true for some, experience dictates that the desire to win and to excel is far more potent a motivator than pharmaceuticals in this endeavor.

It must be pointed out that, while empirical evidence is often very strongly supportive of many of these reported effects of anabolic steroid use in sports, the scientific literature does not interpret such evidence this way. The use of steroids, then, must be classified as an inexact science at this point owing to the sparseness of truly objective data that would support the listed beneficial effects.

Thus, the methods of use, dosages used, and the exact steroids to be taken are factors that must be decided upon in "guesswork" fashion. Indeed, it is clear that a vast majority of athletes using steroids are forced to guess. They simply have no understandable source of information to guide them.

BLOOD TEST RESULTS AND STEROID USE

The table on page 271 lists the various blood (serum) constituents that are typically included in blood tests prior to steroid administration or steroid therapy. "Normal" ranges for each of the constituents are listed, but very little data are available that would indicate some of them to be classified as normal for the athlete engaging in heavy weight training. Extreme stress (such as that imposed through weight training) as well as muscular hypertrophy (increased muscular size) tends to elevate some of the readings—greater than "normal" ranges are therefore appropriately applied to athletes, but these altered ranges have not been established as yet by any scientific studies. In particular are the typically high LDH and SGOT levels among athletes undergoing stressful training. It is not uncommon to have readings of 10%–20% above the "normal" ranges for these two serum enzymes, the elevated readings stemming from metabolic stress—not from steroids.

Calcium

While increases or decreases in plasma calcium can signal many different factors, of significance to the athlete is the fact that frequent use of diuretics (such as Lasix) can cause a decrease in calcium. Abnormally high calcium concentrations can be caused by ingestion of high doses of vitamin D. Anabolic steroid use does not seem to be a factor.

Inorganic Phosphates. Since phosphorus and calcium are working partners in most metabolic functions, increases or decreases in one will cause a commensurate change in the level of the other. Of note to the weight-training athlete is that elevations in blood phosphorus may be associated with hyperthyroidism and elevated secretions of human growth hormone. Anabolic steroids appear to be a nonfactor.

Fasting Glucose. Users of anabolic steroids should be aware that such drugs can often significantly alter blood sugar tolerance. Normal to extremely elevated blood glucose levels can be a signal of a diabetic or pre-diabetic state. Too, lowered blood sugar (hypoglycemia) can signal liver disease (rare).

Blood Urea Nitrogen

Urea is the byproduct of protein breakdown in the liver. It is excreted in the urine. High Blood Urea Nitrogen (BUN) levels can signal renal (kidney) failure. Of significance to the athlete is that unusually high intake of protein can cause a slight to moderate elevation of BUN, as can excessive protein catabolism.

Uric Acid

Elevations in uric acid can signal gout, renal failure, or congestive heart failure. For the athlete, perhaps the most important considerations are that hyperuricemia may be the result of fasting (starvation diets) or diuretic use. Anabolic steroids appear not to alter uric acid concentrations.

Cholesterol

With noncomitant elevations in bilirubin and alkaline phosphate, hypercholesterolemia can signal liver disease. Anabolic steroids can often cause elevations in cholesterol while causing a decrease in high density lipoproteins. This in turn increases the risk of atherosclerosis (coronary artery disease).

CLINICALLY NORMAL RANGES FOR SELECTED SERUM, WHOLE BLOOD, OR PLASMA CONSTITUENTS*

Item	Normal Ranges	Item	Normal Ranges
Calcium	8.5–10.5 mg/dl	CPK (Creatinine Phosphokinase)	55–170 U/L (male) 30–135 U/L (female)
Inorganic Phosphates	2.5–4.5 mg/dl		
Glucose (Fasting Level)	70–110 mg/dl	Alkaline Phosphatase	30–85 mU/dl
BUN (Blood Urea Nitrogen)	10–26 mg/dl	LDH (Lactic Dehydrogenase)	100–225 mU/dl
Uric Acid	2.1-7.8 mg/dl (male) 2.0–6.4 mg/dl (female)	SGOT (Serum Glutamic-Oxaloacetic Transaminase)	8–33 U/ml
Cholesterol	150–300 mg/dl	SGPT (Serum Glutamic Pyruvic Transaminase)	1–36 U/ml
Total Protein	6.0–7.8 gm/dl		
Bilirubin	0.1–1.2 mg/dl		
Triglycerides	10–190 mg/dl		
		Testosterone	246–1328 mg/dl (male) 30–120 mg/dl (female)
		Sodium	136–142 mEq/L
		Potassium	3.8–5.0 mEq/L

*Depending upon the source for these normal ranges, the values can fluctuate as much as a few percentage points, indicating the inexact nature of the estimates of "normalcy."

Total Protein

Through a process of electrically charging the serum solution (electrophoresis), blood proteins tend to layer themselves, thereby making it possible to determine precise ratios. The normal ratio of albumin to globulin in 3.2–4.5 g/dl and 2.3–3.5 g/dl respectively. Elevated globulin and depressed albumin (i.e., a reversed A/G ratio) can be suggestive of chronic liver damage.

Bilirubin

While a normal level of total bilirubin rules out any significant impairment of the excretory functions of the liver, an elevated total bilirubin level can be (and often is) indicative of obstructive jaundice. Bilirubin is a byproduct of hemoglobin metabolism, and is excreted by the liver.

Triglycerides

Like cholesterol, the triglycerides can be related to coronary artery disease. Electrophoresis is used to distinguish the different classifications of hyperlipidemia. Cholesterol, triglycerides, and phospholipids are classified as lipids, and circulate in the blood while bound to protein—thus the term *lipoproteins*. Of note are type 2 in which there is elevated cholesterol and mildly elevated or normal triglycerides, and type 4 in which the cholesterol is normal and the triglycerides are elevated. These types may signal coronary disease.

CPK

There are many causes of elevated creatinine phosphokinase (CPK) including: intramuscular injections, vigorous exercise, skeletal muscle disease, cerebral and myocardial infarctions, and muscle hypertrophy. It appears to be normal for weight-trained athletes to have significantly elevated CPK values, although in the presence of other symptoms or blood reading such elevations should be checked out.

Alkaline Phosphatase

When there is an extremely elevated alkaline phosphatase reading with elevated liver function tests, liver disease is generally indicated. If the alkaline phosphatase reading is high without a concurrent elevation in liver function tests, bone disease may be indicated. Anabolic steroids have been reported to decrease alkaline phosphatase, even after the steroids have been discontinued.

LDH

Lactic dehydrogenase is an enzyme that is involved in the oxidation of lactic and pyruvic acids. It is therefore found in many tissues of the body, particularly the skeletal muscles. Almost any damage to tissue causes LDH readings to be elevated. The exact source of the elevated readings can be discerned through electrophoresis. Since many disease entities can be associated with LDH elevations, further tests should be looked into (particularly liver and heart disorders).

SGOT

Serum glutamic-oxaloacetic transaminase (SGOT) is an enzyme that catalyzes the conversion of amino acids and vice versa. It is found in the heart, liver, skeletal muscle, kidneys, and bone. Damage to cells causes elevated SGOT readings, and the exact site of damage can generally be determined via other elevated readings of tests. It is not unusual for SGOT levels to be elevated among athletes in heavy training since skeletal muscles undergo considerable trauma (strains, bruises, etc.) Readings generally peak within 36 hours following injury and return to normal within six days or so. Repeated trauma over days will tend to keep the SGOT level elevated.

SGPT

Serum glutomic pyruvic transaminase (SGPT) is liberated upon damage to liver cells. In the absence of cardiac or other muscle injury, extremely elevated SGOT and SGPT are often indicative of hepatocellular damage (anabolic steroids can cause such hepatocellular damage). Generally, elevated alkaline phosphatase, cholesterol, and bilirubin accompany such liver damage.

Testosterone

Anabolic steroids mimic normally occurring testosterone, thereby inhibiting its secretion. It is not uncommon for testosterone levels to dip to levels well below normal while using steroids (in men and women). This effect is almost always reversible following discontinuance of the use of anabolic steroids.

Sodium and Potassium

Electrolytes in general can fluctuate in the body depending upon many factors (environment, various drugs being used, certain disease entities, etc.). Of significance to the athlete is the fact that the use of steroids as well as extreme heat (sweating) can cause mild to severe electrolyte imbalances. Diuretic use also causes loss of electrolytes as can anti-inflammatory drugs (e.g., Butazolidin). Since electrolytes play a major role in muscle function, loss of strength is not uncommon upon use of such anti-inflammatants and diuretics.

METHODS OF STEROID USE

Some of the nomenclature that has become prevalent among body-builders using steroids includes words like *stacking, blending,* and *staggering.* Other words or phrases are *cycling, descending dose pattern, ascending dose pattern, plateau, steroid bounce, tapering,* and *shotgunning.* These words were born essentially out of practical experience rather than any scientific text.

Stacking

Stacking refers to the practice of using more than one anabolic steroid at a time. Many long-time users of steroids feel that a synergistic effect can be achieved by doing this. *Synergy,* in this context, means that the desired action of one drug is aided by the other—sort of a helper if you will. Many drugs—not just steroids—exhibit this kind of synergism when used in combination with another substance.

Plateauing

When the steroid doesn't seem to be affording the user with the desired gains in strength or size, it can be safely predicted that the steroid is no longer working maximally. It is believed that this kind of plateau in progress is caused by the steroid receptor sites shutting down. The first place one ought to look, however, is at his or her training program and diet. Increasing the overload (if undertrained) or decreasing it (if overtrained), or limiting your caloric intake can often be the culprit responsible for the plateau in progress, as can insufficient nutrients in general (e.g., vitamins or protein). If the problem is indeed receptor site shutdown, then no amount of additional steroid should work to overcome the plateau.

Staggering

To avoid plateauing on a drug, or to avoid plateauing on two (stacked) drugs, long-time users have often opted to get off the drug(s) and go on another. It is felt that this allows the system to pick up where the last one left off. This practice works for some, but not for others. It may be that hitting a plateau incited the user to double his efforts, or to change his workouts—or even to eat more (some drugs cause a reduction in appetite, and switching to another may bring it back, thereby allowing further improvement in size or strength). In any event, it doesn't seem likely that one steroid uses different receptor sites than another, so the receptor shutdown theory doesn't seem to hold water. No one knows for sure what mechanisms are at work in allowing such staggering of drugs to push an athlete past a plateau, or if indeed it does.

Tapering

Research clearly shows that abrupt discontinuance of anabolic steroid use is not the best (safest) method to get your system back to normal. It's better to slowly reduce your dosage over a period of weeks (the longer the cycle, the longer it takes to taper off effectively).

Shotgunning

Taking a host of drugs in the hopes that what one misses the other will get has been a popular method of steroid use (or abuse) in the past. There is no sound rationale for this line of reasoning, either in the scientific literature or in the practical world. It simply doesn't

EFFICACY LISTING OF INJECTED AND INJESTED SUBSTANCES OFTEN USED AS ERGOGENIC AIDS

Ergogen (listed alphabetically)	Increased Performance While in Competition			For Precontest Training Increased Recovery or Therapy		
	Yes	No	Questionable	Yes	No	Questionable
adrenaline (epinepherine)	SE		Z			SEZ
alkalies		SZ	E	SEZ		SEZ
*alcohol		EZ	S	SEZ		
anti-inflammatants (Butazolidin)	SEZ			SEZ		
amino acids beyond the normal daily requirement		SEZ		SEZ		
*anabolic steroids (Dianabol, etc.)		SEZ		SEZ		
antiestrogens (Novadex, Clomid, Teslac)		SEZ				SEZ
asparates		SZ	E	SEZ		
B-12 injections			SEZ			SEZ
barbiturates		SEZ		SEZ		
blood doping		S	EZ	SEZ		
beta blockers		SZ	E	SZ		E
camphor			no responses			
*caffeine	SE	Z				SEZ
*central nervous system stimulants (strychnine, etc.)	E		SZ			SEZ
digitalis		SZ	E	SEZ		
**diuretics	Z	E	S	SEZ		
ether		SEZ		SEZ		
**electrolytes	SEZ			SEZ		
glycogen loading	E	S	Z	SEZ		
gelatin		SEZ		SEZ		

Key: S = strength; E = endurance; Z = muscular size or bodybuilding

* drugs banned by the IOC in international competition (or other sport groups have banned these and other drugs as well); caffeine and alcohol are banned on a discretionary basis in certain sports of the IOC.

** diuretics are often used to cut water weight in order to make weight for contests in boxing, weightlifting, powerlifting, and wrestling. Bodybuilders use diuretics and other drugs to "cut up" or achieve greater definition for contests. Electrolyte replacement is a must.

Note: Some of the efficacy ratings listed depend upon whether certain preconditions or concommittant conditions are met. For example, certain ergogens don't work unless heavy training or adequate nutrition is implemented. Further, some are extremely dangerous and should be administered only under expert supervision, while others should **never** be used owing to extreme danger.

EFFICACY LISTING . . . CONTINUED

Ergogen (listed alphabetically)	Increased Performance While in Competition			For Precontest Training Increased Recovery or Therapy		
	Yes	No	Questionable	Yes	No	Questionable
glycine			SEZ			SEZ
human chorionic gonadotropin (HCG)		SEZ				SEZ
lecithin		SEZ			SEZ	
liver extracts		SEZ			SEZ	
levidopa (ex. Sinemet)		SEZ				SEZ
marijuana		SEZ			SEZ	
minerals or vitamins (supplements)		SEZ		SEZ		
nicotine		Z	SE		SEZ	
nitroglycerin		SZ	E		SEZ	
*narcotic analgesics (ex. morphine)	E	SZ		E	SZ	
*psychomotor stimulants (ex. amphetamines)	SE	Z			SEZ	
phosphates		SEZ			SEZ	
pain killers (analgesics)	SEZ			SEZ		
periactin (antihistamine)		SEZ			E	SZ
sulfa drugs		SEZ			SEZ	
somatotrophic hormone (STH)		SEZ		SEZ		
sugar		SEZ			SEZ	
*sympathomimetic amines (ex. ephedrine)	E	Z	S		SEZ	
wheat germ		SEZ			SEZ	
**wydase	Z	SE			E	SZ
yeast		SEZ			SEZ	

Key: S = strength; E = endurance; Z = muscular size or bodybuilding
    * drugs banned by the IOC in international competition (or other sport groups have banned these and other drugs as well); caffeine and alcohol are banned on a discretionary basis in certain sports of the IOC.
    ** diuretics are often used to cut water weight in order to make weight for contests in boxing, weightlifting, powerlifting, and wrestling. Bodybuilders use diuretics and other drugs to "cut up" or achieve greater definition for contests. Electrolyte replacement is a must.
Note: Some of the efficacy ratings listed depend upon whether certain preconditions or concommittant conditions are met. For example, certain ergogens don't work unless heavy training or adequate nutrition is implemented. Further, some are extremely dangerous and should be administered only under expert supervision, while others should **never** be used owing to extreme danger.

EFFICACY LISTING OF NON-INJECTED AND NON-INGESTED ERGOGENIC AIDS (SUBSTANCES AND PRACTICES)

Ergogen (listed alphabetically)	Increased Performance While in Competition			For Precontest Training Increased Recovery or Therapy		
	Yes	No	Questionable	Yes	No	Questionable
acupuncture	SE	Z		SEZ		
analgesic balms		Z	SE			SEZ
cold (wet or dry)		Z	SE	SEZ		
carbon dioxide		SEZ			SEZ	
disinhibition conditioning	SE		Z	SEZ		
DMSO			SEZ	SEZ		
electrostimulation		SEZ		SEZ		
heat (infrared, wet or dry)			SEZ	SEZ		
hypnotism	E		SZ	SEZ		
manipulation (chiropractic or naturopathic)	SE		Z	SEZ		
massage or vibration			SEZ			SEZ
music		SEZ		SEZ		
motion pictures		SEZ		SEZ		
meditation	SEZ			SEZ		
noise (loud and explosive)	SE	Z		SEZ		Z
Pavlovian disinhibition	SE		Z	SEZ		
oxygen	E	Z	S	E		SZ
transcutaneous electrical nerve stimulation (TENS)		SEZ		SEZ		
ultraviolet light		SEZ				SEZ
ultrasound		SEZ		SEZ		

Key: S = strength; E = endurance; Z = muscular size or bodybuilding
Note: Some of the ergogenic practices listed here may work or be beneficial only if certain preconditions or concommittant conditions are met. Further, some can be dangerous and should only be administered under expert supervision.

work that way. While there are obviously differences in anabolic steroids, the aspect that athletes are interested in—namely the nitrogen-retaining aspect for muscle growth—works basically the same for all anabolic steroids. The receptor sites are the same, the RNA and DNA are the same, and the protein-manufacturing ribosomes are the same. Or so it seems, given the present state of the art.

Other Drugs Often Used By Athletes

In the quest for that winning edge—the advantage over one's opponent—many athletes have opted to dig deeper into their pharmaceutical grab bag. Probably the most frequent users of these other drugs are the bodybuilders, although weightlifters, powerlifters, and other athletes do as well. The tables on pages 275–277 list many of these ergogens, classifying them into two categories: (1) ingested and injected ergogenic aids; and (2) other practices and substances (non-injected and noningested).

33

DRUGS AND SOME PREDICTABLE INTERACTIONS

I stand in awe over athletic feats that shatter those of yesterday's heroes. All of us do. But utter awe is too placid a term for the incredible practices of some athletes regarding their drug habits. I don't want to preach. I do want to enlighten. There is a matter that all of us in the world of sports have to come to grips with.

It concerns the matter of drugs. No, not the same old tune about the dangers of steroids. This problem is even bigger than that, although it concerns steroids as well. Many of the top stars enter sports competitions and place in the top echelons one year, but don't even place in the top ten the following year. They come back for a third try and again place high. There seems to be no continuity in their preparation procedures, no sign of progress from one year to the next, and certainly no logical explanation has been forthcoming from scientists or coaches. I know what the problem is. I know because I've interviewed dozens of athletes at one time or another, and have personally assisted many of them in their training, nutrition, and preparation procedures.

The problem is the indiscriminate use of several different, and often antagonistic and dangerous, drugs.

Many writers over the years have alluded to athletes and coaches of athletes having to be as expert in pharmacology and nutritional biochemistry as they are in training methodology. I don't mind the training and nutrition expertise requirement, but it's plain to me that none of our top athletes is anywhere near expert in how they're handling whatever drugs they're taking to assist them in their training and peaking procedures. It shows, and it shows all too plainly year in and year out. Not only is their ignorance losing them contests, but it could very well kill them.

I've looked into the kinds of drugs that supposedly intelligent athletes are taking and have taken in the past, and it's so scary that I almost dare not speak about it.

I said "almost."

In looking at the drug situation, I learned many startling facts about how most of them interact with one another, how they act, and what kind of indications and contraindictions there are involved in their use (or, should I say abuse). I have become painfully aware of the warnings associated with each. I want to share this information with you.

Why should you be concerned with what's happening at the upper levels of sports? Simply because many athletes are attempting to emulate the drug habits of the stars. The "If it does that to them, it can do it for me" attitude is a farce, a lie, and a cop-out that I don't want perpetuated year after year.

And I know for a fact that high standards of sports excellence can be achieved without resorting to the pharmacological grab bag.

Before getting into some of the drugs being used, let me give you a short background on how this drug fiasco got started. After all, the stars (and most probably most of you) are clean living men and women who believe in God, country, and family. They all are moral people. How could they have fallen prey to such a demeaning and dangerous practice?

No, it wasn't the injection of money into sports once called amateur. Drugs were being used long before that ever happened to be sure. Neither was it lust for gold medals, an insatiable appetite for glory, or a need to take unfair advantage over the other guy. These are reasons posited by pencilnecks who simply don't understand the peak performer's lifestyle. No, it was none of these. Instead, it was because taking drugs was an acceptable thing to do.

Medical doctors gave drugs to athletes. Strength coaches and gym owners gave them out like candy. Everybody talked openly about their methods of cycling, new drugs on the scene, and how to avoid detrimental side effects just as openly as if they were discussing their training routines.

The media and the public gave it little notice, largely because it was generally accepted that drugs were here to stay. Drugs had become part and parcel to the very idea of sport, and almost everyone was using drugs in one form or another.

Then came Caracas.

Since the Pan Am Games in 1983, the din and hue of both the media and the public has been such that the word "drugs" has once again become a dirty word. In most cases this is right and justified. The question is not whether drugs have a place in sports, however.

Rather, the important issue is what can we do about it?

I suggest two things to be done: Continue testing, and educate the youngsters coming up in sports on not only the physical dangers of drug use but also the moral responsibility of a civilized person to tread a higher road. In my opinion, it is the latter that will ultimately restore sport to an exalted position. Here I speak of sport in a people sense, not just in the sense of a childlike pastime. At its highest level, sport symbolizes the unfettered, pure spirit of man striving for perfection. In the twinkling of an eye, drugs remove all semblance of that purity.

WHO'S USING WHAT?

Friends, take it from me, the list of drugs I've tabled here is only a small fraction of those being used out there in the world of sports. The lists of warnings and side effects aren't hype. They're very real and potentially lethal. At worst they can kill you. At least they demean you and sport. Study the table and take care to note these dangers. Once noted, put them in the back of your mind. You needn't remember them all verbatim. The chances are that you're not well enough versed in pharmacology to fully understand all of them anyway. And, God knows there are all too many amateur pharmacologists out there among you.

SOME OF THE CONSEQUENCES OF PLAYING PHARMACOLOGIST

Drugs interact. They interact with one another, and they interact with your body's own biochemicals. The possible number of interactions stemming from just one or two commonly used drugs by an athlete in the process of peaking for a contest can be in the dozens. Do you know what they are? Do you know how to control them? Do you have total confidence that your drug practices will win contests and peak you perfectly, or do you have doubt, never knowing whether you're doing the right thing?

Chances are, you're doubtful. If you're smart you would be. And if you're *really* smart you'd stop this nonsense!

Here are some of the more apparent interactions you can expect. You can read them and weep, or you can read them and LEARN!

Side Effects and Interactions

Anabolic Steroids with Human Chorionic Gonadotropin (HCG). Androgenic drugs which aromatize (e.g., Anadrol 50, Testosterone, Deca-Durabolin) react with HCG to promote water retention and gynocomastia (so-called "bitch tits").

Cortisone Derivative Drugs and Anabolic Steroids. Cortisone pro-

DRUGS ATHLETES USE . . . AND THEIR CONSEQUENCES

Name	Clinical Use	Bodybuilders Use	Contraindicators	Side Effects
Testosterone (propionate, enanthate, cypionate, methyltestosterone)	Male hypogonadal states	"Strength/size" drug, "androgenic phase" of steroid program	Male breast cancer, prostate cancer, liver disease, kidney disease, pregnancy	Acne, hirsutism in females, water/sodium retention, decreased sperm formation, increased arteriosclerosis, liver disease, neoplasm promotion, gynecomastia
Nandrolone decanoate (Deca-Durabolin)	Weight gain promotion after surgery, severe trauma, offset protein catabolism associated with corticosteroids	Injection anabolic, used primarily before contests to promote size/muscularity	As in #1	As in #1
Nadroline Phenylpropionate (Durabolin)	Shorter acting version of Deca-Durabolin	As for Deca-Durabolin	As in #1	As in #1
Oxandrolone (Anavar)	As in #2, plus relief of bone pain in osteoporosis	Anabolic "cutting" drug, power drug supposedly increases strength	As in #1	As in #1
Oxymetholone (Anadrol 50)	Treatment of anemias due to deficient RBC production, bone marrow failure	Androgenic strength/ bulking drug, adds size and strength	As in #1	As in #1

STEROIDS

Stanzolol (Winstrol, Stromba Set, Winstrol V)	Hereditary angloedema (hereditary immune system malfunction)	Anabolic cutting-up drug	As in #1	As in #1
Methandrostenolone (Dianabol)	As for Durabolin	Anabolic to promote weight gain, size increases	As in #1	As in #1
Methenolone (Primobolin)	As for Durabolin—not available in USA	Anabolic to promote weight gain, size increases	As in #1	As in #1
Boldenone Undecylenate (Equipoise)	Post-op convalescence of older HORSES (veterinary drug)	Size, strength increase	As in #1	As in #1
Sustanon 250 (testosterone injection)	4 testosterones in one injection; promotes even blood androgen level	Size/strength bulking drug	As in #1	As in #1
Human growth hormone (protropin, asellincrin, cresorman)	Treatment of growth disorders in children due to genetic lack of hGH	Anabolic agent to promote size/strength increase, lipolytic (fat burning) agent	Prepubertal use may produce "giantism," known neoplasms, pituitary tumors	Acromegaly (excessive growth of jaw, hands, feet, tongue, forehead, etc.) diabetes, promotes neoplasm
L-dopa	Parkinson's disease	To promote release of growth hormone	Skin cancer (melanoma)	Cardiac effects, gastrointestinal discomfort, psychosis

GROWTH HORMONE STIMULATORS

DRUGS ATHLETES USE . . . AND THEIR CONSEQUENCES (CONTINUED)

Name	Clinical Use	Bodybuilders Use	Contraindicators	Side Effects
THYROID				
Triacana (thyroid)	Hypothyroid states (low thyroid)	Cutting-up agent used to hype "metabolism"	Hyperthyroidism, heart disease	Excessive cardiac stimulation, nervousness, tremors, excessive sweating, muscle loss
Cytomel (T3 Thyroid)	As for Triacana	Cutting-up agent used to hype "metabolism"	Hyperthyroidism, heart disease	Excessive cardiac stimulation, nervousness, tremors, excessive sweating, muscle loss
Synthroid (TY Thyroid)	Longer acting version of thyroid	Cutting-up agent used to hype "metabolism"	Hyperthyroidism, heart disease	Excessive cardiac stimulation, nervousness, tremors, excessive sweating, muscle loss
AMPHETAMINES				
Dexedrine (Dextroamphetamine)	Narcolepsy, attention deficit disorder, anti-obesity	"Speed" energy enhancement, anorexic to reduce appetite	Arteriosclerosis, cardiovascular disease, hypertension, hyperthyroidism, glaucoma	Increased body heat, high blood pressure, amphetamine "psychosis," cardiovascular effects, acute mental confusion
Methamphetamine	Narcolepsy, attention deficit disorder, anti-obesity	"Speed" energy enhancement, anorexic to reduce appetite	Arteriosclerosis, cardiovascular disease, hypertension, hyperthyroidism, glaucoma	Increased body heat, high blood pressure, amphetamine "psychosis," cardiovascular effects, acute mental confusion

Category	Drug	Clinical Use	Athletic Use	Contraindications	Side Effects
	Ritalin (Methylphenidate)	Narcolepsy, attention deficit disorder, anti-obesity	"Speed" energy enhancement, anorexic to reduce appetite	Arteriosclerosis, cardiovascular disease, hypertension, hyperthyroidism, glaucoma	Increased body heat, high blood pressure, amphetamine "psychosis," cardiovascular effects, acute mental confusion
DIURETICS	Lasix (Furosemide)	Diuretic-edema, hypertension, pulmonary edema	Diuretic to eliminate sodium and water retention especially before a contest	Kidney failure	Hypokalomia (low blood potassium), nausea, vomiting, dizziness, vertigo, cardiovascular complications
DIURETICS	Spironolactone (Aldactone)	Diuretic-hypertension hyperaldosteronism	Diuretic blocks sodium retention	Kidney failure, high blood potassium levels	Gynecomastia, cramps, diarrhea, high potassium levels
ANTI-INFLAMMATORY	Non-Steroidal Anti-inflammatory (aspirin)	Reduce inflammation, pain, arthritic states	Same as clinical use	Allergic reactions to these drugs	Gastrointestinal pain, edema, tinnitus, nervousness
CORTICO-STEROIDS	Cortisone (Decadron, Aristocort, Depo-Medrol, etc.)	Adrenal insufficiency, rheumatic disorders, collagen diseases, skin diseases, allergic states	Pain/inflammation, use to treat joint/tendon injuries	Systemic fungal infections, drug hypersensitivity	Sodium/water retention, potassium/calcium loss, muscle catabolism, peptic ulcers, pituitary suppressant

DRUGS ATHLETES USE . . . AND THEIR CONSEQUENCES (CONTINUED)

	Name	Clinical Use	Bodybuilders Use	Contraindicators	Side Effects
HCG	Human chorionic gonadotropin (Pregnyl)	Cryptochidism, hypogonadal states, female infertility	Promotes fat loss (unproven); stimulates endrogenous testosterone production	Precocious puberty, prostate cancer, other androgen-dependent tumors	Headache, irritability, fatigue, restlessness, depression, edema, gynecomastia
ESTROGEN BLOCKERS	Nolvadex (Tomoxifen Citrate)	Anti-estrogen agent for breast cancer, male infertility	Prevention and ameloriation of gynecomastic "bitch tits"; cutting agent for females	None known	Promotion of eye diseases; in women, "chemical menopause" hot flashes, nausea, vomiting
	Testlax (Testolactone)	Anti-tumor agent for breast cancer	Estrogen blocker prevents "bitch tits"	Breast cancer in males	High blood pressure, edema, nausea

motes sodium and water retention, and with steroids the effects are cumulative and often result in severe swelling of serous fluid in connective tissues.

Nolvadex and Male Hormones. This combination can promote a sort of chemical menopause in women, manifested by hot flashes, vaginal thinning, and may promote infection, osteoporosis, polycystic ovarian syndrome, and infertility.

Thyroid Drugs and Steroids. Steroids decrease blood levels of thyroid hormones (as does excessive or severe dieting and low-carb diets), while exogenously administered thyroid promotes rapid breakdown of those same steroids. Excessive thyroid use will result in muscle tissue loss and it will not be offset by steroid use.

Aldactone and Androgens. Spironolactone (aldactone) is an androgen blocker. It blocks androgen receptors, thereby preventing androgens from entering the cells. In doing so, however, your body's estrogen levels are greatly increased, causing gynocomastia (enlargement of breasts).

Anabolic Steroids and Tagamet. Tagamet, a popular ulcer drug, competitively inhibits androgen uptake, resulting in water retention and gynocomastia.

Amphetamines and Corticosteroids. Amphetamines increase blood corticosteroid levels, resulting in rapid muscle tissue loss, potassium loss and increased sodium levels, and a concomitant hypertensive state (edema).

Amphetamines and Steroids. Amphetamines promote increased mental aggressiveness as do androgenic hormones. A combination of these two drugs could result in acute paranoiac aggressive states and stress reactions leading to aldosterone secretion and water retention.

L-Dopa and Amphetamines. Both drugs promote excessive limbic activation in the brain, resulting in paranoiac delusions akin to schizoid states.

Veterinary Steroids. Examples include Winstrol-V, Parabolan Equipoise, and Finejet. These drugs may contain impurities (up to 5%), resulting in anaphylactoid reactions (hypersensitivity) and suspected damage to vascular beds.

Thytropar (TSH) and Thyroid Drugs. Together in the body, these two drugs interact producing excessive thyroid stimulation. This in turn results in toxic goiter and possible cardiovascular problems such as arrythmia. In addition, it causes rapid muscle tissue loss.

Insulin Used to Offset GH Hyperglycemia. Insulin promotes fat buildup, water retention, and hypoglycemia.

Anabolic Steroids and Insulin. Both drugs have a hypoglycemic effect, resulting in abnormal glucose tolerance curves. This, in turn, could result in excessive glycogen loss from muscle tissue, resulting in a "flat" look, loss of energy from hypoglycemia, and inability to achieve a pump.

Esciclene. Bodybuilders use this drug to make localized tissue swell, making it appear as if their muscle is larger. Esciclene causes localized inflammation resulting in loss of definition.

Anadrol 50 and Human Growth Hormone. This combo can cause neoplastic changes in your red blood cells' production, which can in turn cause leukemia over the long term.

Using Lasix Right Before a Contest. Lasix and other diuretics cause a "rebound" effect in water retention. You'll lose water all right, but then your body hoards it, causing a smooth appearance very rapidly.

Withdrawal from Nolvadex Before a Contest. Getting off Nolvadex (an estrogen blocker) right before a contest results in a "rebound" of estrogen levels, particularly in women. This results in an increase in aldosterone which causes severe water retention and a smoothed-out look.

Sodium Loading and Steroids. Steroids cause sodium retention. During the depletion phase of a sodium-loading protocol, you can't deplete your sodium levels because of the antagonistic effect of the steroids. The result, of course, is excessive water retention.

Carbohydrate Loading and Androgens. It's very likely that using steroids at the same time you're loading glycogen will result in severe water retention in the interstitial spaces and subcutaneously. Getting off steroids a week early doesn't work either, because most oral and injected steroids remain active in your body much longer than a week.

Aldactone Use Before a Contest. Withdrawing from aldactone use before a contest may promote aldosterone secretion, particularly during a carbo-depletion cycle. This in turn causes severe water retention.

These are but a few of the problems you'll face in resorting to a pharmacological approach to sports preparation. Isn't it easier to do things right? Isn't it easier, and more reliable, to stay away from drugs that you have no knowledge of, and have no understanding of regarding the harm they can do?

Sure, you think you're so smart! "Well, I'll just experiment a few times with these drugs until I get it right. Then I can rely on them to get me strong or big precisely when I want them to." Boy, are you in for a letdown. Can't you see what I see? Can't you see that the best in the world don't even know how to control the potent and possibly dangerous effects of these drugs? Your body is an ever-changing, dynamic organism. You don't know how these changes affect your ability to use these drugs from contest to contest, and you certainly shouldn't be expected to know. Even physicians don't know—believe me, I've asked over a dozen about these interactions in preparing this chapter, and most of them shook their heads in both disbelief as well as self-admitted ignorance. No one knows.

34

DRUG-FREE:
Peaking for Strength Sports Competition

In the preceding chapter, I wrote about the incredible array of biochemical interactions that can, and most often do, interfere with your contest-peaking efforts when you rely on drugs. The drug mentality is so embedded in the fabric of sports that it is going to take a monumental effort for the next generation of athletes to come around to the truth of the matter.

The truth is, simply stated, sports excellence is a lifestyle. It is a commitment to health, fitness, and excellence. In such a lifestyle, using dangerous drugs has no place. Yet, this knowledge is not enough apparently to stem the tide of athletes resorting to pharmaceutical assistance for that elusive edge they all seek.

Because I know this to be a fact—just as plain a fact as are the high ideals of the sports excellence commitment—I have worked hard to try and find viable alternatives to these drugs. I assumed in my search that if athletes had a way they could achieve the status of an Olympic athlete without drugs, they'd take advantage of it.

There is a way. It's hard, but fruitful. It takes dedication and discipline, but it's worth it—every bit. It's up to you.

PEAKING BEGINS WITH OFF-SEASON DISCIPLINE

So many times I notice athletes allowing their body weight to climb far beyond their contest weight during the off-season. Sometimes as much as 30 or 40 pounds have to be shed in order for that athlete to be sharp enough to compete.

This practice is most often a result of two very silly indulgences: the gross abuse of anabolic steroids, and lack of discipline. The drugs, as you all know by now, cause tissue bloating. When the bloat is reduced through unnecessarily rigorous fasting, muscle tissue is lost in the process, negating any so-called benefits of taking steroids. And, the lack of discipline is the cause of overeating that puts on layers of hard-to-remove fat.

It makes infinitely more sense to me to stay within 5%–6% of your contest body weight during the off-season training cycle. During this cycle of training, you should try to put on more muscle, of course, but never mistake bloat and fat for muscle.

If you are gaining in muscle mass during the off-season, your body weight will climb naturally—perhaps as fast as one or two pounds every two weeks. It's not possible to gain more than that in solid muscle, so if you're gaining faster, back off from your caloric intake slightly at each meal to compensate.

Remember, discipline is the key in the off-season. If you exercise discipline in your caloric intake, you'll come into the contest more prepared than ever.

HOW MUCH, WHAT, AND WHEN YOU EAT ARE ALL IMPORTANT

Every top athlete has his or her own secret nutritional regimen. People are different. They have different tastes in food, they have different metabolic rates, and they have different training regimens that dictate caloric needs. However, there are some rather universal guidelines that should be a part of anyone's dietary regimen if you expect to step onto that field in peak form.

- You should eat at least four, and preferably five or six meals each day.
- Never eat between meals, as doing so will disrupt the ongoing cycle of digestive processes already at work on your last meal.
- Each meal should be planned carefully. Most athletes have found that about 10%–15% of each meal's caloric value should be from high-quality unsaturated fats, at least 20%–25% from complete proteins, and the remaining 50%–60% from complex carbohydrates. Sugars and animal fats should be kept minimal.
- Continually monitor your body weight and percent body fat. Doing so will both guide you in your muscle-building progress as well as control your caloric intake so that you can gain muscle or lose fat accordingly.
- The number of calories you consume each day should be determined according to your activity level. On days when your training is light or absent, reduce your caloric intake to bare minimums. On training days, increase your caloric intake to match

your muscle-building and energy needs. The same holds true for the time of day; pretraining meals should be somewhat larger than the others.

- Remember that extra calories are stored, and are not reclaimed as easily as muscle tissue during times of fasting or increased energy requirements. That's why you should vary your caloric intake from meal to meal and day to day.
- Never try to gain or lose weight any faster than one or two pounds every two weeks. Remember that one pound is gained or lost for each 3,500 calories above or below your energy requirements.

TAKE ADVANTAGE OF THE SCIENCE OF NUTRITIONAL BIOCHEMISTRY

Over the years I have tried to provide athletes with information on the best food supplements science had to offer so that muscle growth and overall health would remain optimal. Over the past few years, the science of nutritional biochemistry has uncovered several remarkable substances that aid athletes far beyond mere health or muscle size.

- Improved short-term (anaerobic) energy
- Improved long-term (aerobic) energy
- Decreased pain
- Improved recuperation from training fatigue
- Improved recuperation from injuries or trauma
- Improved mental concentration
- More rapid fat loss
- More rapid muscle building (protein synthesis)
- Improved overall health, vigor, and fitness

As you know, I have written several articles and books on the subject of nutritional supplementation. I invite you to reread the chapters on nutrition in this book.

Substances like inosine, amino acids in their free-form, carbohydrate energy enhancers, multivitamin/mineral supplements, growth hormone releasers, and many others fulfilling the above-listed needs of athletes like yourself in heavy training really do work. Make no mistake about that. And, I know that when used as directed, many of these substances can greatly improve your performance as well as your off-season preparation.

YOU MUST ADOPT A POSITIVE MENTAL ATTITUDE WHEN PEAKING

Before all the major contests, many top athletes come to my office to visit, chat about their training, and get some tips on how best to train, supplement, and diet. I see them when they're engaged in off-season training and I see them during the final stages of their peaking programs.

What an incredible metamorphosis many of them suffer! Some go from soft-spoken, gentle introverts to raging megalomaniacs in a few short weeks! Why? Partly because of the aggressiveness-causing drugs, that's for sure. But also it's due to their unnecessarily rigorous fasting and the attendant lack of energy-giving blood glucose.

If only these guys would learn the meaning of the word *discipline* during their off-season training, they'd never have to drop 30 or 40 pounds in the space of a very short few weeks.

I often ask these top athletes to show me their training and nutrition log when they come to see me. "What log?" they ask as if I popped a surprise quiz. "I don't keep a log—I don't have time. I can't see the need for one. I already know how to train and what to expect."

These are excuses made by lazy men not fully dedicated to their craft. A training diary is a labor of discipline, and discipline is part and parcel of the most productive mental mindset needed to achieve greatness in sports. A disciplined, well-kept training diary will help you uncover weaknesses in your training, inadequacies in your diet, and how best to supplement your diet with the many nutritional aids science has been uncovering of late. You can't remember everything, but a training log definitely can!

ATTENTION TO DETAIL PAYS OFF

Would you ever consider going into business without first carefully establishing a plan of action? A business plan includes all of the obstacles, pitfalls, resources, methods, and timetables you'll need in order to make a profit. A complete spreadsheet listing exactly where every penny is coming from and going to will ensure that your efforts are maximally efficient.

It's the same in any endeavor, and it's the same in training. If you carefully sketch out your master plan for the coming year, you will stand a much better chance of succeeding. To illustrate my point, take a look at the table I've constructed here. You'll notice that I have carefully integrated your training intensity, your caloric intake, and your body weight in such a way that the following chain of events happens:

- Each five-week period is coordinated so that your training intensity is constantly upward with peaks and valleys so you can avoid overtraining.
- Your caloric intake remains constant over the entire 20 weeks, except that you take in fewer calories during low-intensity training periods, and more calories during high-intensity training periods.

HOW TO COORDINATE TRAINING, CALORIC INTAKE, AND BODY WEIGHT BEFORE A CONTEST

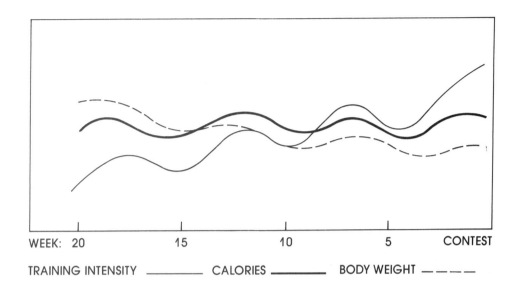

WEEK: 20   15   10   5   CONTEST

TRAINING INTENSITY ———— CALORIES ———— BODY WEIGHT — — — —

- The overall result is that, as training intensity increases as you draw closer to a contest, your body weight will slowly decrease due to the relatively stable caloric intake.

This is but one method of literally dozens to ensure that you lose fat, not muscle, as the contest draws near, and that you do it safely, in a disciplined approach, and come in fully prepared.

Doesn't it stand to reason that you'll put on a bit of fat during a day that training is light but your food intake remains as high as if you were training heavy? This kind of erratic thinking is the cause of putting on too much fat over a long period of time, and that fat is very difficult to remove without causing you to suffer muscle loss in the process.

So, these are the kinds of details you must account for if you wish to master your performance goals. Leave nothing to chance.

35

hGH: BREAKFAST OF THE SASQUATCH

Sasquatch. Big feet. Lordy me, what next!

Sasquatch was/is an acromegalic. His or her growth hormone levels gone wild, this throwback to Pleistocenian antiquity would be SOL if he came to town to buy shoes. In the wonderful world of sports, I've noticed with no small measure of concern, we have a few throwbacks ourselves. But Sasquatch has an excuse for his acromegalic features.

Scientists, just now involving themselves in the use of such ergogens by athletes, tell us that the jury is still out regarding the efficacy of human growth hormone (hGH) in producing strength or size among otherwise healthy athletes. That they're having a tough time of it in sorting out this question is understandable due to the varied responses reported by athletes using the stuff. It appears to work for some but not for others.

Now, I do not want to sound like the anti-drug crusaders and bore you with scare stories such as they are wont to do. My position regarding the use of drugs is well known by now—I'm staunchly against the practice. But this hGH stuff scares me more than a trifle. It scares me even more than steroids do. My opinion is that it ought to scare you, too.

Herein I shall contain myself on that subject, and report only the facts as they're represented in the research literature. I think it's time some of you knew the **rest** of the story!

SOME OF THE DANGERS OF hGH USE

Acromegaly is an insidious, irreversible disease that long-term hGH users must face. Many athletes (some of whom all of us know) are beginning to show signs of acromegaly; coarsening of the skin, thickening of the bones of the face, hands, and feet are some of the outwardly visible signs. But other complications have been noted as well. Diabetes, arthritis, and a shortened life span are included. Complications can arise, too. For example, growth hormone antibodies can be formed, making you growth hormone deficient.

As users of injectable steroids know, it's just a matter of time before you inadvertently use a contaminated needle. It's almost inescapable, and one day you will get a dose of hepatitis. What scares me the most is that AIDS is spread the same way.

Unlike many of the scare stories being spread around by crusaders regarding the dangers of using anabolic steroids, these hGH-related dangers are all too real.

WHY IS hGH SO SOUGHT AFTER BY ATHLETES?

What is it that makes athletes want to risk these inherent dangers anyway? Does hGH offer sufficient rewards that these risks are worth it? Obviously, the many athletes using the stuff think so. Otherwise they wouldn't be using it.

Many find, to their dismay, that they've wasted their money (a *lot* of money, incidentally—the stuff is expensive), having experienced no benefits at all. Scientists tell us that there may be good reasons for this. First, let's look at the list of things hGH is supposed to do for athletes.

1. The most important function of hGH is to increase somatic growth among hypopituitary children. It stimulates skeletal and soft tissue growth and also has profound metabolic effects in day-to-day homeostatic functioning (Macintyre, 1987).
2. Growth hormone shifts oxidative metabolism toward the use of fatty acids, thus sparing glycogen and protein for anabolism (Campbell & Rastogi, 1969; Kostyo & Reagan, 1976).
3. Total daily insulin production is markedly increased by growth hormone use, and the increased affinity for insulin by the enzyme systems results in improved protein synthesis (Campbell & Rastogi, 1969).
4. Growth hormone stimulates the mobilization of lipids from stored fat, resulting in decreased peripheral fat stores, decreased respiratory quotient, and increased plasma-free fatty acids (Hunter, et al., 1965; Kostyo & Reagan, 1976).

5. Cartilage is stimulated to grow by growth hormone (Isaksson, et al., 1985).
6. Growth hormone markedly increases protein synthesis, but the type of protein synthesized as a result of growth hormone administration is markedly different from that synthesized as a result of muscular work (Grodsky, 1982; Root, 1972; Bigland & Jehring, 1952).
7. Muscle hypertrophy resulting from growth hormone administration appears to be a result primarily of collagen formation, and not contractile protein (Lewis, 1972; Naugelsparen, et al., 1976).
8. The research literature reports that hGH is *possibly* effective in: catabolic changes resulting from aging and debilitating diseases (Macintyre, 1987), primary and secondary osteoporosis (Northmore-Ball, et al., 1975), and accelerated healing of bone fractures (Lindholm, et al., 1977).

So, it's easy to see why athletes have opted to use this drug. Simply put, injectable hGH, whether the type recovered from human cadaver pituitaries or the newer biosynthesized version, stimulates increased size and reduces fat stores. Some users claim that it performs these two functions better than any other class of drugs, steroids included.

The majority of users, however, notably athletes in sports requiring increased strength, beg to differ. No such gains have been noted by the majority of users, either in size, fat reduction, or strength. Essentially, the self-experimentation was a monumental waste of money, and the risks to which they exposed themselves were, in the final analysis, not worth it.

There are no clear statistics that reveal the exact ratio of those benefiting from hGH injections and those not. However, it is clear that something is causing this curious discrepancy. Assuming that you can rely on the anecdotal evidence afforded us by current and past users who have or have not benefited, we can make some wild guesses as to why this happens.

WHY DO SOME BENEFIT AND OTHERS DO NOT?

There are a lot of reasons why using injectable hGH wouldn't work for some yet deliver significant results for others:

1. Working out in a cold gym and/or residing most of the time in cold temperatures is known to inhibit hGH release; it's possible that this condition could also reduce the effectiveness of exogenously administered hGH (Buckler, 1973; Christianson et al., 1984; Frewin et al., 1976).
2. Glucose ingestion reduces hGH response (Shepherd & Sydney, 1975), meaning that if you train with high blood glucose or if you

administer hGH injections while hyperglycemic the anabolic effects of the hGH may be reduced.

3. Several hormones inhibit or altogether nullify the desired anabolic effects of hGH: somatostatin, progesterones, and glucocorticoids are examples (Daugheday, 1985; Merimee, 1979; Refetoff, 1979; Reichlin, 1985). The same is true of many neurotransmitters and their analogues: phentolomine, isoprenaline, methysergide, cyproheptadine, and atropine. Other drugs such as chlorpromazine, imipramine, morphine, and theophylline also inhibit hGH release, giving rise to the possibility that they could also be involved in reducing the effectiveness of exogenously administered hGH.

While the above classes of physiological or pharmacological inhibitory factors represent speculation as to their potential effect on injected hGH, they are known to inhibit endogenous hGH release under certain circumstances. For example, the physiological factors that cause hGH release, such as sleep, exercise, stress, high temperatures, and hypoglycemia all are reduced in their effectiveness in the presence of the classes of hGH-release inhibitors listed above.

In fact, the release of hGH through the use of amino acids such as arginine, ornithine, lysine, and others is inhibited by the above factors. Indeed, arginine, the best known of the hGH-releasing amino acids, is rendered useless in releasing hGH in the presence of beta-endorphins. Beta-endorphins, as you no doubt know, are released into the body through extreme exertion and pain, two conditions that go hand in hand with heavy training (Reid & Yen, 1981).

Of course, it may also be true that strength cannot be improved through injecting hGH. It's certain that size (through collagen formation rather than through myofibrillarization or mitochondrial proliferation) as well as decreased peripheral fat stores can be, provided that inhibitory factors are inoperative (Kostygo & Reagan, 1976; Grodsky, 1982; Lewis, 1976).

WHAT ALTERNATIVES DO ATHLETES HAVE?

I still believe that natural means of stimulating hGH release are the most beneficial alternative to shooting up.

1. Exercise stimulates hGH release. So do high temperatures. I recommend training in a warm gym—above 74°–76°.
2. Pain and extreme stress both release beta-endorphins into the bloodstream. Thus, make your training more productive in its hGH-releasing capacity by avoiding pain and unnecessarily high-stress exercises. Extreme effort and extreme stress are not the same. Effort yes. Pain or unnecessary stress, no.
3. Avoid training or going to bed with a belly full of carbohydrates.

High blood glucose will inhibit hGH release exactly when you need it most.

4. Try avoiding doing the same old exercises or training protocol all the time. Changing routines will inject new adaptive stress, of the positive kind, into your training, and in so doing will promote hGH release. If your body has adapted to your training methods it will not register intensely enough to stimulate an anabolic effect.

5. Use arginine/ornithine supplements before training and before going to bed (about one hour before training and immediately before going to bed).

6. Go to bed with little to eat, especially carbs, in order to keep blood sugar in the normal-to-low range.

7. Train with just enough blood glucose to get you through your training and to replace spent stores immediately after training. Training with high blood sugar, remember, inhibits hGH release.

8. The fatter you are, the lower your hGH response to exercise will be (Daugheday, 1985; Galbo, 1983; Merimee, 1979). So, if you're fat—with a percent body fat above 15% (men) or 20% (women)—get rid of the baggage, and you'll begin making better muscular gains.

9. Women tend to have higher hGH responses to exercise than men, presumably because of their higher estrogen levels, because they're generally less fit than their male counterparts, or because they respond psychologically to exercise with more stress than men (Shepherd & Sydney, 1975; Galbo, 1983).

The bottom line is this: If you think you need pharmacological assistance to make it to the top, you're mistaken. You can, through smart scientific training and nutritional supplementing, achieve far more than you realize. You may have tried some of these well-known alternatives to drugs before but came away less than satisfied, but did you try them in the best possible manner? Use the above guidelines and give them a good, honest try again. I believe you'll come away convinced that drug-free training is indeed possible.

At the very least, you'll have more money in your pocket, your forehead will remain pretty, and your feet will not grow to Sasquatch proportions.

REFERENCES

Bigand, B., and Jehmng B. Muscle performance in rats, normal, and treated with growth hormone. *Journal of Physiology* 116: 129–136, 1952

Buckler, J. M. The effect of age, sex and exercise on the secretion of growth hormone. *Clinical Science* 37: 765–744, 1969

Campbell, J. and Rastogi, K. S. Actions of growth hormone: enhancement of insulin utilization with inhibition of insulin effect on blood glucose in dogs. *Metabolism* 18(11): 930–944, 1969

Christenson, S. E., Jorgenson, O. L., Moller, N., and Orskov, H. Characterization of growth hormone release in response to external beating comparison to exercise induced release. *Acta Endocrinologica* 107, 295–301, 1984

Daugheday, W. H. The anterior pituitary. In Wilson & Foster (Eds) Williams textbook of endocrinology, 7th ed. pp. 577–611, W. B. Saunders. Philadelphia, 1985

Frewin, D. B., Frantz, A.G., and Downey, J. A. The effect of ambient temperature on the growth hormone and prolactin response to exercise. *Australian Journal of Experimental Biology* 54: 97–101, 1976

Galbo, H. Hormonal and metabolic adaptations to exercise, pp. 1–116 Georg Thierne Verlag, New York, 1983

Grodsky, G. M. Chemistry and function of the hormones IV pituitary and hypothalamus. Martin et al (Eds) Harper's Review of Biochemistry. Lange Medical Publications, Los Altos, 1982

Hunter, W. M., Fonseka, C. C., and Passmore, R. The role of growth hormone in the mobilization of fuel for muscular exercise. *Quarterly Journal of Experimental Physiology* 50: 406–416, 1965

Isaksson, O. G., Eden, S., Jansson, J. O. Mode of action of pituitary growth hormone on target cells. *Annual Review of Physiology* 47: 483–499, 1985

Kostyo, I. L., and Reagan, C. R. The biology of growth hormone. *Pharmacology and Therapeutics* 2: 591–604, 1976

Lewis, P. D. Neuromuscular involvement in pituitary gigantism. *British Medical Journal* 2: 499–500, 1972

Lindholm, R. V., Koskinen, E. V. S., Puranen, J., Nieminen, R. A., and Kairaluoma, M., et al. Human growth hormone in the treatment of fresh fractures. *Hormone and Metabolic Research* 9: 245–246, 1977

Dr. J. G. Macintyre. British Columbia Sports Medicine Clinic, University of British Columbia, 3055 Wesbrook Mail, Vancouver, British Columbia V6T 1WS (Canada)

Marimee, T. J. Growth hormone secretion and action. In DeGroot et al. (Eds) *Endocrinology.* Vol. 1. pp. 123–132, Grune and Stratton Inc., New York, 1979

Naugelsparen, M., Trickey, R., Davies, M. J., and Jenkins, J.S. Muscle changes in acromegaly. *British Medical Journal* 2: 914–915, 1976

Northmore-Ball, M. D., Wood, M. R., Meggitt, B. F. A biomechanical study of the effects of growth hormone in experimental fracture healing. *Journal of Bone and Joint Surgery* 62-B (3) 391–396, 1980

Refetoff, S., Frank, P. H., Roubebush, C., and De Groot, L. J. Evaluation of pituitary function. In De Groot et al. (Eds) Endocrinology, Vol. 1, pp. 175–214. Grune and Stratton, New York, 1979

Reichlin, S. Neuroendocrinology. In Wilson & Foster (Eds) Williams textbook of endocrinology, 7th ed., pp. 514–531, W. B. Saunders, Philadelphia, 1985

Reid, R. L. and Yen, S. S. C. The effect of beta-endorphin on arganine-induced growth hormone and prolactin release. Life Sciences 29 (25) 2641–2647, 1981

Root, A. W. Human pituitary growth hormone. Charles C. Thomas Publisher, Springfield, 1972

Shephard, R. J. and Sidney, K. H. Effects of physical exercise on plasma growth hormone and cortisol levels in human subjects. In Wilmore & Keough (Eds) Exercise and sport science reviews, p. 1–30, Academic Press, New York, 1975

36

MUMIE:
Space-Age Substance
from Antiquity

Stealthily she stole past the athletes' dorm guards, past the track, over to the men's dormitories. That's where she was to meet a member of the U.S. contingent to the World Championships. Purpose: to raise money to support herself while in training by selling a new super-drug.

Let's call her Tanya. She's a Bulgarian. And she has in her possession an ancient Oriental substance that recently found its way into the pharmacological grab bag of the Soviet athletes. She needs the money because Communist bloc athletes don't get to keep their winnings at such meets.

And, money in hand, she tiptoes back to her dorm. Task accomplished. That's how it's done in the real world of one-upmanship sports, fellow iron freaks. Just like back home, no?

And our American athlete who was the recipient of the stuff? Why, in storybook fashion, he went on to win a gold medal the following year, leaving Western coaches literally amazed at his magnificent progress over the last year's training.

That was before Chernobyl. That singular disaster, which left untold scores of Soviet citizens poisoned, dead, or disfigured—and the rest of the world bitter—also had a devastating effect on the world of sports. You see, the stuff of which I speak, as the story goes, was one of the substances of choice in treating the radiation victims left in the wake of the Chernobyl disaster. The supply practically vanished overnight.

I'm talking about mumie, a resin-based substance that looks like

301

black pitch in its raw form. And it's mined from the bottom of the Black Sea along a certain ridge of mountains long ago submerged from the ever-shifting earth's movement.

Ancient Orientals used the stuff for a variety of ailments. In scientific terms, mumie is an ancient humus matter contained in marine sediment. As submerged trees and other plant life begin to decay over eons, the resin (sap) is the last of such vegetation to mineralize, or petrify. They scoop up the humus matter and drag it up into the mountains to some lab and, through a process of electrophoresis, the matter stratifies, leaving one of the strata in the form of mumie.

Of course, the Soviets analyzed the stuff. Through a variety of chromatographic techniques, they were able to surmise the elemental compounds in mumie. As expected, mumie contained all the things one would expect decaying vegetation to contain. A dash of copper, iron, and bromide. A smidgeon of benzoic acid, a pinch of magnesium and calcium, and a bit of salicylic acid. A trace of p-hydroxybenzoic acid for taste. You get the picture. Unreplicatable in the lab.

I got wind of the stuff through my contacts with the athletes using it. The Soviet bloc athletes apparently go on the stuff for 10 days, then off for 10 days, and back on for the final two weeks prior to competition. Other athletes around the area of Tibet, India, and Turkey appear to have a more sophisticated method of administration. All swear by the stuff as an exceptional adaptogenic aid. It helps them to recover fast.

I dug deep to find the info on this new (yet ancient) remedy, folks. But don't bother yourself trying to find out about it. Much of the info "disappeared" after the Chernobyl disaster. Makes me wonder if they're keeping it under wraps.

There are some alternate names mumie goes by. There are also different varieties of mumie. Kopal (oriental name), lofor, colcother, or Prussian Red are a few of the names I've been able to uncover. Some of the species are Transbaikal Bagshune, Caucasian mumie, and balsam mumie.

Paleozoic though it may be, mumie has some rather interesting uses in our modern world.

1. Treatment of myocardial infarction (presumably because of its iron and copper content)
2. Increased melon growth (apparently a foliar spray of the stuff stimulates melon growth through effect on plant hormones)
3. Inhibition of tumor growth (neoplasm)
4. Liver function (liver mass, liver mitochondrial respiration, increased concentrations in the liver of protein, RNA, glycogen, and an inhibition of phosphorylation in the liver—all this amounts to a profound detoxification process in the liver)
5. An antidote to pesticide poisoning (related to improved liver function)

6. Treatment of stomach ulcers (through diffusing levels of adrenaline and nonadrenaline on the stomach walls)
7. A dehydration catalyst (significance as yet uncovered)
8. Protection of spleen following irradiation poisoning (depresses acid nuclease activity in the spleen)
9. Blood disorders (mumie apparently is able to normalize blood composition in experimental subjects suffering from anemia, leukopenia, and thrombocytopenia)
10. Bone regeneration (stimulates bone regeneration and enhanced DNA and RNA of bone cells—also stimulatory of bone healing in irradiated animals)
11. Blood-forming organs following acute doses of radiation (mumie stimulates blood formation and in general prevents irradiation poisoning)
12. As a general tonic (mumie improved the permeability of vessel walls, increased proliferation of reticuloendothelium, and produced measurable immunomorphological changes in the organism)
13. Antibacterial agent (mumie was found to be chemotherapeutically superior to penicillin in treating purulent and inflammatory diseases).

Wow! Does this stuff sound like an elixir from the Gods, or what! As for its usefulness in the general field of medicine, especially in treating radiation sickness, there can be no doubt as to its efficacy. As for athletes, well, as they say, the proof is in the pudding.

Only time will tell, however, whether this stuff is dangerous for otherwise healthy people. I, for one, have an abiding fear of trying to fool Mother Nature by ingesting anything that has the array of effects mumie appears to have. I suspect that, if this stuff ever becomes available here in the USA, you're going to see a lot of black marketeers tripping over themselves to procure the stuff.

37

DIBENCOZIDE:
New Kid on the Block

Ah, the Soviets! How many times have I written about some new training technique or an ergogenic substance, and had to give origin credit to the Soviets? Most of the time. Back in 1983 I traveled to Moscow to attend the Institute of Sport. I had heard so much about their training and had witnessed so many earth-shattering performances by their athletes that I simply had to go see for myself.

I befriended a couple of the weightlifters there and was fortunate to come out of the Soviet Union with some pretty esoteric stuff by 1983 standards. One of those substances was inosine, and you all know the tremendous impact that substance has had here in the U.S. since I uncovered it in *Muscle & Fitness.*

Another that I didn't uncover, because I thought it was a drug, was dibencozide. Apparently, it's either not considered a drug here in the U.S. or it simply hasn't been classified as yet by the FDA. In either case, it's now surfacing around the world of sports. In fact, it's being sold through mail order channels in some publications.

So, the Soviet lifter said to me, "Take this. Is good!"

"Good for what?" I asked, urging him to be specific.

"Is good for *you!*"

"Why?"

"You want to lift, no?"

"Yeah. *Heavy* iron. None of that peewee weight you Ruskies lift, either! I'm a *powerlifter!*"

"OK. You take this. Is good!" he reassured me, making a gesture like he was pumping a hypodermic needle into his butt.

End of discussion. So, I went to the only place I could find relevant information at the time: the package insert.

Activity: The metabolically active form of vitamin B_{12}. It favors protein biosynthesis (especially at the liver level). This drug is used as an anabolic agent in treatment of diseases of nutrition and during convalescence. It is used as a growth factor for children.

Dosage: orally. 1 mg once or twice daily.

Other names dibencozide goes by: cobamamidum (P), cobamamide (INN) (DCI) (DC.IT), coenzyme B_{12}.

Of course, each of the forms of dibencozide carries specialty names, depending on the manufacturer. Some of the more commonly found brands are: Aima, Anabasi, Betarin, Cobazina, Coben B_{12}, Extrabolin, Fortezim, Glade, Indusil, Marvizim, Maximal, Neocobol, Nutricon, Premier, Radiozima, Trillovit, Trofamide B_{12}, and Zidovit. That's just half the list you'll likely find if, like so many of the black marketeers around the world who deal in ergogenic drugs, you go abroad for the stuff.

Does it work? Well of course it does, specifically for the purposes for which it was intended. Whether it assists athletes (especially bodybuilders) in achieving augmentation of either protein synthesis or some form of growth factor, no one knows yet. The proverbial jury is still out. Chances are, the jury is in permanent recess, owing to the restrictiveness of the laws governing the use of human subjects. You'll only have someone's word that it works or not.

One thing is clear. The drug is being used by athletes in the belief that it masks steroids in the radio-immunoassay tests. Where a "spike" appears on the scope, the presence of dibencozide is reported to be overlapping with that of the steroid molecule, thereby "masking" it. Does it really work? I don't know for sure—just ask one of the scores of athletes who have attested to using the stuff for that purpose. But note, too, that sooner or later the testers will deduce that its existence in tests means steroid masking.

For that matter, ask them if their training has been any better while on it. Don't, however, assume that it works because they say it works.

Me? I'll try it, now that it's on the market. But bet that I'll do so only in close collaboration with my doctor. If it's deemed to be a drug by the (sometimes slow to act) FDA, I'll forget it and simply stick to the other forms of supplements out there that are tried, true, and (most importantly) safe.

As for contraindications, there are none reported in the existing literature, although the foreign pharmaceutical companies and the respective FDAs of those countries would probably not have opted to classify dibencozide as a drug were there not some inherent dangers associated with its misuse or abuse. I'd be careful.

Finally, another warning: As of this time, I know of no company, pharmaceutical or otherwise, that is manufacturing this substance in this country. That means one of two things: It's smuggled into the country illegally, or it's a bathtub brew. Again, I'd be careful.

38

EC FROM SIBERIA

Eleutherococcus senticosus (EC for short) is, by proclamation of the federal government, referred to in all health food stores and advertisements as "Siberian ginseng." This is unfortunate. Too many athletes have heard of, and have used, ginseng of various origins and species for countless millenia, and have profited little from its use.

This has given ginseng a bad name. Nowadays, only the diehard health food freaks use the stuff or attribute miracle status to its benefits. Few athletes interested in peak performance have opted to leave it on the list of supplements they must take because it simply doesn't deliver measurable (or more pointedly, immediate) benefits.

EC is different. I won't get into a pro/con polemic on ginseng in general. But I'd like to talk about EC because I feel strongly that it has some important, and immediately recognizable, benefits for bodybuilders and other athletes.

So, here we go again with the Soviet Connection. Why is it that every time I turn around, there's new stuff coming out of the Soviet Union? Are they that far ahead of the Western world? Or is it that they keep more of an open mind when it comes to sports-related protocol for training and nutrition? One thing is clear to me, after having traveled there and studied there. The Soviets want to win, and they want to win *badly*!

The Soviets derive an extract from a thorny creeping plant known as *Eleutherococcus senticosus*, which belongs to the family *Araliaceae*, the same family (although a distant cousin) of the ginseng root. That's why it's erroneously referred to as Siberian ginseng.

Its acceptance into the sports world was the culmination of many years of research at the USSR Academy of Science's Institute of Biologically Active Substances located in Vladivostok. The substance now is listed in the Russian Pharmacopeia along with a wide range of tonic drugs derived originally from Far Eastern traditional medicine, including ginseng, pantocrine, and schizandra.

The Russians discovered that EC increased stamina and performance, yet had fewer side effects than any other known stimulants. Prof. I. I. Brekhman, Director of the Vladivostok Institute, gave EC extract to a large group of athletes before a 10-mile race. Those taking EC chopped a full five minutes (average) from their times in comparison to a placebo group in the same race.

Encouraged with these findings, Brekhman then gave the EC extract to 1,500 athletes at the Lesgraft Institute of Physical Culture and Sports in Moscow. He reported that his earlier findings relating to endurance were corroborated. Further, he found that EC extract also improved reflexes and concentration, particularly in longer events. He also found that it was especially helpful in assisting athletes in tolerating greater training loads.

Further testing on mice (bearing far greater training loads and greater concentrations of the EC extract) was performed with similar results as those found in humans. The question as to what the active ingredient was remained unanswered, however, until Prof. G. B. Elyakov of the Moscow State University got his hands on the stuff.

Elyakov discovered that the main active ingredients of EC were glycosides containing phenolic or coumarinic groups. That is, the specific molecules were linked to a sugar molecule. Ginseng glycosides contain triterpenoid groups, which are analogues of steroids. Thus, EC is far less toxic than ginseng. Other antifatigue substances containing glycosides as the main active ingredient are:

- Aralia manshurica
- Acantopanax sessiliflorum
- Schizandra berries
- Rhodiola rosea
- Pantocrine from young deer antlers

I've taken EC for a while now, in the form of a tea (marketed as SPORTea by Ultimate Performance Products, Inc., from Denver). I find the substance to be rather remarkable in its effects on my training stamina. The stuff works. Since I'm about the farthest thing on this planet removed from an endurance athlete, I can't attest to its ability to chop seconds (or minutes, as the case may be) off my time in the mile. (I couldn't even *walk* that far!)

PART 6
THE PSYCHOLOGY OF POWER

39

THE OLYMPIAN MIND:
The Key to Athletic Success

One's goal in any sports endeavor obviously is to do as well as possible. Of course, there may be other sub-goals, such as fun, travel, socializing, and the like, but the single common denominator for all athletes is maximizing performance. Anything detracting from this goal, or tending to block one's attainment of it, is termed a *constraining factor*. The dedicated athlete, must, in the interest of successful competition, do all that is justified to remove these obstacles from the path toward success.

Indeed, it is said of the serious athlete that he or she will go to great extremes in the quest for methods or practices that assist in top level performances. Isn't it strange, then, that many athletes overlook some of the more pervasive constraining factors? Isn't it strange that many athletes haven't yet learned the basic fundamentals of efficient training? Stranger still is the fact that few athletes understand the true power of the mind. For, it is within one's psychological structure that some of the more devastating constraining factors reside. Yet, reflecting on some of the amazingly naive practices engaged in by many athletes, perhaps they aren't as ignorant of the power of the mind after all. For example, witness the fact that many athletes engage in the use of all sorts of stimulants, such as amphetamines, mood elevators, and the like. Witness the strange, ritualistic practices of some athletes prior to a competition such as having their face slapped silly, stomping up and down, screaming in mock anger, and the like. Presumably, these athletes have advanced to a primitive understanding of the fact that one's mental state plays an important part in successful performance. Primitive indeed, for, while the essence of understanding is there, for the most part, the average athlete hasn't a clue as to how to cope with these powerful constraining factors. In fact, in Western culture in general, there seems to be a marked tendency to avoid practices such as meditation, self-hypnosis, introspection, and other practices dealing with mind control. The average Western athlete is all too ready to take the lead of "legitimate" science and use the products of that science—drugs, fancy equipment, vitamins, to name a few. They tend to reject the so-called "Eastern" philosophies as either bunk or pseudoscientific methods, or, at the least, inapplicable to their efforts in sport.

Less than two decades ago, a tremendous amount of interest began to develop in the area of sport psychology. Much research (by "legitimate" scientists) has ensued, to the point where much is known about the functions of the mind insofar as they relate to athletic performance. The list on page 311 is a partial listing of some of the more applicable areas that sport psychologists have researched. All of these areas, and many more, are to be regarded as potential constraining factors, and therefore worthy of scrutiny by the truly dedicated athlete.

Needless to say, many of the above constraining factors are interrelated. When it comes to performance in sport, they are all interrelated in the sense that all of them weigh upon the individual to some extent, with the results being a mixture of positive, negative, and neutral factors in performance. All that an athlete does, including lifestyle, training methods, eating habits, sleeping habits, familial relations, choice of training partners, precompetition regimens, backstage behavior, and virtually all avenues of one's life, come to bear eventually upon performance. It is the truly astute athlete who is able to harness these states of being and to make them all positive forces.

Lest the reader misunderstand me, or misinterpret what I'm attempting to say here, let me state my position another way. Your psychological makeup (including all the factors listed in the table) determines how you approach training. These factors determine how you approach competition. They will modify your efforts in the gym and on the platform. They will, in large measure, determine the extent to which you succeed in sport. And, perhaps most importantly, they *can* be modified. The concept of behavior modification is not new—it has been practiced for as long as humans have been on this planet. There are many techniques that have been applied in the process of modifying behavior, ranging from Freudian psychoanalysis to Skinnerian and Pavlovian conditioning techniques. From drug therapy to transcendental meditation. Biofeedback to hypnosis. Meditation to mental rehearsal, lobectomy to stress reduction techniques. The list is endless.

POTENTIAL CONSTRAINING FACTORS IN SPORT THAT ARE RELATED TO PSYCHOLOGICAL STATES

Personality	Overarousal
Attitude	Underarousal
Attentional factors	Emotional state
Discipline	Depression
Social influences	Self-esteem
Anxiety	Self-concept
Fear of pain	Perception
Fear of failure	Intrinsic motivation
Fear of success	Extrinsic motivation
Group affiliation	Level of aspiration
Aggressivity	Cultural factors

ANXIETY AND OVERAROUSAL

Athletes unaffected by precontest jitters are rare indeed. The reasons for the onset of such anxiety are many, and include fear of pain, fear of failure, fear of success, fear of group (i.e., training partners) reprisal, and a host of other factors. Often too, just the mere thought of all-out exertion causes tremendous physiological responses to occur, such as increased heart rate, adrenaline flow, tenseness, and sleeplessness. Lumped together, and considered from the point in time just preceding a contest, these anxieties are called the *pre-start phenomenon*. Naturally, there are as many reasons for such a response as there are athletes. However, there are a few overriding considerations that one may address in attempting to eliminate such problems. Collectively, these methods are referred to as *stress reduction techniques*, or, more specifically, *arousal control techniques*.

Some stress (or anxiety) is inevitable (and perhaps desirable) in any sport endeavor. The trick, of course, is to control the dysfunctional aspects of stress and to attenuate the functional aspects. One must strive to mobilize his or her mental forces at the appropriate point in time.

Long-term tension (weeks or months before competition), *pre-start tension* (days before competition), and *start tension* (following competition) are all important in maximizing coming performance(s). Each is dealt with differently. The following guidelines should be given careful consideration by athletes preparing for competition:

1. Be careful not to peak too soon.

2. Be wary of activation during the pre-start period.
3. Avoid emotional contagion from one athlete to another in the start period.
4. Be aware of the emotional state of the athlete upon completion of a contest, because this level will ultimately affect readiness for the next contest.

Psyching refers to what is done in the start period, immediately preceding competition. Psyching an hour before, or for some athletes, even 15 minutes before, can be devastating. Tremendous tension builds to the point of escalating fatigue, and should be avoided at all costs. Simply removing oneself from the warmup area (or staying to oneself), and concentrating on some of the techniques of "mind control" is the best way I know for avoiding start tension.

Immediately before competition (within five minutes, and preferably during the last two minutes), an athlete must psych himself or herself maximally in readiness for the effort to come. Again, athletes everywhere have their own techniques for doing this. It is critically important to maximal performance that the appropriate amount of arousal is welled up in the athlete. For the few who may have technique problems, too much arousal will be detrimental to performance, and "calming down" procedures may be advised.

Dr. Joseph Oxendine (1970) lists sports according to the amount of arousal necessary in each in the table on page 313.

I have found that, among the truly great athletes, the psyching technique of choice is almost always exemplified by outward calm. No jumping, face-slapping, growling in animal-like fierceness, or howling. Inside, however, a raging storm is taking place. Inside, in the confines of the subconscious, trickles of primordial jungle instinct become raging torrents, escaping into the conscious. So intense are the resultant emotions that there is no room for any other thoughts— surrounding noise, other people, the weight on the bar, and even pain are all but mere shadows of reality, and the singleminded effort of movement predominates.

The constraints mentioned in this article are powerful. They can cause success or failure, and can impinge to an extent even greater than any physical preparedness. It is largely up to the athlete to alter states of mind to positively affect performance.

A powerful constraint is met in considering the *emotional state of the athlete*. All athletes are familiar with the term "psych" and each has his own peculiar method of achieving this state of arousal. Whether the increased arousal is induced by thinking of sex, getting mad at the weight, feeling the impact of the audience's presence, or doing it for Old Glory is inconsequential. They all appear to work. Other methods include getting slapped on the face, smelling ammonia, the use of all forms of uppers, and other strange, ritualistic

OPTIMUM AROUSAL LEVELS FOR SOME TYPICAL SPORT SKILLS

Level of Arousal	Sport Skills
5 (extremely excited)	football blocking and tackling weightlifting running 220 and 440
4	sprints and long distance running shot put broad jump wrestling judo swim racing
3	basketball most gymnastics high jumping boxing
2	baseball pitching and batting fancy diving fencing quarterback soccer
1 (slight arousal)	archery and bowling field goal kicking golf putts and short irons basketball free throw
0 (normal state)	

Adapted from Oxendine, J., Emotional arousal in sport, *Quest*, 13, p. 23-30, 1970. Oxendine elaborates on each state, indicating that #1 is only slightly above normal arousal, and #5 approaches "blind rage."

practices. Generally, the mechanisms behind the faciliatory response are increased secretion of adrenaline, intensification of nervous discharge of the muscles, and irradiated nervous impulse from surrounding muscles not actively involved in the movement.

Extreme depression, over-arousal, or fear are emotional responses that often tend to inhibit maximal performance. It goes without saying that the astute athlete will find his or her own means to achieve appropriate levels of arousal.

Self-esteem is yet another powerful constraint that must be dealt with. Success begets success. Some forms of sport call it "momentum." Self-esteem, in such sports, is incredibly flexible. One minute an athlete hates himself (or his team), and the next minute, perhaps as a result of an exceptional play, his self-esteem shoots way up, thereby facilitating his subsequent performance. The increased confidence appears to have "disinhibited" him.

For the athlete, however, self-esteem is far less transitory, and is developed over months, even years! For some, it never comes. Most of you will recognize this example: Picture the lifter entering a meet, confident of success, only to learn later that Bridges was entered! Wow, what a blow. The lifter says to himself, "Well, I can't win now. I'm nowhere near good enough to beat that guy." . . . and so it goes. Better that he had said, "Well, I'll take a close second *THIS* time, but he won't beat me next year! I'm potentially better than he is, so now I'm gonna prove it!" The reader can, I'm sure, see the point of this discourse. The challenge is, that if you have the guts to utter the second response, you *must* truly believe it yourself! The reality of being beaten is omnipresent in sport. For every winner, there are many losers. Most losers push on because they *truly* believe that soon they'll be the champ. Others may continue because they enjoy what they're doing, win or lose. That's all right too. But, while self-esteem may be present in abundance, it is not the kind that will someday tender a winning attitude.

Self-esteem has a marked tendency to result in disinhibition. High self-esteem will cause a mobilization of various forces designed to avoid loss of face (to the audience or to oneself). This "fear of losing" syndrome is a major force behind every champion I have ever known.

Fear, in general, however, causes generally inhibitory responses, much unlike that kind of fear experienced by the champion. When a weight is lifted, sensory input tells one whether it "feels light" or "feels heavy." In fact, even before the weight is lifted, past experience tells one whether the weight on the bar is capable of jeopardizing one's integrity. Strength is increased if the importance of the lift is great, or if the effort involved is recognized (from prior experience) to be nondestructive. Most other situations result in inhibition, especially if one fears for his or her well-being.

Concentration is another constraining factor, for without the ability to lift maximum weights without conscious thought of the movement patterns, the weight on the bar, or the actions of surrounding judges or spotters, the lifter is doomed to failure. The athlete cannot be thinking of such extraneous factors while putting forth maximal effort. Such cerebration is referred to as "paralysis by analysis."

The best performances are nearly always those that are executed below the threshold of total consciousness. Lifters breaking records consistently report that they lifted without knowing quite what took place, or without any conscious reaction to their surroundings. They had, essentially, retreated to their own inner mind, where there is no pain, no discomfort, and where only positive forces loom. All other factors require cerebration to some degree, and this is exactly what the champion must not do. Such intense concentration comes only to those who are totally self-confident, have high self-esteem, are motivated, and well-trained. Such a state of mind is an eclectic response to well-devised mental conditioning practices.

40

SUSTAINING MOTIVATION IN TRAINING

"C'mon, let's go train!"

"Naw, got a date."

"But, you *have* to train because my car isn't running and I need a ride to the gym!"

And so it goes in the typically mundane world of the strength athlete. Hundreds of similar scenarios could be constructed to get the point across that there are more motivating forces in your life than just getting to the top in the bodybuilding world. Sex, friendship, will to excel, obligation—these are the competing factors from the above scenario. There are, of course, an infinite number in any athlete's life, and the exact course of action taken at any given time depends on the relative strengths of the many competing factors operating simultaneously. Your job, if sports greatness is paramount in your life, is to ensure that the incentive to train is the strongest of all the competing factors in your life.

This is no easy task, even if you are already highly motivated to excel. The demands on you are great, and involve so many factors—such as diet, sleep, medical assistance, money, scientific training, and much more—that it's a safe bet that no athlete has ever achieved the ideal state of training because of the competing factors in his or her life.

There is a very healthy amount of scientific research behind motivation in sports. Much of it pertains directly to you as an athlete. Many athletes and aficionados (coaches and exercise physiologists) of the sport see *motivation* as the *primary problem* in achieving peak athletic performance. This chapter deals with one aspect of motivation—incentive.

WHAT IS INCENTIVE?

David Birch and Joseph Veroff, two internationally prominent psychologists, teamed up in 1966 to write what is widely regarded as one of the most definitive studies of human motivation. They identified seven major incentive systems that collectively account for almost all of man's goal-directed behavior. Through an extensive review of the research on motivation to that date, they postulated that a motive, the incentive itself, will direct a person's *immediate* goal-oriented activity only if that motive is the strongest of all other competing motives. Birch and Veroff's incentive systems are as follows:

- Regulation of bodily experiences (sensory incentive system)
- Reacting to new stimuli (curiousity incentive system)
- Depending on social contact with others (affiliative incentive system)
- Reacting to frustration by others (agressive incentive system)
- Evaluating their own performance (achievement incentive system)
- Withstanding the influence of others (power incentive system)
- Operating on their own (independence incentive system)

Strength athletes, like any other class of athletes, need to train. They need to carefully regulate their diet, and they must also tend to other aspects of contest preparation that trancend the confines of the gym. They are therefore subject to the above-listed incentives, and the one that is the strongest wins. The important job of regulating these incentives so that the appropriate one surfaces as the strongest at the right time can be a real challenge. It is a challenge that only the most disciplined athlete can meet.

But it can be done—it *must* be done if championship status is your long-range goal. And that brings up an interesting point of discussion. Implicit in Birch and Veroff's paradigm of goal-directed behavior is the notion that long-range goals can only be achieved if short-term (immediate) goals are regulated effectively.

The above notion bears repeating: You cannot expect to become all that you can become unless you set short-term goals and manipulate your life to the extent that you systematically achieve each one. Each immediate goal must be fully realized, and the sequential attainment of these immediate goals will, if thought out carefully, lead you down the path to championship status. A closer look at each of Birch and Veroff's incentive systems will illustrate how you can effectively manage your day-to-day goal orientation.

The Sensory Incentives

Tasting, hearing, smelling, seeing, and feeling are the main sensory experiences for man. Pain is perhaps the most negative sensation for athletes because it generally causes an *avoidance* response. In the gym, under heavy iron, pain is commonplace. You put up with it because you know the outcome will be more pleasant than the temporary discomfort. But, in truth, don't you sometimes shy away from exercises because of an avoidance reaction to what you know will be painful? If you're normal you probably do, and more often than you'd like to admit.

Hunger is another negative sensory experience that all athletes have experienced. So hunger, like pain, is often avoided. Other sensory experiences (both positive and negative) common to athletes are the pumped sensation, physical effort, fatigue, and tension. Top athletes learn how to make these sensory experiences work for them rather than against them. They learn how to make them positive rather than negative incentives.

Curiosity Incentives

Curiosity plays a major role in children's pursuits of new activities, and research shows that the same curiosity stays with most adults, albeit in the form of an incentive to optimize stimulus complexity. Relating this concept to sports is quite simple and straightforward. Continually engaging in a boring, simple training regimen becomes a negative incentive over a short time. Get into the *science* of your sport! Make it challenging! Alter your routine periodically; take advantage of what science has to offer and avoid boredom!

Achievement Incentives

Sport psychologists generally agree that the incentive to achieve in sports is probably the "master" incentive. Two important achievement orientations show up. The first and most common is the drive to enjoy success. The second is the drive to succeed. In the first case, an athlete who experiences success (at the local contest level, for example), is spurred on to greater things. Even after attaining success, he (or she) continues because the orientation is to continue to experience success. The other is the drive an athlete displays in getting to the top and then quitting. This drive to succeed is immediately quenched upon achieving success, and further participation is no longer meaningful to the athlete. He or she has finished the task.

There appear to be three main categories of achievement incentives in sport: competence, a sense of effectiveness, and masculine identity. *Competence* in sports is generally judged on the basis of comparison with others in the group, and success is dependent upon what the individual's goals are. So, while related, competence to win at any given level in sports may not signal success. It is important to keep your goals clear, and to avoid the pitfall of letting winning or losing cloud your own judgment of your level of competence.

Your *sense of effectiveness* can be modified by success and failure. It is important for you, particularly if you are a beginning athlete, to know your own level of competence and to set your sights on long-range goals through successfully achieving short-range goals. In this way, your own sense of effectiveness will remain positive.

Many sports in our culture achieved the popularity they have because they provide the participants a chance at improving their *masculine identity.* Girls in our culture have been told for generations that successful women are not achievement oriented—they must learn to do the things women do. Boys, on the other hand, have been told that achievement is closely linked with masculinity, and that success as a man depended heavily upon their fostering a masculine image. For good or bad, this age-old stereotype is changing, and more and more women are entering the sport area expecting the *feminine* image to be enhanced. Boys and men, of course, continue to participate for reasons associated with the masculine image they were taught was important.

Affiliation Incentives

The need for reassurance is perhaps the strongest incentive for a person to train with another person because they can offer a measure of self-worth and social acceptance. Forming this kind of a "mutual admiration" arrangement is good, and fosters greater achievement incentive as well.

It is a well-known paradox in sport psychology that those of us who are unable to love or like another person are those who seek affiliation the most, whereas those who are loved or liked the most are those who do not depend on affiliation for a source of reassurance or feelings of self-worth. Most good coaches know this, and try to accommodate the person who needs affiliation as well as the person who doesn't.

You should try to remain aware and sensitive to the needs of your training partner (s) because ultimately their achievements will reflect on your own. If you're in it together, then work together!

Aggression Incentives

In its purest form, aggression is defined as being present when the intentional destruction or injury of another person occurs or is sought. Of course, such aggression has no place in sports, and in fact is rare in organized athletics. Frustration, resentment, or pain are typical causes for negative forms of aggression to appear in the gym.

HOW TO SUSTAIN YOUR MOTIVATION

Perhaps the most effective means of ensuring continued motivation in sports is to set short-term goals. Your short-term goals should ultimately lead you to your long-range goal, but be prepared to cope with occasional setbacks in the way. Here's how:

- Know yourself. Learn about the major motivating forces in your life, and adjust them to complement each other rather than to act negatively or continually compete with one another.
- Establish a schedule for training and avoid interrupting influences.
- Learn how to make pain a positive factor in training—key on the end result rather than the temporary discomfort.
- Feel the exhilaration of the pumped sensation, the joy of effort, and the enjoyment of all-out training fatigue—they are signals of goal attainment.
- Make your training a challenge in itself. Allow the fascinating complexity of the art and science of your sport to totally captivate your interest. Get into it! Construct and reconstruct your regimen as your knowledge of the sport grows. This will help you to avoid boredom and also to get the most out of your training for faster goal attainment.

Text continues on page 320.

A form of "instrumental" aggression is useful, however, where behavior is intensified in order to achieve a particular goal. Keep your short-term goals in mind, and pursue them vigorously.

Independence Incentives

The need some athletes feel to "do it on their own" is referred to as independence. However, a complex interplay of situational factors often occurs that tends to modify this behavioral pattern. Independent athletes often interrupt their concentration or independence incentive when they feel a need to be evaluated—as in a contest. Also, curiosity incentives often replace independence incentives when the athlete is confronted with a different (competing) incentive. Highly independent athletes tend to lose interest in the sport more easily than those who have a greater affiliative incentive. Thirdly, highly independent athletes who continually fail (in their own self-evaluation) even-

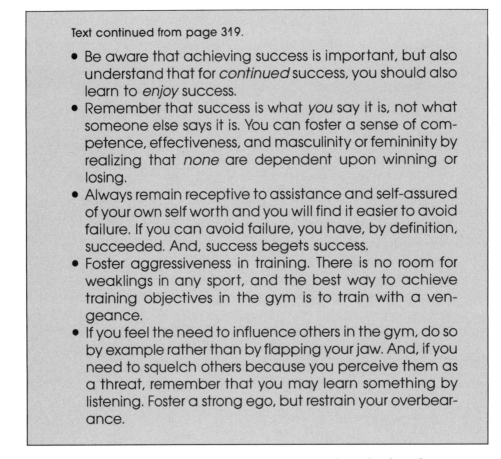

Text continued from page 319.

- Be aware that achieving success is important, but also understand that for *continued* success, you should also learn to *enjoy* success.
- Remember that success is what *you* say it is, not what someone else says it is. You can foster a sense of competence, effectiveness, and masculinity or femininity by realizing that *none* are dependent upon winning or losing.
- Always remain receptive to assistance and self-assured of your own self worth and you will find it easier to avoid failure. If you can avoid failure, you have, by definition, succeeded. And, success begets success.
- Foster aggressiveness in training. There is no room for weaklings in any sport, and the best way to achieve training objectives in the gym is to train with a vengeance.
- If you feel the need to influence others in the gym, do so by example rather than by flapping your jaw. And, if you need to squelch others because you perceive them as a threat, remember that you may learn something by listening. Foster a strong ego, but restrain your overbearance.

tually seek assistance from others, allowing their high achievement incentive to come to the fore. If they were more attuned to their needs, such assistance could have been available to them long before failure became such a problem.

Power Incentives

It is a cliché in sports that athletes have whopping egos. The need to exert influence over others and the need to remain insensitive or unreceptive to the advice of others is, by definition, a power incentive. Personality clashes in the gym are frequent, and they often arise from athletes who resist advice as well as impose themselves on others.

Perhaps a more pervasive example of the power incentive operating in sports is when, for reasons of peer acceptance, familial acceptance, or public acceptance, a person engages in the sport. Status, recognition, or prestige are powerful motivators, and if that's your bag, so be it. But being dependent upon some form of social evaluation must ultimately cease—self-evaluation is also critical, and must be fostered for continued success and perhaps especially for continued enjoyment in the sport.

CONCLUSIONS

Your physical ability as an athlete can be likened to a machine. But the power that makes it work is *motivation*! Although seven different incentive systems were treated in this chapter you must bear in mind that they are not independent—they often work both for and against one another in determining your course of action. While skill, ability, or genetic predisposition are important factors in your athletic success, the intangible factor that makes them work in winning is motivation. Just as there can be no performance without ability, there can be no performance without motivation.

Judge yourself on the basis of these seven incentive systems, and know yourself better, and how to achieve your long-term goals in sports.

41

CONCENTRATE TO WIN

I ain't talking orange juice when I say concentrate to win. This is an age of fast foods, fast sex, fast travel, fast credit. For you to also make it a time of fast workouts because of your short attention span may be a tempting solution to your boredom with training.

Your ability to concentrate is just as controllable as is your ability to get big. Moreover, you won't have to subject yourself to agonizing mental gymnastics or to Siegelesque mental programming. Concentrating is an easy thing to do. So, concentrate for a few minutes, and I'll tell you how you can concentrate better during training.

Let's see. Where was I? (*I'm* not concentrating.)

Oh yeah, the brain. Your brain is constantly screening information sent there by your senses of sight, smell, touch, and so forth. Your brain is responsible for deciding what's important and what's not. That's how you stay alive. The ability to concentrate, then, is only of secondary importance to your survival, and most of you can only do it for about 20–30 minutes at best.

Your ability to concentrate, to focus, to pay selective attention to specifically targeted stimuli, involves many levels of brain functioning. It's not simply a task of your brain's "thinking" centers.

This recent discovery is an important one in understanding how best to improve concentration skills. The arousal center in your brain—a bundle of nerve fibers called the reticular activating system—likes variety in the incoming stimuli. It hates being bored, so to speak, and therefore does not work very well with routine or regimented tasks.

322

Going to the gym and performing well-learned reps and set patterns isn't the best way to stay aroused, according to recent research on the brain's arousal centers. Consider that in industry, where such routine and boring tasks are more the norm than the exception, it is important to understand the dynamics of improving concentration skills. Doing so would dramatically improve productivity and decrease the incidence of mistakes and industrial accidents.

The same is true in the gym.

SEVEN COMPONENTS OF CONCENTRATION

Scientists have discovered the psychological components that influence one's ability to concentrate well beyond the 30-minute norm. These factors are hunger, noise, anxiety, time of day, pace, complexity, novelty, and feedback.

Hunger

Remember how tired and lethargic you felt after your last big meal? Not a very conducive state for concentrating, is it? No, it isn't, and scientists have found as much as a 16% drop in performance of repetitive tasks following meals.

Noise

Noise can be very distracting. However, just the right amount of noise can improve your vigilance. Noise, according to several studies done recently by industrial psychologists, creates a mild stress, which your brain's arousal center tries to overcome.

Anxiety

Noise is anxiety-producing stress. So is excessive room temperature. In fact, the very act of having to concentrate is anxiety-producing. According to one study, this fact explains why people in general tend to avoid tasks that require concentration and instead opt for a quick and easy way through the task at hand.

Time of Day

Your body operates on an internal clock. Bodily processes such as core temperature, hormone release, perception of pain and arousal, all operate according to a rather predictable rhythm called the *circadian cycle*. Psychologists have categorized concentration tasks into two groups: successive tasks and simultaneous tasks. A successive task, one that relies on your memory, is best performed in the morning hours. Simultaneous tasks, which do not require memory functions, are best done in the afternoon.

Pace, Complexity, and Novelty

Performing a task too quickly leads to errors, while going too slowly initiates boredom. Similarly, if a task is too easy or difficult, productivity breaks down. Keeping a routine day in and day out promotes boredom too; but too frequently altering routine causes errors and confusion. It seems that by finding an equitable blend of working speed, difficulty, and change you can improve your ability to concentrate on your task.

Feedback

When you have instant information about your effectiveness while performing a task, you will tend to perform that task much more effectively.

HOW TO UTILIZE THESE COMPONENTS

Not wishing to tax your ability to concentrate (save it for the gym), let me spell out how you can benefit from this information.

- Stay psychologically stressed during training. You can do this by establishing a deadline for your workout (say, for example, one hour or less).
- Work out with noxious music or other kinds of anxiety-producing noise. Avoid Bach or Sinatra like the plague unless they're noxious to you.
- In addition to its beneficial effect on growth hormone production, a very warm gym (near 80°F) will produce anxiety and thereby force you to concentrate.
- Most athletes already know that eating big meals before training is stupid. However, since it also makes it difficult for you to concentrate, it bears repeating to avoid them before training (or any other time for that matter). What's the phrase? Stay hungry!
- Do your training primarily in the morning if possible. Your "motor memory" is stimulated to remember your previous workouts, your strength levels, and other important clues and cues as to how best to derive benefit from your training efforts. Afternoon workouts are OK for mundane, otherwise boring work such as midsection or calves.
- Change your routine as often as practical, and inject variety into your training. Heavy weights, light weights, high reps, low reps, fast movements, slow movements—this is the best way to train anyway, because you'll get maximum stimulation of all cellular

Hatfield "zones in" for the big lift.

elements for maximum growth. And the bonus is that you'll find it easier to maintain a high level of concentration.

- Talk to yourself. If you think that you'll look foolish doing so, then have your partner talk to you. Constant feedback on how your form is, how your effort is, reminding you of important techniques, and so forth is the kind of feedback that will improve your powers of concentration.
- Use the mirrors for feedback. When performing a very heavy squat or clean and jerk, most lifters find that their concentration is broken by watching themselves in the mirror. But for most athletes, this kind of stimulation will improve your concentration, not break it.

42

THE STRESS RESPONSE:
A Nutritional Approach to Coping

"Argh-h-h-h!" you mutter. "Time to go train!" Not an uncommon response in the high-pressure world of one-upmanship sports competition. Training gets tedious, and stresses related to having to improve week by week are immense.

Very soon such a response has a profound impact on your training readiness. Your energy levels are of critical importance before, during, and immediately following training because it takes high energy to inflict high-intensity stress on your muscles, your rate of recovery, and your ability to replace spent energy stores. Growth can only occur if you've been successful at replacing spent energy substrate.

So, stressed out over the impending severity of your training session, you drag yourself to the gym. There you encounter other zombies going through the ritual of up, down, up, down, up, down. It pisses you off that your training partner is late, there's a kid using the weights you want to use, and your cuts aren't showing as well as you'd like. Then there's the guy over in the corner hitting on the woman you've had your eye on for the past two weeks.

Take stock of what's happening, man! Let me sum it up for you here. It's called the stress response, and it takes a deathly toll on training energy, recovery, and growth over time.

1. Your brain sends impulses throughout your body to create a state of preparedness.
2. Your heart pumps faster and with stronger beats so that your body will have more fuel.

3. Your muscles (especially those required for fast movement or great strength) fill with oxygenated blood.
4. Your spleen contracts, forcing increased blood circulation.
5. Your eyesight sharpens because of optic nerve stimulation.
6. Your sense of smell sharpens because of stimulation of your olfactory nerve.
7. Your adrenal gland pumps adrenaline throughout your body.
8. Your peripheral blood vessels contract, especially in your face (causing a "flushed" appearance).
9. Further stimulation of your adrenal gland (especially the adrenal medulla) causes a heightening of blood sugar for quicker energy.
10. Air passages dilate, allowing deeper breathing.
11. Your pupils dilate.
12. Muscle chemicals are released that reduce fatigue.
13. Chemicals in your blood accelerate the coagulation function (in case you're injured).
14. Nerve impulses from your cerebral cortex signal your bladder to evacuate.

This mobilization of bodily functions all adds up to what scientists call the "fight or flight" syndrome. The nasty thing about it is that your body doesn't recognize that the psychological stress you're experiencing isn't potentially damaging to your person. All it knows is what the brain tells it. You're stressed out, and you've been stressed out for a very long time.

Can you imagine what sort of long-term effect these manifestations can have on your energy levels? Your ability to train? Your ability to recover from training? Your growth?

Take a look at the accompanying table, and you'll observe the many signs of stress. Go through them and determine if you've been under stress. You may not even know that you're stressed out, you've been living with it for so long. It may be that you have assumed that "that's the way I am."

It ain't, fellow iron freaks, and it's time you did something about it. The long-term effects of stress are damaging to your health, of course. Everyone knows that. But the short-term effects of stress are damaging to your training, and that's what this chapter is all about. Let's look at your energy requirements for training with an eye toward the effects stress can have on them.

Energy for Training

In all the world of creatures and critters out there, the only substance that can make them move is ATP. It is the universal spark that ignites. It is what makes muscles contract. Period. Nothing else can do it, and without it you are rendered virtually immobile.

SIGNS OF STRESS

Physiological signs of stress include:

- Increased cholesterol level in the blood (detected by laboratory results)
- High blood pressure
- Rapid pulse
- Loss of appetite
- Tendency to overeat (especially in response to stressful situations)
- Queasiness in the stomach ("butterflies")
- Nausea
- Heartburn
- Eyestrain
- Fluttering motions of the eyes
- Tightened muscles in the neck and jaw
- Grinding of the teeth
- Clenching of the jaw
- Cold hands
- Sweating palms
- Excessive sweating elsewhere on the body
- Contraction and tightness of general body muscles
- Jerky movement
- Irregular or shallow breathing
- Strained voice, often becoming high-pitched
- Hunching posture (resulting from excessive tightening of shoulder muscles)
- Rigid spine, preventing fluid movement
- Tight forehead muscles, causing change in facial expression
- Contraction of muscles in fingers and toes, causing them to curl
- Headache
- Twitching and trembling
- Dryness of mouth
- Lack of interest in sex
- Frigidity
- Impotence
- Menstrual disorders
- Nervousness, including the tendency to be frightened or startled easily
- Excessive belching
- Chronic diarrhea
- Chronic constipation

- Chronic indigestion (including belching, heartburn, and nausea)
- Weakness and fatigue
- Dizziness
- Tendency to faint easily
- Fainting spells preceded by nausea
- Difficulty in falling asleep
- Inability to remain asleep during the night
- Inability to sit still
- Tendency to tire easily
- Muscle spasms
- Feeling of fullness without eating
- Inability to cry
- Tendency to burst into tears at slight provocation or for no reason at all

Mental symptoms of stress include:

- Depression
- Irritability
- The desire to escape from people or things or situations
- Strong urge to cry
- Impulsive behavior that is incompatible with normal patterns of behavior
- Feelings of anxiety, sometimes vague or ill defined
- Inability to think clearly
- Inability to make simple decisions
- Inability to solve simple problems
- Lack of desire to participate fully in life
- Feelings of self-destruction
- Impatience
- Tendency to be extremely critical of others
- Meticulousness about surroundings and possessions
- Tendency to be a perfectionist
- Tendency to lose temper
- Inability to relax physically
- Feelings of mild panic
- Frustration and concern over health (especially worries over minor aches and pains)
- Fear of death
- Fear of disease (especially cancer)
- Fear of insanity or mental illness
- Fear of being alone

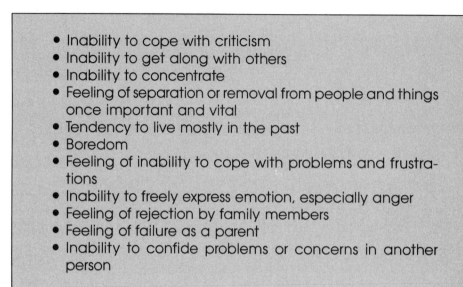

- Inability to cope with criticism
- Inability to get along with others
- Inability to concentrate
- Feeling of separation or removal from people and things once important and vital
- Tendency to live mostly in the past
- Boredom
- Feeling of inability to cope with problems and frustrations
- Inability to freely express emotion, especially anger
- Feeling of rejection by family members
- Feeling of failure as a parent
- Inability to confide problems or concerns in another person

Fortunately for you, there are more ways than one to coax your stressed-out body to manufacture ATP. Some are efficient and some are not. For workout energy, and the period immediately following workout, it makes sense to tap into those methods that are most efficient.

To get a rough idea how your muscles manufacture ATP, have a look at the table on page 57. You will see that the processes that utilize the raw materials for both anaerobic energy and aerobic energy hinge on two critical materials: oxygen and muscle glycogen. In bodybuilding, where short, intense training bouts are more often recommended, the aerobic pathway of energy supply is of little importance. But the anaerobic pathway (ATP) and the glycolytic pathway (glycogen) are crucial.

Muscle glycogen supplies will not be abundant enough for your grueling workouts if you've been tense and stressed out over several hours, or you haven't been eating the right foods or supplements. There are ways of coping with stress so that tense muscles and mobilized bodily resources won't deplete you of precious energy.

Let's take a close look at both how and what you should eat to fuel your furnaces for workout energy so your workouts will yield dividends in growth.

WHAT TO EAT

First, you know that carbohydrates are necessary for a truly efficient source of muscle glycogen. But did you know that all carbohydrates are not the same? No indeed! Some convert to blood glucose too rapidly, causing your insulin to spiral upward with it. Then, in the middle of your workout you crash. Bam! No energy, lethargy sets in, and your workout loses intensity. Worse, however, you have lost your ability to recover from your workout, and that will affect your growth hormone output in the hour or so immediately following training. That means little or no growth, and your training efforts have literally been in vain.

Other carbohydrates, however, convert to blood glucose slowly, and your blood sugar levels remain constant and supply your muscles with needed glycogen throughout your workout. As you begin slowly to replace spent muscle glycogen during the period immediately following training, your blood sugar levels begin to come down and you are able to achieve a far more effective growth hormone response. That's because your insulin levels have come down, too.

The result is far greater growth potential from your training efforts.

The rate at which foods are converted to blood glucose is called the *glycemic index*. This method of rating foods was developed to assist diabetics in their efforts to control blood sugar and attendant insulin response. It works for nondiabetics the same way, and has become one of the cornerstones of modern training methodology for serious athletes.

Here's the scenario for those of you who are just beginning to benefit from weight training:

1. Your preworkout meal should be eaten about 1½–2 hours before workout.
2. It should consist of low glycemic index carboyhydrate sources (e.g., beans, fruit) and high quality protein.
3. About one hour before workout take your growth hormone releasers (e.g., L-ornithine and/or L-arginine).
4. Before workout take inosine for rapid ATP regeneration.
5. Immediately before or during training you may wish to supplement your workout energy stores with a good quality energy workout drink, but not too much of it.
6. Somewhere during this process of preworkout preparation, or immediately following training, use the BCAAs to boost your amino acid pool for enhanced recovery.
7. Wait at least 45 minutes after training before eating again, to ensure that you have benefited from a GH response. (Remember, eating will send blood sugar levels upward, thereby inhibiting a GH response, so it's necessary to wait.)

The bottom line is this, folks: Stress can limit the effectiveness of your training. You should take steps to reduce the stress in your lives. When you can't, it's even more critical than usual to ensure that your preworkout energy stores are tended to.

43

WHY GREAT ATHLETES FAIL

A trip to any top gym in the nation will convince you that there are guys out there who should be counted among the superstars. But they aren't. There's some real talent in the world of competitive sports, and even more in the gyms. Yet the list of "could've beens" never diminishes. Why?

"Who cares!" you may challenge. "Why waste your time with guys who ain't got the guts to put their egos on the line?"

You may ask the same question of a guy who races cars. He has a car that could have beat anything out there, except that it needs a tune-up. So he doesn't race it. Sound stupid? Maybe he doesn't know that it needs one. I truly believe that there are just a few small details that some of the potentially great athletes may not have recognized, and which, once tended to, could put them over the top.

Perhaps you're one of those guys. Read on with an open mind. Be introspective. Be self-analytical. Maybe you're the guy who can knock off a current world champion..

Why Smart People Fail is a recent book by Carole Hyatt and Linda Gottlieb (Simon & Schuster, 1987). The authors traveled across the United States interviewing people who survived major career defeats. From what I read, it became very clear to me that most of the athletes I've known who truly should've become great didn't because of one or more of the six major reasons for defeat written about in this insightful book.

LACK OF SOCIAL SKILLS

Your sports career will invariably involve other people—judges, magazine interviewers, lawyers and agents, training partners, and coaches. People who have a high social intelligence know how to take criticism, admit mistakes, and to be sensitive toward the views of others. That doesn't mean you have to humble yourself or to defer so completely to the whims or views of others that you become a wimp. What it means is that you should acknowledge your mistakes and learn from them. If people don't like you, they'll go out of their way to help you fail.

The very common "I don't need them!" certainly won't endear you to those who could very well assist you in your career. Don't let a mammoth ego get in your way. A strong ego, yes—but keep it in check with intelligence and good manners. It's easy to see how many athletes fall into the trap of feeling godlike because, in the eyes of admiring bystanders, they are. Don't fall into that trap.

WRONG FIT

Examine everything you do. Examine who you train with, who your coach is, the gym you train in, the kind of training program you follow—everything. Look at your diet. Look even more carefully at the peaking routine you use to prepare yourself for competition. Perhaps you're suffering from ill-fitting surroundings, training regimen, or social climate. For you to be a success at anything in your life—not just in sports—you'll find the way easier if you fit your abilities, your personality, your values, your work ethic, and your physical strengths to your environment.

ABSENCE OF COMMITMENT

You may, when old and gray, say "I could've been great." By then, however, it'll be too late to ask yourself whether you cushioned yourself against failure by not really trying. If you don't put yourself on the line *now*, you can expect to hear yourself utter those words later.

Often the reason for not trying is that you don't really believe you can make it in the big time. This lack of self esteem breeds halfhearted training. All sorts of imaginary fears of failure creep in. If you continue to compete in the "little league" you'll never have the spark needed to take the chance and compete against the big boys.

TOO SCATTERED TO FOCUS

It never ceases to amaze me how many guys fall prey to gym mythology about what kind of exercises to do. Often I see guys doing literally every exercise in the book for each body part. This practice stems from the mistaken belief that what one exercise misses, the others will get. In itself, this may not seem bad, but actually several bad things happen. First, you forget that intelligent training demands that you focus on weaknesses. Second, doing so many exercises means you're probably overtraining. Third, you're spending too much time in the gym and therefore probably not benefiting from any significant growth hormone reponse to your training efforts.

Lack of focus is often seen in other training realms as well. Maybe you're too wrapped up in your job. Perhaps you're spending too much time on other things when you should be training. Maybe you're just trying to do too many things at once.

Focus! Set your priorities straight! Recognize your limitations and organize your life (and training) in order to eliminate weaknesses and emphasize your strengths.

HIDDEN BARRIERS

The most damaging of all problems that potentially great athletes face is the belief that they're already good enough. They don't recognize their weaknesses. They don't see the need to change their training regimen or their diet. They simply don't see the hidden barrier keeping them from success, and can't figure out why.

Hanging on to the status quo, even after you have failed to win, is comfortable because it's an easy way to preserve your ego.

To avoid such barriers, force yourself to explore options. Be truthful in your analysis of your situation. Regain control of your future.

BAD LUCK

Bad things happen: You injure yourself, lose your job, your car is stolen, you encounter financial difficulties, your girl friend up and leaves. We all suffer such bad luck from time to time.

You do have options, however, even in the midst of uncontrollable circumstances. Remember these things: Don't blame yourself for bad luck (assuming that it was indeed luck and not of your own doing), and look for alternatives that will help you to recover from ill fortune.

Remember that despite adversity in your training or competition, whether it be in the form of lousy officiating or lack of financial support, you can find a way. You *must* find a way. Excusing yourself because of bad luck is convenient, but it's totally unnecessary and *never* excusable.

Perhaps the most important point I can make is that everyone fails from time to time. Don't let that worry you. Intelligent people learn from failure.

EPILOGUE:
Training Wisdom

Vince Lombardi was a helluva man. Why, in his day, Ol' Vince's very presence would inspire an entire platoon of quasi humans to perform magnificent feats of sport prowess. He was a winner. By today's standards, however, Vince was a dinosaur.

Consider this. Vince is known for his statement, "Winning isn't everything, it's the *only* thing." That's what he said. Perhaps they were prophetic words back when he was alive, and Lord knows many top coaches believe those words to this day.

But we've learned much since then, a point to which I shall return later. Let's peruse the gym wall slogans around the country, and have a look at what else Vince and his disciples have had to say about sports, training, and success in general over the years. You won't be bored. Your training efforts, after all, are "ten percent perspiration and ninety percent inspiration."

The wisdom of the ages is contained in the Bible. I suspect Vince was a student thereof.

> In a race, everyone runs but only one person gets the prize. So, run the race to win.—*1st Corinthians 9:24*

Could Vince have been a great athlete with an attitude like that? Maybe, but he was a gifted leader. He had a lot to give. However . . .

> When a man has a great deal given to him, a great deal will be demanded of him.—*Luke 12:48*

335

The question is, can you become a great athlete by wanting to win badly? Remember that a vast majority of athletes want to win. The will to win is not enough. You must first truly believe you *can* win!

Belief is the thermostat which regulates success.

The above was no doubt written by an inspired heating equipment salesman. Vince, on the other hand, took belief a step further. He believed that *commitment* was all-important in traveling the road to winning.

We know how rough the road will be, how heavy here the load will be, we know about the barricades that wait along the track but we have set our soul ahead upon a certain goal ahead and nothing left from hell to sky shall ever turn us back.—Vince Lombardi

Ah, character. Vince was one. Character is a blend of commitment, discipline, and pride. In equal parts. With a dash of ambition:

If what you did yesterday still looks big to you, you haven't done much today.

Notice that I didn't say anything about those fortunate few who are gifted but never realize their true potential because of complacency.

Some men are bigger, faster, stronger, and smarter than others—but not a single man has a corner on dreams, desire, or ambition.—Duffy Daugherty

Or, more pointedly,

Talent will get you to the top, but it takes character to keep you there.— John Wooden

No, talent alone isn't everything, to paraphrase Vince. Neither is being disciplined.

Discipline is the refining fire by which talent becomes ability.—Roy Smith

But let's not forget the dash of ambition in our stew that comprises the strength athlete's lifestyle.

Progress comes from the intelligent use of experience.

Well, perhaps for some. Perhaps that was true in Vince Lombardi's day. Experience is, at best, a poor teacher by today's standards. For,

You are today where your thoughts have brought you. You will be tomorrow where your thoughts take you.—James Allen

Now, I don't mean to pick on poor ol' Vince. If he were alive today, he'd surely take exception to my ribbing. But, in truth, Vince had some strange ideas about what a man must do to win. And he had some stranger notions about why men fail. Said he, "Fatigue makes cowards of us all." As in a previous chapter, I disagree. Fatigue is the spark that ignites. It is the means to an end. It is the vehicle to success. Fatigue only makes cowards of the uncommitted.

Sure it's "tough." I like that word. I see it in practically every gym that hangs slogans on the wall. For example:

Nobody said life would be easy . . . and you only make it tougher if you feel sorry for yourself.—Morley Fraser

When the going gets tough, the tough get going.

If it ain't tough to get, it ain't worth having.

Fatigue and tough both conjure images of hard work, and in truth, hard work is what it takes to become a champion.

If hard work is the key to success, most people would rather pick the lock.—Claude McDonald

The difference between good and great is just a little extra effort.— Duffy Daugherty

But it isn't just hard work that ensures success. It's *smart* work. To work hard you have to be enthusiastic, but to truly get anything accomplished in your quest for the stars, you'll also have to be a little smarter than the other guy who's intent on making the same journey.

Enthusiasm without knowledge is like running in the dark.

What your predecessors, great men all, did to become great is no longer enough. You, my friend, have to do battle with men infinitely more knowledgeable than the greats of yesterday fought with.

A closed mind is usually empty . . . because it won't allow anything to enter.

Complacency is often the culprit in cases where athletes think they know enough to become the greatest there ever was. And complacency often is preceded by vanity and misplaced pride.

Too many fellows think they can push themselves forward by patting themselves on the back.

Such men have made the cardinal mistake of losing sight of what the possibilities are.

There is no mistake so great as the mistake of not going on.

In all sport, there can be only one winner. That makes losing all the tougher to take. In team sports, you have your teammates to blame or to be consoled by when you lose, and it isn't as personally demeaning.

Ol' Vince must've hated to lose. That he lost on occasion—with pride and dignity, no less—is what life is all about. But he was seething inside. Fair enough, but the more socially oriented among us may relate to the following poem more than to despising failure.

> FAILURE doesn't mean I'm a failure.
>   It does mean I haven't yet succeeded.
> FAILURE doesn't mean I have accomplished nothing.
>   It does mean I have learned something.
> FAILURE doesn't mean I have been a fool.
>   It does mean I had enough faith to experiment.
> FAILURE doesn't mean I've been disgraced.
>   It does mean I dared to try.
> FAILURE doesn't mean I don't have it.
>   It does mean I have to do something in a different way.
> FAILURE doesn't mean I'm inferior.
>   It does mean I am not perfect.
> FAILURE doesn't mean I've wasted my life.
>   It does mean I've an excuse to start over again.
> FAILURE doesn't mean I should give up.
>   It does mean I should try harder.
> FAILURE doesn't mean I'll never make it.
>   It does mean I need more patience.
> FAILURE doesn't mean you have to abandon me.
>   It does mean you must have a better idea.
>   Dr. Robert H. Schuller

Failure should not be a word that applies to the human species. It certainly doesn't apply to bodybuilders.

Men do not fail. They just give up easy.

A lot of people seem to be preoccupied with the possibility of failure. That's another word I see often on gym walls. If I owned a gym, the word would never appear anywhere. Just look at the stuff I see!

Winning is a foregone conclusion if you have prepared with *passion*.

Success is never permanent. And fortunately neither is failure.

When success turns a person's head, he's facing failure.

Defeat must be faced, but it need not be final.

Failure is something you know in your heart. Success is something that lies in the eye of the beholder.

Failure is the line of least persistence.

Even Vince Lombardi had failure on his mind when he uttered his famous statement quoted first in this chapter. You cannot comprehend the concept of winning unless you first know of failure.

No, Vince didn't have the answer. Indeed, there is not a single gym wall on which the true answer is to be found. You can take all these quotes recorded here and elsewhere and stuff them. They're cute, but "cute" doesn't cut it. Only passion does. For, *passion* is the ultimate ingredient in becoming the greatest there is, or ever will be.

PASSION
. . . and Peak Performance!

NOT need to achieve . . .
    Instead, a burning desire to exceed all bounds!
NOT commitment to excellence . . .
    Rather, utter disdain for anything less!
NOT endless hours of practice . . .
    Instead, PERFECT practice!
NOT ability to cope . . .
    Rather, total domination of all situations!
NOT setting goals . . .
    Goals too often prescribe performance limits!
NOT doing what it takes to win . . .
    Instead, doing what it takes to EXCEED!
NOT force of skill or muscle . . .
    Rather, the explosive, calamitous force of WILL!

If you believe these things, then for you winning is neither everything nor the only thing. It's a foregone conclusion!

But if, along the way, you somehow stumble, *profit* from the experience!

And vow, by the power of Almighty God, it'll NEVER happen again!

Dr. Squat

INDEX